To Jacky –

fellow member of the
exclusive Trinomial Authors Club –
including ... well you start.

Michael Alan Park

LIVING WITH ANIMALS

BONDS ACROSS SPECIES

EDITED BY
NATALIE PORTER AND
ILANA GERSHON

CORNELL UNIVERSITY PRESS
Ithaca and London

First published 2018 by Cornell University Press

Printed in the United States of America

Library of Congress Cataloging-in-Publication Data

Names: Porter, Natalie (Natalie H.), editor. | Gershon, Ilana, editor. | Container of (work): Musharbash, Yasmine. Yuendumu dog tales.
Title: Living with animals : bonds across species / edited by Natalie Porter and Ilana Gershon.
Other titles: Living with animals (Cornell University Press)
Description: Ithaca : Cornell University Press, 2018. | Includes bibliographical references.
Identifiers: LCCN 2018004048 (print) | LCCN 2018005724 (ebook) | ISBN 9781501724848 (epub/mobi) | ISBN 9781501724831 (pdf) | ISBN 9781501724817 | ISBN 9781501724817 (cloth; alk. paper) | ISBN 9781501724824 (pbk.; alk. paper)
Subjects: LCSH: Human-animal relationships. | Animals and civilization.
Classification: LCC QL85 (ebook) | LCC QL85 .L578 2018 (print) | DDC 591—dc23
LC record available at https://lccn.loc.gov/2018004048

*For Nancy Lightfoot, who loves animals and authors
and Robert Porter, a naturalist and a gentle soul*

❧ Contents

🐿 ACKNOWLEDGMENTS

This book is the outcome of friendships—both between humans and between humans and other animals. Over the years the authors in this volume have been engaged in a growing community of scholars bound by a shared interest in animals—human and otherwise. For our part, we as editors have gotten to know our contributors through conferences, workshops, and email correspondences and through the simple act of reading and admiring their scholarship. We would like to thank each of our contributors for their companionship and for embracing our request for playful, readable, and unconventional modes of writing about nonhuman animals and their relationships with human animals. We are quite simply delighted by the results. We could not have imagined the degree of responsibility, commitment, and grace with which the authors have tackled thick, complex, and often difficult relations between beings. Of course, the beings in these chapters deserve our greatest thanks, for being our friends, our companions, our pets, our models, our food, and our teachers; for suffering and forgiving us our constant questions and observations, our interventions and manipulations, our oversights and neglects. It is with a feeling of gratitude that we donate the proceeds of this volume to the Xerces Society, a nonprofit environmental organization based in Portland, Oregon, that focuses on the conservation of invertebrates considered to be essential to biological diversity and ecosystem health; and to the Chimpanzee Sanctuary in Cle Elum, Washington, which provides sanctuary for chimpanzees discarded from the entertainment and biomedical testing industries.

LIVING WITH ANIMALS

With Animals

An Introduction

NATALIE PORTER AND ILANA GERSHON

I

Being human means being with other animal species every moment of every day. Perhaps you have a dog at your feet or a cat on your lap as you read these words. Or maybe you've just encountered a squirrel on your walk across campus, or a pig in your breakfast sausage. Haven't seen a nonhuman animal today? Rest assured that you have at least a dozen or so demodex spiders living on your eyelashes at this very instant, and you very likely swallowed one or two in your sleep last night. You may have heard that 90 percent of "human" cells are actually bacteria. Seem outrageous? Take it from the BBC: "You're not totally human. . . . You're really more of a bug city, teeming with different species." (See: http://www.bbc.com/future/story/20150402-why-you-are-more-bug-than-human.)

To be human, then, is to be with animals. As people go about their daily lives, they are consciously and unconsciously navigating their relationships to countless creatures; not only those in and on people's bodies but also those in homes and on the street, in parks and safaris and zoos, in classrooms and laboratories, and in restaurants, markets, and dining halls. The sheer number and diversity of nonhuman animals people encounter on a daily basis should be enough to give us pause and encourage us to reflect on what it means to live, and live well, with animals.

Many of our most pressing political and ethical questions revolve around our relationships with other species. We are currently living in the Anthropocene, an era in which humans are irrevocably transforming, and endangering, the earth and its myriad species. In the midst of ecosystem crises, mass extinctions, and the intensification of animal production and exploitation worldwide, scientists, scholars, and activists from many fields are beginning to consider alternative ways of thinking about and relating to animals—to *being with* animals.

As a part of this trend, a growing interdisciplinary field of animal studies has emerged to tackle these problems. Scholars in this field are exploring a range of relationships between species, including those where other animal species figure as prey; as technologies; as environmental subjects and objects; as workers; as food; as nonhuman persons; and as companions. Animal studies scholars come from a variety of disciplines—anthropology, biology, psychology, sociology, history, and philosophy—and most ask questions such as: What are the social, biological, and historical conditions that lead human and nonhuman animals to live with each other in particular ways? How do shared histories and environments shape the bodies and behaviors of humans and other animals? How do humans and nonhuman animals respond to each other and their conditions of coexistence, and to what effect?

Animal studies does not always start with the question of whether a particular way of being with other animals is right or wrong. Scholars often begin by examining the bewildering number of ways that humans live with other animals, try to understand why they live that way, and ask what it might mean for the future. In other words, this approach asks first what it is actually like to live with animals and then considers how we might live otherwise.

Developing new ways to live with animals requires developing new approaches for thinking and writing alongside them. This book brings together nineteen chapters that describe various ways that humans live and do things with other animal species. The chapters are all based on the authors' extensive research, but many are told from the perspective of fictional characters. Still others are written for fictional or imagined audiences, namely individuals and communities engaged in the particular social tasks involved in living with animals. They should be considered ethnographic fictions, written as accurately *and* as engagingly as possible (Narayan 1999: 142).

By adopting different voices and addressing different audiences, these authors bring fresh perspectives to the question of what it means to be with animals. Writing in the voice of people engaged in tasks with animals, such as a professional horse breeder or an industrial pig farmer, opens up space to examine what it actually looks and feels like to carry out such activities.

Similarly, adopting the voice of a laboratory mouse or ferret prompts a reconsideration of the objectives and effects of scientific research and brings a degree of empathy to accounts of animal experimentation.

These chapters thus capture the imaginative thinking exercises that we all go through when we confront scenarios that puzzle us, give us pause, and make us uncomfortable. We often step into the shoes of others when trying to work through a problem or a difficult relationship. These chapters embrace this kind of thinking as they grapple with some of the most urgent questions of our time. By experimenting with different ways to think *and write* with other animals, they offer innovative angles from which to view conundrums like the ethics of animal killing, laboratory testing, and ritual sacrifice and provide new conceptual tools for engaging with ongoing debates about animal conservation, disease control, and domestication.

Together, these chapters take up Donna Haraway's (2016) exhortation to "stay with the trouble," to embrace the uncomfortable question of how to live and die with other species on a compromised planet. Haraway suggests that staying with the trouble is a way to build more livable futures for humans and nonhumans alike. The chapters that follow present many uncomfortable questions with no easy answers and many troubling scenarios with no clear designations of right or wrong, good or bad. On the contrary, these chapters show us that if we adopt different perspectives, activities we may have assumed to be good—like bird conservation or animal rescue—can actually involve doing violence to other animal species. Activities that we may have assumed to be bad—like animal slaughter and experimentation—do in fact display moments of mercy and even love. In this volume, staying with the trouble means bringing different voices to the conversation and considering the possibility that the most important problems of our time will not be solved by scholars, or even humans, alone.

In keeping with the spirit of innovative and creative thinking, we invite you to read this volume in a number of ways. We have divided the chapters according to various kinds of tasks with animals, but the beauty of these chapters is that each stands on its own as an imaginative glimpse into multispecies worlds. You may, for instance, want to begin with chapters about your favorite animal. Or you might choose to start with social tasks that take place in a particular region of the world that attracts you. You might be curious about a particular topic, like health, habituation, or even the process of conducting field research. Experiment; sniff around; see what grabs your attention; lump the chapters into your own set of themes and interests. In what remains of this introduction, we identify a few key issues that tie the chapters together and comment on what each chapter can teach us about them.

II

People often talk in ways that set humans apart from animals, but the stories collected here all show that thinking about species difference blinds us to a whole host of other more interesting questions about how humans live with and among nonhuman beings. Instead of proceeding from an assumption about species difference, these chapters explore how species differences are made, remade, and sometimes unmade in the everyday social tasks that humans do with other animals. Even though humans and nonhuman animals live together, they are rarely equal, or even voluntary, partners in their shared tasks. Navigating inequalities and differences, it turns out, is hardly an easy, pretty, or comfortable process. You are staying with the trouble.

One of the key differences that humans and other animals navigate together is their lifespans. Humans live much longer than many of the animals with whom they socialize, which means that death and how to deal with death is a significant part of human-animal relationships. Several of the authors find themselves in situations where humans are trying to avoid or delay the death of an animal. Whether in the work of dog rescue, bird or elephant conservation, or wild bird release, they tell stories of humans attempting to do things *for* animals. The authors describe how dog trainers, community organizers, and Buddhist monks identify particular animals and animal characteristics worth saving and show how they select for, refine, and even cultivate those creatures under the auspices of salvation and preservation.

There is not a little bit of hubris operating here, for the very idea that humans can somehow control the fate of their chosen animal suggests an unequal distribution of agency across species. And the inherently selective work of rescue, release, and conservation signals how the death-defying human-animal relation is always imagined in terms of a larger human audience, whose preferences dictate the task at hand. Natalie Porter's volunteer organization doesn't rescue any old dog; it saves only those who can be transformed into plug and play canine companions. The community organizers Nicholas D'Avella works with don't just conserve any old birds; they choose the ones seen as beautiful who inhabit endangered urban spaces. The Buddhist monks whom Frédéric Keck observed engaging in ritualized bird releases do so according to religious principles laid down by their particular orders, the very human notions of merit making, and what is available at the live bird market. Even in instances where nonhuman animal behaviors save lives, there is an assumption that humans can both apprehend and control such behaviors toward their own ends.

The work of salvation is not easy, and this set of stories narrates the incredible labor and improvisation that it takes on the part of both humans and other animals to avoid death. Rescue volunteers must accommodate or alter nonstandard canine personalities to achieve adoptability in American pet keeping culture. Activists in Buenos Aires must locate at-risk birds in their appropriate urban ecologies and document and circulate them in the appropriate political networks in order to preserve them. Merit makers and conservationists must recalibrate bird releases to account for potential animal pathogens, shifting bird migration patterns and market dynamics in southern China. Researchers must track chimpanzees through forests without ever letting them know that they are watching (in case the chimpanzees become too comfortable with humans), doing so by mobilizing cameras, storytellers, and assistants who learn to collect feces while hewing to standardized, lab-worthy procedures. Expeditious animal classifiers must confront snakes, crocodiles, infectious diseases, and foot rot to find unique and beautiful specimens, knowing all along that some of them will go extinct before they can be classified systematically. An entire family, a jeep, an after-hours vet, and a lot of prayers must come together to save an ailing feline.

Of course animal death is not always something to be avoided. Sometimes it is planned. We might think of this approach to death as doing things *to* animals. Tasks like food production and animal experimentation constitute calculated interventions into animal life that more often than not result in death. Alex Blanchette's standard operating procedure for industrial hog farming, for example, illustrates a meticulous micromanagement of every aspect of a pig's life process and environment—which means also standardizing every interaction between laborer and lively commodity. Such procedures ensure that, in death, the pig achieves maximum efficiency and profitability. Or take the adventures of the laboratory mustelids and rodents, those feisty ferrets and musing mice whose every move is measured and carefully (though differentially) controlled in the name of scientific objectivity. Their deaths, too, are premeditated and methodical, though it turns out that there are some things these critters can do either to hasten or to delay culling (and perhaps even momentarily to enjoy themselves). Those that do die on schedule perhaps do not suffer meaningless deaths, for as Nicole Nelson and Kaitlyn Stack Whitney's murine narrator reminds us, postmortem data is highly valuable in academic circles. Zebu cattle in Madagascar, too, attain meaningful death—at least from the human perspective. Acting as proxies for humans, Genese Marie Sodikoff describes how they are sacrificed as a means for men to curry favor with powerful, ever-present ancestors.

Even though the animals' value in these relations is imagined in terms of human outcomes, it does not mean that humans ignore how nonhuman animals feel and think. As Atfield, Blanchette, and Sharp demonstrate, built into these killing strategies are techniques to comfort animals, the enrichment activities like playtime for the ferret named Lucifer, or the standard (and often unintuitive) labor practices meant to avoid startling a hog. Considering how different animals think and feel and deciding on the extent to which killing is an acceptable human intervention are not comfortable processes, especially when we confront critters who defy ideas about their animal natures and keep us uncertain about the terms and morality of our relationships. Take oysters, categorical curiosities that are classified as animals but share most of their characteristics with plants. These creatures beckon Eva Hayward, a vegan who savors the taste and feel of their flesh with full knowledge of the contradictions in her consumptive behavior. To eat a live oyster, Eva suggests, is to feel uncomfortable. It is to confront murderousness and the uneasy contours of killing particular life-forms, rather than justifying killing with some abstract notion of species difference.

III

The essays all challenge readers to think anew about how people experience the human/nature divide in this contemporary moment. Often the authors discuss humans' efforts not just to control nature but also to standardize nature, either by creating uniform experiences or creating uniform animals. These attempts to standardize tend to go awry because too much work is involved in trying to get a potentially wide range of contexts or beings or interactions all to seem just like each other. As Aleta Quinn's discussion of systematics shows, animal classifications can follow a number of different logics and forms of evidence, sparking fierce debates about the relationship between different animals and their ancestors. In these moments, "nature" writ large becomes the site of resistance to humans' longings for unvaried consistency. Indeed, the quest for consistency can be misleading. Not only, as we have already argued, are categories such as human and nature operating at too great a level of generality, which has the effect of obscuring valuable insights, but it is also a peculiarly Western and modern take to see the human/nature divide as centered on standardizing and obstacles to standardizing. This take is drawn partially from the needs to standardize inherent in our current form of capitalism and our current models of scientific research.

You begin to see different logics motivating efforts to standardize when you put the stories about why industrial farmers require standardized animals next to the stories about why scientists require standardized animals. Long-reaching markets cause businesspeople to care about creating the most uniform product possible so that it can be distributed more easily around the world; thus, when animals become commodities, they need to be standardized because consumers have learned to value predictability. Pork eaters want to know what taste they are about to experience, dog adopters would like to be able to imagine how a dog will fit in to their life (almost always a life filled with other standardized objects and standardized processes). Nineteenth-century physicians, as Robert Kirk shows, wanted to obtain particular species of medicinal leeches, the very best bloodsuckers able to treat scores of patients in succession. Contemporary scientists, by contrast, want to standardize in order to be able to make believable claims that what happens in their labs can be replicated in other labs with similar results.

Sometimes businesspeople use the techniques scientists have developed to benefit market needs for standardized processes. When businesspeople try to turn animals or animal parts into commodities that can travel, they turn to practices developed and authorized in labs. Several chapters in this collection describe humans and other animal species scientifically recreating and supposedly improving on natural processes. Jeannette Vaught and her colleagues mimicked and mirrored and intervened during each step of the stallion's orgasm—from using one's arm as a proxy penis to calibrate the artificial vagina, to steadying the mounted beast and encouraging his climax, to collecting his semen and measuring its motility. This illustrates the very literal ways in which humans have a hand in controlling the means and products of reproductive animal labor. The stallion's spent and exhausted body and the sheer numbers of semen canisters being shipped to breeders is but one example of what animals are forced to be when asked to serve market demands.

As people try to standardize an animal's body and an animal's experiences, they often try to take into account that animal's species "nature." This often helps to support the belief that different animal species do in fact have a shared nature that unites all members of that species. Yet when the essays turn to how this works in practice, creating standardized practices to accommodate a species-specific animal nature becomes a tricky task indeed. Scout Calvert's juxtaposition of artificial reproductive practices for cows and humans exposes just how curious, and *non*-universal, efforts to enhance nature can be. In describing the kinds of traits that can be selected for in the reproductive process, she reveals that efforts to improve upon nature are rooted in culturally and historically specific ideas about what an ideal species body looks, feels, and acts like. The stories of rendering a rodent suitable for experimentation, a dog for adoption, a gorilla for observation, a hog for factory production, a horse or cow for reproduction all reveal how on the ground human-animal interactions, which are sometimes unpredictable, often emotional, and always unequal, create obstacles for standardization. In addition, as humans, we can never know for sure that a ferret would prefer a grassy hill to contrived conditions of the laboratory, but Heather Altfeld and Lesley Sharp in imagining Lucifer make a strong case for it. And while the managers at Berkamp Farms would have their employees and customers believe that a standardized hog is a productive, healthy, and therefore fully actualized hog, the very material conditions of its existence that Alex Blanchette describes do much to undercut that promise. In short, these stories raise politically and ethically charged questions about why standardization is an ideal in the first place, and for whom.

IV

There are also less interventionist ways of encountering animal "nature," and some chapters describe humans attempting to relate to other animals in ways that encourage animal improvisation and creativity. Andrew Halloran and Catherine Bolten, for instance, want to document how chimp communities in Sierra Leone adapt to and thrive in dwindling habitats, where they compete with humans for scarce resources. These chimp communities are defying scientific understandings of their species nature by surviving and reproducing in difficult conditions, in large part because they express a healthy fear of their aggressive human neighbors. And so Andrew and Catherine's task of conservation requires that they suspend notions of how chimps are supposed to behave and instead assemble a toolkit to collect intimate details of chimps' daily practices and life processes as unobtrusively as possible.

Other forms of animal improvisation emerge in Marcus Baynes-Rock's work with the hyenas of Harar. Marcus spent quite a lot of time looking at and interacting with a hyena pack, namely its most courageous member, Willi. But Willi showed Marcus that the terms of hyena habituation were not entirely under his control, and Marcus struggled to negotiate his pack position according to *hyena*-specific notions of rank and hierarchy. This process of mutual habituation, it turns out, opened up space for the hyenas to interact with Marcus on their own terms and to treat Marcus according to their own set of values, rather than one imposed upon them by an intermediary species.

The different approaches to habituation in these pieces signal a productive tension that emerges when humans and other animals inhabit shared worlds.

Pete, the service dog in Leslie Irvine and Sherri Sasnett-Martichuski's chapter, illustrates this tension beautifully. Here is a dog who is fully and purposefully habituated to his vision-impaired companion Amy. As Pete explains, the task of guiding a human animal starts from birth (or even breeding) and requires an intensive, years-long training regimen that erodes a puppy's canine proclivities—to bite, to play, to be distracted—and fully attunes his senses and sensibilities to the particular capabilities, needs, and daily rhythms of his companion. Now, this may seem like an instance of the most extreme form of habituation and standardization in the service of human needs. Indeed, there are benchmark standards that guide dogs have to meet in order to carry out their work. But it turns out that Pete is also expected to use his innate response systems to help navigate Amy through her daily tasks. Service dogs must improvise when the unexpected ferret runs over their head, and they must trust their instincts when their human unwittingly commands them to step into oncoming traffic. Habituation sometimes means acting in unstandard ways to keep human animals safe.

When humans get involved in animals' lives, it is not only human animals to whom animals have to habituate. Christena Nippert-Eng's account of zoo gorilla introductions illustrates the accommodations that individual gorillas have to make for one another in captivity. Much like students assigned to share college dormitories, primate cohabitants must learn to live together, establishing social hierarchies among themselves, navigating their built environments, and negotiating their relationships with the human animals who determine the conditions of their captivity (or residence).

And so living together requires constant negotiation and improvisation. Depending on the unique landscapes they cohabit, humans and other animal species establish both proximity and distance between their bodies and perceptions. In other words, they move in and out of each other's worlds. Dog walking provides Agustín Fuentes and Michael Alan Park with an opportunity to see their world anew and to contemplate the evolving contours of human-dog companionship—something that has transformed from a collaborative hunting endeavor into a task done primarily *for* the animal: taking the dog out. Both species benefit from this task. When the authors walk their dogs, they can train their attention to the sights, smells, and sounds that fill canine worlds and pique their senses. The dogs, too, transit in and out of human worlds: Shelly knows that the suburbs are not a space for hunting, but she still enjoys using her nose to explore the sensory landscape of suburban America. In between chasing turkeys in the woods of Connecticut, Michael's pups also mediate his social encounters with other human animals.

V

All the chapters address how humans and other animals interact when there are different species-specific understandings of what the interaction is all about. Seeing these interactions from the points of view of anthropologists shows us that cultural differences can also be at play in these moments. Not everyone understands human-cat or human-dog relationships in the same way, and as anthropologists interact with companion animals based on their own culturally specific understandings of what *companion* means, the reactions of others to their unexpected and unfamiliar actions shed light on all the cultural assumptions at play. Alex Nading's Nicaraguan hosts and friends were baffled to learn that he hand-fed and -bathed Floyd, and they protested that such activities would erode the cat's inclination to hunt—a necessary skill on the streets of Managua. Alex, who had his own beloved cat at home in the United States, tried to cultivate the kinds of detachment common to human-feline relations at his field site, but when he spectacularly failed, he revealed a part of himself and his cultural disposition to those around him, ultimately bringing him closer to his host family and neighbors.

When Yasmine Musharbash tried to teach her dog Kunyarrpa to walk on a leash or to come when she called, her Australian aboriginal (Yapa) friends were perplexed. For them, every being is autonomous, whether the being is a dog or a person. And just like you do not order a person to do something, you do not order a dog. But what a cultural difference! By contrast, Yasmine grew up around people who felt free to order other people to do things and extended their own prerogative to dogs without thinking much about it. Human-animal interactions can also be about human-human interactions. And all these interactions are shaped by culturally specific beliefs and strategies about how one should behave with others, including what autonomy means and what it means to treat others as autonomous beings. When cultural differences are at play, even everyday practices that you thought everyone did suddenly have to be thought anew—like naming a dog. Why, if you are Yapa, would you name a dog if you are never going to tell a dog to come to you or to go away or not to pee on your bed? Why, Yasmine realizes, to talk about the dogs with other humans, of course.

VI

What does it mean, then, to be with animals? Well, it means many things, because being with animals is a condition of our humanity. It is therefore curious that studies of human-animal relationships have come under fire recently for being "anti-humanist," for pondering the perspectives of animals while failing to do the apparently more important work of criticizing social conditions. Such a critique, however, is based on simplistic assumptions about inherent species difference and the universal ascendancy of human-kind that all of the essays in this volume roundly reject. To suggest that considering animals is anti-humanist is to deny all of the inextricable ways that human lives are bound up with other animal lives and all of the ways that humans use their understandings of animals to accomplish consequential social tasks.

Tracing the local and global traffic of animal commodities offers a window onto viewing and critiquing the ways in which capitalism has infected all of our social systems, how it enrolls both humans and other animals into unequal labor relations, consumption patterns, and health risks. On the surface, helping a horse have an orgasm may seem like a trivial pursuit, but in fact this activity illuminates how scientific practices intersect with global commodity flows to shape the ways in which we imagine and render different lives. Describing the standard operating procedures of pork production shows how capitalism calls on science to discipline the bodies not only of hogs but also of particular classes of people who engage in extremely risky work on the farm. Linking the golden age of leeching to the birth of modern medicine shows the deep-seated roots of new advances in health care, which, like longstanding practices of sacrificing cattle, enroll the bodies and labor of nonhuman animals in the service of human well-being. Observing a ritualized bird release may seem like a frivolous, academic flight of fancy, yet it shows how different ways of valuing other creatures can have an impact on the health of an entire planet.

Studying the daily work of animal conservation reveals still more about contemporary social conditions: how the privatization of urban space both threatens and empowers entire groups of humans and other animals; how war, poverty, and political unrest push different species to their limits and provoke them to forge new ways to coexist in harsh environments. Understanding the advantages and disadvantages of these contingent and improvisational human-animal relations will only become more pressing as climate change continues to stress the earth's ecosystems.

By sharing what may seem like mundane, even inconsequential details about the manner in which human animals and other animals engage with, learn from, and rely on one another, these chapters move away from philosophical abstraction and instead reveal what it is to live and perhaps even live well with other beings. The humans and other animals we meet in this book aren't ruminating on what it means to be human (or animal) or on what distinguishes humans from other animals. And they aren't drawing on such distinctions to debate "right" or "wrong" ways of living with one another. Instead, the humans and other animals we meet in this book are forging ways to coexist and cooperate—to occupy and thrive in the same spaces, to breathe the same air, to get things done—often in less-than-ideal conditions. And in doing so, they are learning about themselves and each other.

Suggested Readings

On the question of the human, and animal, see:

Gilles Deleuze and Félix Guattari. 1987. "1730: Becoming-Intense, Becoming-Animal, Becoming-Imperceptible." In *A Thousand Plateaus: Capitalism and Schizophrenia*. Minneapolis: University of Minnesota Press.

Vinciane Despret. 2016. *What Would Animals Say If We Asked the Right Questions?* Translated by Brett Buchanan. Minneapolis: University of Minnesota Press.

Donna Haraway. 2007. *When Species Meet*. Minneapolis: University of Minnesota Press.

Donna J. Haraway. 2016. *Staying with the Trouble: Making Kin in the Chthulucene*. Durham, NC: Duke University Press.

Linda Kalof and Amy Fitzgerald. 2007. *The Animals Reader: The Essential Classic and Contemporary Writings*. Oxford: Bloomsbury Academic.

On ethnographic fiction, see:

Kirin Narayan. 1999. "Ethnography and Fiction: Where is the Border?" *Anthropology and Humanism* 24: 134–47.

On animal death, see:

. . . In livestock production

Timothy Pachirat. 2013. *Every Twelve Seconds: Industrialized Slaughter and the Politics of Sight*. New Haven: Yale University Press.

Noélie Vialles. 1994. *Animal to Edible*. New York: Cambridge University Press.

. . . In conservation

Human Animal Research Network. 2015. *Animals in the Anthropocene: Critical Perspectives on Non-Human Futures*, edited by Human Animal Research Network Editorial Collective. Sydney: Sydney University Press.

Eben Kirksey. 2015. *Emergent Ecologies*. Durham, NC: Duke University Press.

Jamie Lorimer. 2015. *Wildlife in the Anthropocene: Conservation after Nature*. Minneapolis: University of Minnesota Press.

Celia Lowe. 2006. *Wild Profusion: Biodiversity Conservation in an Indonesian Archipelago*. Princeton: Princeton University Press.

On standardization, see:

. . . In science

Gail Davies. 2012. "What Is a Humanized Mouse? Remaking the Species and Spaces of Translational Medicine." *Body and Society* 18: 126–55.

Carrie Friese and Adele E. Clarke. 2012. "Transposing Bodies of Knowledge and Technique: Animal Models at Work in Reproductive Sciences." *Social Studies of Science* 42: 31–52.

Robert E. Kohler. 1994. *Lords of the Fly: Drosophila Genetics and the Experimental Life.* Chicago: University of Chicago Press.

Sabina Leonelli and Rachel A. Ankeny. 2012. "Re-Thinking Organisms: The Impact of Databases on Model Organism Biology." *Studies in History and Philosophy of Science Part C: Studies in History and Philosophy of Biological and Biomedical Sciences* 43: 29–36.

. . . In capitalist systems

Alex Blanchette. 2015. "Herding Species: Biosecurity, Posthuman Labor, and the American Industrial Pig." *Cultural Anthropology* 30: 640–69.

Henry Buller. 2013. "Individuation, the Mass, and Farm Animals." *Theory, Culture, and Society* 30: 155–75.

Marianne Elisabeth Lien. 2015. *Becoming Salmon: Aquaculture and the Domestication of a Fish.* Berkeley: University of California Press.

Nicole Shukin. 2009. *Animal Capital: Rendering Life in Biopolitical Times.* Minneapolis: University of Minnesota Press.

On habituation, see:

Marcus Baynes-Rock. 2015. *Among the Bone Eaters: Encounters with Hyenas in Harar.* University Park: Pennsylvania State University Press.

Matei Candea. 2010. "'I Fell in Love with Carlos the Meerkat': Engagement and Detachment in Human-Animal Relations." *American Ethnologist* 37: 241–58.

Rheana "Juno" Salazar Parreñas. 2012. "Producing Affect: Transnational Volunteerism in a Malaysian Orangutan Rehabilitation Center." *American Ethnologist* 39: 673–87.

On what other animals can teach us about culture, see:

Laura A. Ogden. 2011. *Swamplife: People, Gators, and Mangroves Entangled in the Everglades.* Minneapolis: University of Minnesota Press.

Hugh Raffles. 2011. *Insectopedia.* New York: Vintage.

Hoon Song. 2013. *Pigeon Trouble: Bestiary Biopolitics in a Deindustrialized America.* Philadelphia: University of Pennsylvania Press.

🍎 PART 1

Fieldwork

🐾 CHAPTER 1

Yuendumu Dog Tales

YASMINE MUSHARBASH

For every Warlpiri myth, fable, or folktale about a child left in camp by its parents while they go hunting, a child who then gets adopted by dingoes, who treat it as one of their own, there is a myth, fable, or folktale about a dingo pup left behind in camp by its parents, who are off hunting, a pup who then gets adopted by Yapa (Warlpiri people), who treat it as one of their own. These stories beautifully reveal the close bonds between Yapa and dingoes (and later, dogs). As Eunice, a senior Warlpiri woman, puts it, "Dogs look after you, they are family, *warlalja*. They get upset, they cry when someone passes away, they are like people in that way, they grieve. They worry for their humans, and they are happy when you are happy, they are relatives for you. They make us happy like family."

And for every dog tale about dogs who help, there exists an opposite dog tale about dogs who mess things up. Take stories about dogs' hunting expertise ("when I was little, my father had a dog called Wardalapi, and he was the best hunter! We had kangaroo almost every day!"). For each such story Yapa have another one about a dog scaring kangaroos just when the hunters are about to spear or shoot them. Curiously, people tell more stories about dogs helping or messing up a kangaroo hunt than anecdotes of dingoes hunting for smaller game such as goannas or bilbies, which they are much more adept at.

Today, Warlpiri people hardly ever use dogs for hunting any more, but dogs are still everywhere at Yuendumu. Most every camp has a pack of dogs, and their furry, barky, wet-nosy, ever-present company is an elemental if quotidian fact of Warlpiri life. References to dogs permeate Warlpiri speech: When complaining about being left behind after everybody else goes to town, one might say, "I was left like a dog!" And somebody who has indiscriminate sexual liaisons is described as "running around like a dog." And dogs are a favorite topic of conversation in the camps, like they are for dog-owners the world over. Warlpiri people often provide a running commentary on what the dogs are up to right here right now (and each pack is a soap opera in itself). They reminisce nostalgically about dogs who have passed on, including their own dogs, their parents' dogs, or even their grandparents' dogs—memories of dogs reach far into the past. They sing and retell Dreaming dog stories, and they love to recount funny dog stories. In fact, it is not unusual for dog stories to be told in the same register as stories about Yapa, and sometimes—if one isn't familiar with the protagonists—it is hard to tell if Yapa are talking about their family or about their dogs. Some dog stories are even condensed into one sentence. (This is a common Aboriginal practice, called "the word.") Someone will say, "That time when Anton chased Marvin," and everyone will know the story, and laugh, or sigh, or tut, depending on what the appropriate reaction is. One such "word" is "That time when Wardalapi came back from bush camp."

Wardalapi

Barbiedog, one of Yuendumu's first sausage dogs and possibly the bitch with the most puppies—ever—had puppies again. Her puppies were very popular; short-legged dogs were the latest craze. I had asked Barbiedog's owner for two puppies for Celeste and myself, and when they were old enough to leave their mother, we moved them to our camp. We called them Wardalapi, after Celeste's sister's father's famous hunting dog of old, and Kuntangiyi, after Celeste's father's brother's dog. Kuntangiyi died while still a pup, poor thing. Wardalapi lived to a ripe old age and became a bit of a family favorite—more than just Celeste's dog, everyone loved and spoiled him. But Toby was Wardalapi's special human. Toby was a young teenager when Celeste got Wardalapi, and the two grew really close. A year or two later, when Toby was going through initiation, Wardalapi disappeared. We looked for him everywhere but couldn't find him. We were worried about Toby coming out of the bush camp, eventually, a man now, only to find out his favorite dog had been . . . what? Stolen? Injured? Run over?

Then, one afternoon, as we were preparing food to take over to the ritual ground for the men to take to the bush camp to feed the initiates, Wardalapi walked into our camp as if nothing had happened. Except: He was covered with red ochre handprints. We laughed and laughed and laughed and laughed. And didn't really know why we were laughing. Probably a combination of things: relief that Wardalapi was alive after all; the silliness of worrying about how Toby would take the loss of Wardalapi when the two of them had been together all this time; and the shocking incongruity of dog (ridiculous sausage dog no less) and red ochre (which during initiation time especially stands for all that is male, sacred, and secret).

For years after, when anybody said, "Remember that time when Wardalapi came back from bush camp?," everyone would immediately laugh uproariously. Now, that laughter is tinged with sadness as people remember Wardalapi and all the times they shared with him.

Yilyinika

Yilyinika is about six months old, brimming with energy and curiosity. In the camp, she plays with her two brothers for hours on end—chasing them, being chased by them, mouthing, play fighting—only to suddenly fall asleep, utterly exhausted. She is the runt of the litter, skinnier than the others, pups who have been claimed by Yapa and are thrown tidbits during mealtimes by their respective humans. She doesn't look that different from her brother Wati, but where the brown markings on white fur give him a handsome, roguish appearance, her markings are grey, and to be honest, make her look eternally dirty. Wati was claimed by Polly, when he was very little, and was the first to leave his mother, over at Eunice's camp. Polly's grandson claimed Willi, Wati, and Yilyinika's short-legged brother. Yilyinika came to Polly's camp with Eunice, who came to stay with Polly for company one day as her own camp emptied because her co-residents went on a trip south. Eunice brought her dogs, and when she returned home after a week or two, Yilyinika stayed behind in Polly's camp with her brothers.

Not much later, I returned to Yuendumu (same as every year for the past two decades) to undertake research with Yapa. I had come for shorter visits before but this was my first long-term return since my dog Kunyarrpa passed away after ten wonderful years we'd spent together. At Yuendumu (his home place) I felt the loss again, and intensely. Everybody around me had their dogs. Each camp has a pack of dogs, and out of that pack, individual dogs relate to individual Yapa (those who claimed them). As always, I live in Polly's camp, and the pack there knows me well, so when I arrive after an absence they all run up to me, tails wagging, welcoming me with little yelps and jumps. Still, without Kunyarrpa, I felt dogless, so much so that one day, when Marion went to the shop and asked me if I wanted anything, I shouted: "All I want is a dog!" Eunice heard me and called out: "You can have one of mine, that white one!"

That is how Yilyinika, at that point still nameless, became mine (or I hers). I took her to old lady Clara to ask for a name. Every Warlpiri person has a skin name (a subsection term), which is both a term of address and a socio-centric name that allows one to configure relationships to everyone (and everything) around. Yapa also give skin names to non-indigenous people who come and stay in the desert (as service providers, or, as the case may be, anthropologists). My skin name is Napurrurla (which is also pretty much what everybody at Yuendumu calls me). Dogs, which are seen as protectors, are given one's parents' skin names, which made the little runty white dog a Napaljarri (my mother). Clara thought of names of Napaljarris and decided on Yilyinika. So, I now had a puppy, and my puppy had a name and a skin name. Yapa get their skin names via their parents, dogs via their Yapa, which means that had Yilyinika, Wati and Willi been human they would have the same skin name as siblings do, but as they are dogs and belong to Polly (Napaljarri), her grandson (Japangardi) and me (Napurrurla), respectively, they have different skin names. Human kinship overrides canine kinship. In fact one of things dogs are known to be ignorant about is proper kinship etiquette, witnessed yet again just today by everyone here when Ask'im copulated with his mother Nangala.

As Yilyinika and I grew closer, I began to observe her more carefully, and was thrilled to notice that unlike her brothers, she always paid close attention to the rest of the pack, even when the three of them were absorbed in play. When the older dogs run off in formation, barking, she often tentatively joins in (while her brothers continue to play). Following the pack, she joins her high-pitched puppy bark to theirs, watching her elders, trying to figure out what the commotion is all about.

Yapa do not train their dogs at all, except through encouraging toddlers to "cruel" puppies, that is rough play, pinching, throwing around, hitting, and manhandling. Harsh as this may sound, two very good results flow from it: dogs generally having healthy respect for children in particular (I have never seen a camp dog attack or annoy a child) and Yapa, generally; and Yapa in turn are very good at handling dogs and very rarely afraid of them. Even though they have no human training different dogs seem to specialize in different tasks. I often wondered how they worked out their respective responsibilities. Watching Yilyinika is instructive. I can picture her becoming quite skilled at detecting dangers because she pays such close attention and watches the Three Brothers. They are Polly's dog Nangala's sons, all large and the oldest males of this pack. They take turns in leading chases. While, like all dogs, they enjoy having a snooze more than most anything, at least one of them is usually on lookout (or, listen-out, or smell-out), and the other two spring up when one of them barks the alarm.

Yapa often focus more on dogs' hearing than their nose; my friend Tamsin for example said about her dogs: "if you are sleeping and someone or something comes around at night at your place, I think they sense them, they know if something is approaching, that must be why they have the biggest ears, to listen." And there exists a Warlpiri myth about how a husband and wife got so very annoyed by their dogs' barking every night that one evening the husband cut their ears off so that he and his wife could sleep in peace. What he didn't realize was that the dogs had been barking at monsters every night and through their barking had kept them at bay and their humans safe. Once their ears were cut off, the dogs couldn't hear the monsters approach. The next night the husband and wife were killed.

Yapa say they can tell from the tone and intensity of the bark of their dogs whether they are announcing the coming of a stranger, signaling the presence of a snake, chasing horses, or defending the camp from monsters. I remember how Kunyarrpa's bark used to change during nighttime chases with his pack: There was a different timbre to his voice depending on whether he was following or leading, and the pitch and rhythm of the barking changed depending on how close or distant he was from whatever he was chasing.

Yilyinika has much to learn: The other night I woke up only to realize that the others were all awake, sitting up on their mattresses, whispering to each other. When I asked Polly what was wrong she said that there must be a monster lurking close by. "Listen!" What I heard was a single dog at the end of our driveway rhythmically going *barkbarkbark barkbarkbark barkbarkbark*. When I approached a window to have a look, Polly warned me to be careful. What made me curious was that only one dog was barking. Through the window I could see that our dogs were all sleeping peacefully on the veranda near the door—surely, they'd be up, too, barking if anything as dangerous as a monster were trying to approach the camp. Then I realized that Yilyinika wasn't there. I opened the door. The barking stopped, and Yilyinika came running up the driveway—she'd been barking at the huge full moon! Polly wasn't sure whether to be amused or outraged to have been scared so by a pup.

I wish Wanguwangu was still alive and could teach Yilyinika. Wanguwangu was one of the smartest dogs I know, he was an old campaigner already by the time I met him, a long time ago, in one of Yuendumu's women's camps that I lived in. He was a proud dog, his body leather-skinned and crisscrossed by scars attesting to his fighting prowess. I wonder what he would say to Yilyinika, if they could have met, if they could have spoken. I imagine him growling out his story something like this.

Wanguwangu

My name is Wanguwangu, it means "without-without" or "bereft." I'm Wangu-wangu because the Yapa I had special bonds with passed away. The first one, Old Man, brought me up from when I was a pup. We shared our smell and our time and space and care; he threw me food, and I slept on his feet. I chased monsters away from him, and I lived with him and his Yapa mob and my dog pack for many years. I was happy. Then, he got sick, and he didn't get better, and then, he died, poor thing. It was terrible. Human pack was wailing. I was wailing. I felt like my whole world was broken into tiny pieces, and I couldn't find the main smell that held everything together. I wailed and wailed and wailed. I stopped eating. I just lay there, too sad to live. Old Man's daughter felt sorry for me, and she started feeding me by hand. Normally Yapa throw food over their shoulders for us when they eat, but she kneeled down next to me, fed me water and fed me meat, and I started following her. When I felt better, she put my nose in her armpit and her smell became my smell, and I was happy again. One day, she died, in the middle of the night, just like that, under her blankets. Everyone was asleep but I knew, I ran away and hid under a bush, wailing. I felt I could never bear that pain again and thought about joining the others out in the bush, those who had become Wanguwangu and could not face life with a human pack anymore. Losing your human is hard. So some dogs leave Yuendumu when their humans die and live wild. I nearly joined them, but then my pack and my Yapa mob made me re-join the camp. I am the best at detecting and chasing monsters. I came back, and now I get tidbits from all Yapa who live in my camp, and I bark the deepest when we chase monsters and the pack follows me.

I learned about jarnpa when I was maybe your age. All I used to do then was play with my siblings and cousins. All day long we were chasing each other and running around in little crews discovering the world around us. That was my life: my age-mates, the rest of the camp snoozing in the shade under the tree or curling up on the blankets next to the fire at night, frolicking in the afternoon rains, eat-ing kangaroo and lizards and mice. Everything changed the day I saw Milpirri, my father, twitch his nose and then witnessed him make the angriest sound I had ever heard anyone make. Paying no attention to me, he turned and ran, fast like a flash, into the bush. As he did, he barked at the others, and they sprinted after him. I was curious, so I left my siblings behind and followed as well. I raced behind Milpirri and the others, out of the camp and into the bush and then into a little grove of Mulga trees and there it hit me! The foulest stench I ever smelled. Pungently evil, obnoxious, vile! I would never have believed there could be something this terrible-smelling in the world. It reeked of hate, of brutality, of ripping and tearing asunder. That scent was such a shock, I almost got sick, but it also made me wild. All I wanted to do, all I could do, was to chase that jarnpa whose scent Milpirri had picked up. Chase it away from here, from us, from the camp, from my mob. That was the first time I chased a monster, and I have never stopped. It's like my calling. I'm always probing the breeze for that odor. Always.

Those monsters are one of the main reasons we live with Yapa. You see, there are two kinds of humans here at Yuendumu, Yapa and Kardiya (non-indigenous people). We know Yapa best, how they smell, how they move their bodies, and how they sound. Kardiya are different, they smell really different, at first you'll think they don't smell like humans at all, they cover their human scent with soap and perfume and deodorant, they don't smell like smoke from the cooking fires or sweat from hunting. They often come in shiny big cars. And they talk different. They don't speak Warlpiri, they speak English. And then there are jarnpa. They look like Yapa (which is why Kardiya sometimes mistake them for Yapa). But they do not smell human at all. No, they don't cover over their scent, it just isn't human, it's evil, they smell like cannibals. We hate them, we chase them, we keep them away from our Yapa. They are monsters, who come here looking for prey, they hunt Yapa. They are tricky monsters at that, they make themselves invisible so Yapa can't see them. Chasing them is pack work; we can't chase them on our own, they are unbelievably strong, and they are fast, some are as fast as a bullet and they try and trick us, they circle back and try and get us from behind. Sometimes Yapa see the tracks a monster left around the camp and they get really frightened. We can hear and smell those monsters from a long way, so we try and chase them away before they come too near to the camp. Sometimes Yapa realize we are chasing monsters, and then we get extra food.

Alas, Wanguwangu passed away many years ago and so it is the Three Brothers who Yilyinika will learn from. And I will learn from watching them. Anthropologists should really start counting dogs as informants, paying attention to them and their relationships to their humans is so very instructive. Take Eddie's Dog, for example.

Eddie's Dog

Eddie's Dog (which was one of her names) was one of the most independent dogs I have ever met. A brown sausage dog with big "kangaroo ears," one always alertly standing up, the other daintily half-flopped, she was truly "boss for herself," as Yapa say. Striving to be boss for oneself (all the while relating to others) is one of the core attributes of Yapa life, and as is true everywhere, Yapa and their dogs mirror some of their most crucial ways of being for each other.

Just like each Yapa decides for themselves what to do, when, how, and with whom, so each member of the pack in the camp follows its own nose—which shade to lie in, whether to join in a chase, who to sleep next to, who to play with. Each dog makes their own choices, and Yapa do not ever tell them what to do. (OK, Yapa might growl at dogs when they fight or kick them at night when they take up too much room on their blankets, but that's all, really. They don't use touch or words to change the dogs or their behavior; they don't teach their dogs to "sit," "lie down," "drop," or any other command.) While most dogs are happy to execute their freedom within the territory of the camp, Eddie's Dog wanted more from life, and she let no opportunity for excitement go past (nor did anyone ever attempt to stop her).

Originally, Eddie's Dog lived at Polly's camp as Polly's dog (Polly named her Brownie), and she was part of that camp's pack. Genuinely sociable and with a keen interest in others—other dogs, other people, as well as other places—Eddie's Dog traveled everywhere she could. She would jump in my car, following my dog Kunyarrpa (those two were besties) and come on drives with me and the Yapa I was taking: to other communities, hunting, to the shop, or for an evening walk. She was that keen on travel that she once jumped onto the Bush Bus (a bus service between remote communities and the town of Alice Springs, which is 180 miles southeast of Yuendumu). She made it all the way to Alice Springs and lived in a couple of different town camps with different strands of Polly's family before returning to Yuendumu.

However, in all her being-boss-for-herself-ness she never became a loner or a drifter; quite to the contrary, the complementary act of being boss for oneself—that is, relating to others—was just as important to her. And so, quite in the fashion of Yapa themselves, she would live with family—in all her travels she made her home with relatives of Polly's, stayed with them full-heartedly while she stayed with them, so much so that different relatives of Polly's claimed Eddie's Dog and gave her not only food and a place on their blankets but also new names. At some point, she and Eddie (Polly's great-grandson) were thick as thieves. Someone jokingly referred to her as "Eddie's dog" to tease Polly, who'd rebuff "that's not Eddie's dog, that my dog" and as the joke was repeated we'd all chorus "Eddie's Dog is Polly's dog"—which is how that particular name stuck.

In each of the camps that Eddie's Dog lived in, she made other canine friends. Yapa marvel at her adventurousness and her extensive social connectedness, and stories about Eddie's Dog are often told around the fires. As Eddie's Dog was Kunyarrpa's buddy, the conversation regularly flows on to him, and it makes me glad to see the fondness with which Yapa recall him.

Kunyarrpa

There are some Kunyarrpa stories shared by all (how he would howl like a dingo if you lifted your head and cried, how he always sat next to me in my car, how he fought with Anton's dog Trash), and then lots of Yapa, including the children, have their own personal Kunyarrpa stories. While I know them all, witnessed the events that they are based on, some of the Kunyarrpa stories I find most momentous are not the ones Yapa would tell. It slowly dawned on me when I first got him that I hadn't just acquired a new dog, what I had was a cute, sharped-toothed, bumbly but highly energetic research assistant. Warlpiri people insist on learning by doing in their social- ization of their children, their dogs, and their anthropologists. Bringing up a puppy in the camps of Yuendumu taught me new things, taught me how to look at things I thought I knew from new angles, and it added another affec- tive dimension to my research.

The first (emotionally profound) lesson was about cultural relativity: Ku- nyarrpa taught me that it is easy to intellectualize the cruelling of puppies by Yapa toddlers but much harder for me to tolerate when it happens to *my* puppy! The second was inverse, and also about cruelty: Young Kunyarrpa had pooped on my swag, again, and this time I caught him at it. I didn't quite rub his nose in it but held it close to, and I may have raised my voice at him before I threw him outside. "Napurrurla!" everybody yelled at me, "stop cruelling your dog!" What different views on cruelty, what different views on puppy socialization!

The next lesson came when I tried to teach him his name so that he would come when I called him. I asked Nathania for help. We sat fifteen feet or so apart with Kunyarrpa in the middle and alternated in calling him by his name; when he came to one of us we'd feed him a treat. "What *are* you doing?" Polly asked me and shook her head. This made me look more closely at the other dogs. They all had names, I had even recorded them. What I had not recorded was that nobody used a dog's name to call that dog. I had not recorded this because I had not noticed. I had *assumed* that names are there to be used the way I expected them to be. Polly's consternation helped me see that dog names are used to talk *about* the dogs, and sometimes, in greeting or to alert a dog that it is spoken about, and now and then, a senior person sings their name and songlines to their dogs in the evenings.

A friend offered Kunyarrpa and me a lift from Yuendumu to the annual anthropology conference in Adelaide (a good thousand miles to the south). Thinking about pit stops along the highway I thought I better teach Kunyarrpa how to walk on a lead to prevent him from running into traffic. I bought a collar and a leash. He got used to the collar eventually, but when I clipped on the leash a few days later he utterly refused to even move, let alone walk, while it was on. I tried treats, I tried pulling, I pleaded, all to no avail. Helene, who had been observing us, said: "Napurrurla, he doesn't want to!"

What may appear as a statement of fact (clearly, he did not want to walk while on a leash) was so much more, just like Polly's question "What are you doing?" when I tried to teach him to come when called. Baffled, and ever so mildly, they were raising some fundamental questions: What was I doing to the dog? How was I treating him? What was our relationship? Who did I think I was in relation to the puppy? Who was I to force a dog to do something it did not want to do? As Yapa saw it, I was trying to "be boss for" Kunyarrpa, attempting to make him do things he clearly did not want to do, and thus robbing him of his capacity to be boss for himself. Yapa frown on being bossed by others as much as on bossing others. Bossing, I began to understand, is bad when done toward dogs as well. More importantly, by implication, I realized that Warlpiri dogs are credited with autonomy much in the same way that persons are.

As Kunyarrpa grew from a little pup into a young dog, he began to develop a personality with his own character traits and quirks. As he came into his own (I notice now, in retrospect) his name changed, he became Kunyap: highly intelligent, deeply loyal, and just as attached to me as I was to him. He also became more than a "canine research assistant," developing into something of an anthropologist himself. Kunyap, it turned out, was most aware of and keenly interested in difference. First, difference between humans: He was highly alert to the fact that I treated him differently to the way the other dogs in the camp were treated as well as to from whom he could (and as importantly: could not) demand such different treatment: I offered pats, for example, and treats and he could insist on his prime seat in my car. Simultaneously, he endeavored to blend into the pack, making light of his different status. All this served him well when I had to move back to the city. I will never forget our first few visits to Fremantle Dog Beach, how Kunyap received praise from all sorts of dog owners: for being gentle with small dogs usually afraid of larger ones, for playing rough with dogs who loved to play rough, for chasing a whippet who was bored with not having been chased . . . while at the same time I could see him look at me quizzically, every so often, as he was trying to puzzle out the ways in which Dog Beach dogs communicated: so very differently from Yuendumu camp dogs! These dogs were much more keyed into their humans than camp dogs, and some were positively inept at dog communication. He made friends and settled in (he acquired a new nickname: Shmunyap), but it was only on the drive back to Yuendumu a year later that I realized how very much he had missed home. After a couple of days on the road, as the colors of the landscape changed to red desert-y tones, as the sounds and smells must have become more familiar, he began to attentively watch the road through the windscreen. As we took the turnoff to Yuendumu, his tail was wagging wildly and when we reached the camp, after a quick and excited "hello" to Yapa and dogs alike, he sighed happily and lay down in the sun for a snooze, contented.

Some years later, he came to Sydney with me (where he became K-Dog, where he walked headfirst into a pillar as his eyes followed a poodle dressed in a rain jacket and gum boots, and where his dog walker used him to train puppies as he was the most dog-socialized dog she knew). We dipped back to Yuendumu as often as possible, where he slipped back into his Kunyap self with ease and joy.

If I had to boil down our ten-year relationship into one key moment, it is this: Kunyap was still young, maybe a year or so old, and as I was demanding something of him (I don't remember what), he looked at me with utter trust and offered total submission. Somehow, we both knew that this moment was not about the here and now but about our relationship henceforth: If I accepted what he offered, I would have had the best-behaved dog imaginable but I would also have to carry the burden of having "broken" something in him (his will? his autonomy?), even if he offered it willingly. Taking seriously what Yapa tried to teach me, I chose not to accept by not insisting on whatever it was I had demanded of him—and we both knew that we had formed a type of contract. This moment cemented our relationship as one of mutual care and respect, rather than one of hierarchy; from that moment on, he would listen to me only if he felt like it (which was most of the time).

The poignant potency this moment had for our relationship, writing about it and the other dog tales I have told here, make me realize the significance of the dog tales Yapa tell: No matter whether myth, fable, folktale, "the word," or just-so dog story—all contain kernels of truth. Truth about us, about us trying to understand them, about them, about them trying to understand us, and about how to live good lives together.

Suggested Readings

On dogs as companion species, see:

Donna Haraway. 2003. *The Companion Species Manifesto: Dogs, People, and Significant Otherness*. Chicago: Prickly Paradigm Press.

Lynette Hart. 1995. "Dogs as Human Companions: A Review of the Relationship." In *The Domestic Dog: Its Evolution, Behaviour, and Interactions with People*, edited by J. A. Serpell, 161–78. Cambridge: Cambridge University Press.

On dogs in Aboriginal Australia, see:

Deborah Bird Rose. 2011. *Wild Dog Dreaming: Love and Extinction*. Charlottesville: University of Virginia Press.

Betty Meehan, Rhys Jones, and Annie Vincent. 1999. "Gulu-kula: Dogs in Anbarra Society, Arnhem Land." *Aboriginal History* 23: 83–106.

On autonomy and relatedness in Aboriginal Australia, see:

Fred Myers. 1986. *Pintupi Country, Pintupi Self*. Berkeley: University of California Press.

On monsters (and dogs) at Yuendumu, see:

Yasmine Musharbash. 2014. "Monstrous Transformations: A Case Study from Central Australia." In *Monster Anthropology in Australasia and Beyond*, edited by Y. Musharbash and G.-H. Presterudstuen, 39–55. New York: Palgrave Macmillan.

Meryn J. Meggitt. 1955. "Djanba among the Walbiri, Central Australia." *Anthropos* 50: 375–403.

On Yapa at Yuendumu, see:

Yasmine Musharbash. 2009. *Yuendumu Everyday: Contemporary Life in Remote Aboriginal Australia*. Canberra: Aboriginal Studies Press.

 CHAPTER 2

How to Build Rapport with Cats and Humans

Alex Nading

Routines

January 2008. I had been doing fieldwork in Ciudad Sandino, a community on the outskirts of Managua, Nicaragua, for two months. I was doing research on local strategies for dengue fever prevention. Dengue is a mosquito-borne disease, so I was interested in how people in the local public health sector worked to control mosquito propagation by applying insecticides, eliminating standing water, and enacting sanitation policies. So far, I had managed to establish connections with the local branch of the health ministry as well as the local government.

Doing this kind of research can be interchangeably boring, frustrating, and lonely. My strategy for fieldwork was to *stay on task*. I was militant about my routine:

1. Up early in the morning, breakfast
2. Out by 8:00 a.m. to visit either the health center or the city offices; either observe or do interviews with key figures.
3. Lunch at 12:00 p.m.
4. Spend the early afternoon making sure that either the health center or city could accommodate me the next day

5. Spend the later part of the afternoon writing field notes by hand
6. Dinner at 6:00 p.m.
7. "Down time" (reading novels, sending emails) from 7:00–9:00 p.m.

I repeated this pattern every weekday for two months. This made weekends somewhat difficult. By January, my supply of novels was running low.

As long as you stay busy, I kept telling myself, *time will fly by!* When I went to the field, I left not only my human partner but also our pet cat. My partner was doing fieldwork in India, and our cat had been passed off to some friends. The busier I was, I reasoned, the less I would miss them.

So I kept myself busy—and detached.

I was renting a room in the house of Doña Maria. I had met Doña Maria on a previous fieldwork trip. The head of a local NGO, Doña Maria had not only given me a place to sleep but also introduced me to leaders in the city government and the health ministry. Doña Maria was a devout evangelical Christian. On most nights of the week, she converted the front of the house into the sanctuary for a fledgling congregation, led by a charismatic woman preacher whom everyone called "the Pastora."

The Pastora had a reputation for prophetic insight. Doña Maria had become convinced of her powers a few years before, when the Pastora had (correctly) predicted that Doña Maria's oldest daughter would soon become pregnant. The Pastora was also something of a social crusader. The core of her ministry was what she called "the restoration of the family," a process that involved the eradication of alcohol, an end to extramarital sex, and harsh condemnations of homosexuality.

The church had only a few members, but at least three nights a week, the Pastora had them all speaking in tongues, singing songs, and confessing sins at a volume all out of proportion to their size. Doña Maria and the Pastora repeatedly invited me to participate, but I stayed out of it. I am not a religious person. I did not agree with many of the Pastora's teachings, particularly her condemnation of homosexuality, and I often found her "prophecy" to be the result of high-percentage guessing. Of course, this kind of disagreement doesn't stop other anthropologists from going to church when it might be good for fieldwork. But participating in religious services was not part of my research plan. Resolved to *stay on task,* I kept to my room at the back of the house.

I was not totally alone there. While the adults sang and prayed, I often found myself in the company of Doña Maria's younger children, nieces, and nephews. The animals also kept to the back of the house. The family had a dog called Simba, who spent most of the day chained to a post. One of the nieces, Adeliza, a girl of about ten, was a budding naturalist. She trapped insects, kept rabbits, and even had a soft spot for the mice that regularly laid siege to the household rice supplies. Adeliza had a remarkable ability to continue loving animals despite their frequent deaths. Her mice were beheaded by traps (or by Simba, when he got loose). Rabbits, even when they could be protected from dogs, were taken by birds of prey. When Adeliza cried in mourning for the dead animals, the other children ridiculed her for being sentimental. But she was persistent.

It was Adeliza who found the cats. One morning on her way to school, she caught a group of boys slinging rocks at a litter of six or eight kittens who had been discarded in a storm sewer by the owner of a chronically pregnant female cat on the block. This was a typical strategy for dealing with unwanted animals in urban Nicaragua. Adeliza managed to rescue two of the surviving kittens, cradling them in an old shoebox.

Carefully peeling off the lid, she asked me if I would help take care of them. I thought of my cat back home. I looked at the kittens, two multicolored balls with blue eyes and greasy hair, both about the size of my hand.

I caved. While I harbored a silent disapproval of the Pastora's social conservatism and prophecy, I found myself sympathizing with Adeliza's love for animals. Perhaps this was because both Adeliza and I were misfits of a kind—she the hypersensitive nature lover, I the hypersensitive and introverted ethnographer. I cleaned out a second shoebox and lined it with an old T-shirt. In went one of the kittens, its nose covered in dried blood (the result of a direct hit from one of the boys).

In her writing on scientific knowledge, the philosopher Donna Haraway often uses the childhood game of cat's cradle as a metaphor. In cat's cradle, two players create geometric figures with strings attached to their fingers. The fun of the game is the entanglement. The string figures inevitably become messy, unwieldy, and uncomfortable, but the two players also become physically and emotionally attached.

When Adeliza brought home the kittens in the shoebox, I wasn't thinking about Donna Haraway. In fact, this was the first moment since I arrived in which I wasn't thinking at all about theory or data or *staying on task*. And so I was about to learn that to do fieldwork is to enter into a game of cat's cradle—to invite discomfort so as to breed attachment. Instead of string, anthropologists and their interlocutors exchange things, ideas, and values. They might also, it seems, share in the responsibility of caring for animals.

Identities

There's a difference, of course, between taking on responsibility for an animal and bonding with that animal. The annals of anthropology are full of tales of fieldworkers becoming caregivers to cattle, pigs, birds, and horses. Knowing this, my initial strategy for dealing with the kitten was to keep our relationship functional.

This is Adeliza's pet. I am just helping.

This is what I was thinking to myself as Adeliza's mother, Trudi, taught me how to prepare powdered milk. What a month-old kitten needed, naturally, was a bottle with a nipple. Before heading off to the health center, during lunch, and after writing up my field notes, I obliged.

This is not bonding, just feeding. Another sort of "down time." Devoting a few minutes a day to bottle feeding, after all, might help extend the life of my dwindling novel collection.

This is what I was thinking to myself when Adeliza's kitten died, about three weeks into our experiment. While Trudi consoled Adeliza, I went to my computer to Google any literature I could find on the effects of Nestle's Nido infant milk powder on feline development. After an hour or so, I returned to my field notes, but not before stealing a bit of gummy rice and leftover chicken skin, grinding it up into a gruel, bringing it to my room, and placing it in front of the surviving kitten, who, I had concluded, needed to learn to eat solid foods.

Two nights later, the kitten jumped out of its cradle and settled in to sleep between my legs. I stayed awake all night, fearful that any false move would crush it.

Keep it alive. Adeliza will thank you. Get it to the point where it can fend for itself, and then turn it over. There is research to be done.

This is what I was thinking as I bathed the kitten in the bathroom sink for the first time. I had read that baby shampoo was safe for kittens and that it would help keep fleas away. I had seen Doña Maria and Trudi bathe Simba the dog, but as far as I could tell, no one in the household had ever heard of a human bathing a cat. After all, cats were supposed to bathe themselves. But I didn't want fleas in my bed.

By the end of January, the kitten was developing a bit of a personality. Not only was it sleeping with me, it was starting to follow me around the house. It seemed to enjoy pouncing on my legs and arms, as if to get my attention.

"What are you going to call it?" Adeliza asked me as it leapt into my lap.

"Well, I think you should decide," I answered, reminding her that *she* had found it. Adeliza demurred. After all, she told me, we didn't even know if it was a boy or a girl. The name we chose had to be appropriate. If it was a girl, we could call it something like "Princesa," but if it was a boy, we might go with something like "Felix."

I did my best to determine the sex through a visual inspection, but I was at a loss. I had no idea what immature cat genitalia looked like. I decided to look for an expert. Later that week, I packed the kitten into its shoebox cradle and marched it to the man who sold dog food and chicken pellets a few blocks away.

"*Macho,*" he concluded after a three-second inspection of the relevant anatomy. The cat was male. This, he assured me, was a good thing. Male cats were more avid hunters, and they had the added advantage of not getting pregnant.

I relayed this information to Adeliza, who seemed slightly disappointed, either at the prospect of not having more kittens or of not having a female companion animal. By this time, another week had passed, and her devotion to this particular animal rescue project seemed to be waning.

"Really, you should name him," she said, running outside to play with her cousin and younger sister.

As the kitten began showing signs of longevity, more and more people around the house began asking me—not Adeliza—to name it.

"Floyd," I finally declared.

The name seemed suitably whimsical.

The less thought I put into naming this cat, the less ownership I will feel. After all, this is not my pet.

This is what I was thinking, but the name followed me. I began telling people I was interviewing at the health center and in the city offices about Floyd. I had spent three months in the field dreading the kinds of personal questions that Nicaraguans love to ask: about my love life, about my family, about money, or about whether I had accepted Jesus Christ as my Lord and Savior. I was avoiding taking on too much of an identity. Now I found myself identifying who I was through Floyd. Even though most people I talked to would never meet the cat face to face, Floyd was something about myself that I was happy to pitch into their worlds. They seemed to find my stories about nursing Floyd through his first few weeks in our house entertaining.

"You mean you *bathe* him?" (*chuckling*)

"And you let him *sleep* with you?" (*incredulous, gently mocking*)

"Next thing you know you'll be wanting to take him home with you to the States!" (*bursting with laughter*)

Even as I recognized their questions as a form of teasing, I also began to realize how offensive my initial reticence to discuss my personal life must have seemed. Talking about Floyd's vulnerability made my vulnerability easier to share. Talk of Floyd led to talk about my family and my love life, even if I still kept Jesus at arm's length.

Openings

"Do you give him food?" asked one of the nurses in the Office of Epidemiology, in part of what had become a daily mini-interview about the kitten.

"Of course we do," I said. ("We" was not entirely accurate. Floyd still slept, ate, peed, and shat exclusively in my room.)

"Oh," she said forebodingly. "You have to stop feeding it, or it won't hunt!"

Maria, Trudi, and even Adeliza took the same position. I quietly disagreed, and I continued to spirit table scraps to Floyd each night. Besides, the only thing he seemed interested in hunting was my leg. From the earliest age, he was a biter.

Floyd is not my pet, I repeated to myself. He might eat and sleep with me, but like Simba the dog, he belonged to the whole household. I encouraged Floyd to explore. By late February, he was lounging in the sun of the patio, stealing his own scraps of food, and sometimes even napping in the laps of the children as they watched afternoon cartoons.

He also continued to bite. A lot.

If you've never been bitten by a kitten, imagine being pierced by a serviceable but slightly dull hypodermic needle. It hurts even more that you think it should. As he grew, Floyd began to stalk not just my legs but those of others. Sitting in my room in the evening, I would hear shrieks and cries as he burst from behind corners to assault the calves, feet, and ankles of unsuspecting passersby. He even tested his skills on the Pastora as she prepared for nightly services.

People were more accommodating than they probably should have been about this. I began placating Floyd's victims as they wiped their bloody ankles, predicting with confidence that his aggression was a sign that he was destined to be a great hunter.

This juvenile biting drew me into adult relationships within the household that I had been avoiding. Finding that Floyd tended to focus his aggression on *my* arms and legs if I stayed out in the front part of the house, I began spending more time there in the hour or so before the Pastora began her church service. Facts and anecdotes about people whom I had thus far kept at arm's length started to leak out in casual conversations, punctuated by Floyd's antics. I learned about the Pastora's years as an apprentice to a charismatic preacher in Miami, Florida, about Trudi's husband's ongoing efforts to quit drinking, and about a string of parishioners' struggles to overcome abuse, economic hardship, and abandonment. With Floyd as a distraction, I learned how to be both "outside" and "inside" the little congregation. Because of Floyd, my "down time" in the field—the time I had reserved for emails and novels—became social time. Because of Floyd, I learned that fieldwork doesn't stop.

By March, Floyd was venturing outside. Our street was mostly quiet, and even as a relatively clueless kitten, Floyd had no problem wandering underneath the gates of our neighbors' houses. Sometimes he would be shooed away (especially if he greeted a neighbor, as he often did, with his little needle teeth). Other times, I would return home to see him being passed around by groups of children. I should probably say at this point that Floyd was ridiculously cute. The spot on his nose where the boys had hit him with a rock had healed in such a way that it retained a Rudolph-like red mark. And Floyd's sociability must have been a novelty. Most cats in urban Nicaragua live nearly their entire lives on rooftops. At night, you can hear their claws clinking on the metal overhead. They might come down at night to hunt, but they sleep, eat, fight, and mate in this elevated world. They kill mice, which is convenient, but they also mostly stay out of sight. In Nicaragua, human-cat relationships are symbiotic, rather than companionate.

Unusually for any cat—Nicaraguan or otherwise—Floyd seemed to like being held and stroked. Perhaps this is because I had started grooming him with a damp cloth. I had read online that cats who are abandoned before weaning from their mothers need to be taught how to groom themselves. Had Floyd not been abandoned, he likely would have already learned to take to the rooftops with his own kind and to groom himself rather than to seek out human hands.

Whenever the neighborhood children saw the *gringo* marching up the street, or whenever a parent had had enough of the distraction, Floyd was always passed back to me. I took to setting up a plastic chair in front of the house after dinner while Floyd took his stroll. If he went too far or bit the wrong person, I would lock him up in my room. By showing a willingness to be *that* gringo—the one with the weird affection for animals—I was able to cultivate my own identity within the neighborhood.

Then it happened.

Still concerned about the state of my supply of novels, I was seated in my chair flipping through an old *New Yorker* magazine, half-listening as the Pastora harangued me about the scourge of alcoholism in the community. Floyd was sniffing through the weeds in front of the house opposite ours. Then, as he had done at most of the other neighbors' houses, he started to crawl under the gate. This would be new territory for him—he had never gone in this direction before. If I wasn't careful, he would find a fresh set of ankles to attack. Wishing to avoid a confrontation with these neighbors, I crossed over to retrieve him.

When I got to the gate, I found Floyd sitting within inches of the snarling face of Killer, the neighbor's Doberman/pit bull/Rottweiler mix. Killer had in common with Floyd an Anglophone name and a reputation for biting. Otherwise, they were diametric opposites. Killer was the size of a miniature horse. Floyd's head was about the size of one of the dog's testicles, which hung astonishingly low between his hind legs. Killer, like Simba and most of the other dogs in our neighborhood, was an alarm system and bodyguard rolled up into one. And it was obvious that Killer did not like cats.

Floyd, however, did not pick up on Killer's signals. Accustomed to shadow-boxing with me in the parlor of Doña Maria's house and to wrestling with the neighborhood children, he was standing up on his hind legs while slashing blindly with his front claws. This was not a defensive posture. Floyd was trying to play with Killer, who was stretching his chain to its limits.

Then Floyd stepped an inch closer.

Then I blinked.

Then Killer had Floyd's head inside his jaws, thrashing left and right as he had been bred to do. I remember the sound of shrieking and screaming—both Floyd's and mine. I remember seeing the woman and the teenage boy who lived in the house pound Killer with their fists and feet, and when that didn't stop him, with sticks. After a few seconds, Killer let Floyd go, leaving a twitching mass of fur in the dirt, covered in saliva and blood.

The muscles in my chest spasmed as I scooped Floyd up and rushed him back to our house. Everyone had heard the confrontation and had gathered out front. I remember screaming for someone to bring me a hose. In my shock, I wanted to clean the cat. As I did so, I sat in the plastic chair while the Pastora began reciting prayers over Floyd's body, which was seizing violently. Despite the progress I had made in being tolerant of the praying and prophecy, I begged her to stop, to give Floyd and me some room.

Finally Floyd settled in my lap and started to wheeze. Air was coming in and out of a hole in the side of his neck, where Killer's teeth—more like drill bits than hypodermic needles—had pierced him. I was wheezing as well, crying and convulsing. I had lost pets before, though never violently, and I had lost friends and relatives, but this was something different.

It was in this moment that I realized that I had become attached—to Floyd, obviously, but also to my neighbors, to Doña Maria, and even to the Pastora. Throughout this entire scene—probably no more than five minutes from attack to the quiet wheezing—I spoke and acted and even sobbed in Spanish. I whispered apologies to Floyd during what I was sure were his final few minutes.

But he didn't stop wheezing. Air continued to flow in and out of the hole in his neck. Doña Maria ordered her oldest son, Mauricio, to pull the family jeep out of its spot in the patio and clear off the back seat. They were preparing to take us to a veterinarian.

This was a Saturday night. In our neighborhood, some twenty minutes outside Managua, there was no one who would be able to help us. Doña Maria knew of someone closer to the capital.

Doña Maria, Mauricio, Floyd, and I set off as the sun set, coursing through the maze of Managua's streets: a web of four-lane arteries punctuated by a series of grand roundabouts. At this time of day, traffic was light. Just to the west of the California-style shopping mall called Metrocentro, he plunged the jeep into a capillary maze of side streets.

Mauricio, who was about seventeen years old, loved to drive. He loved driving fast even more, laying on the horn as he passed cars on the four-lane roads and giving it staccato blasts to clear the side streets of pedestrians (and dogs). Mauricio was having fun, but this excursion was for my benefit. If it weren't for me, Floyd would have been left to die like one of Adeliza's other pets: the mice, rabbits, and birds who lay in unmarked graves across the patio.

After a few wrong turns, we had still not arrived, so Mauricio began stopping people on the street to ask directions. An old man finally said that he knew the veterinarian we were looking for. He leaned into the door, slightly drunk, and gave us directions in the fashion that is typical of Managuans: "One, maybe two blocks *up*, then maybe half a block *toward the lake*. Look for the Purina sign." In Managua, "up" (*arriba*) means west, toward the mountains. The lake (Lake Managua) is on the north side of town. Directions in the city always sounded vague. To me, with Floyd's breath growing shallower, they sounded downright meaningless.

Nevertheless, there it was: a lighted sign, a flickering red, black, and white checkerboard. Mauricio gave two final blasts of the horn and yanked on the emergency brake handle.

When we got inside, I laid Floyd out on a table, making sure to keep the hole in his neck facing up. A young man wearing sandals and a Chicago Bulls jersey began turning on fluorescent lights and assembling gauze and rubbing alcohol. Then the veterinarian walked in. He was older, and his right arm was in a sling. His left arm twitched slightly. Without prompting, I gave him a short history: foundling kitten, male, three or four months old, attacked by

Killer the giant Doberbullweiler. The man said little as he motioned for his young assistant to steady Floyd's body. Managing briefly to stop his unslinged left hand from twitching, the veterinarian injected something into Floyd's hindquarters. Floyd's body quickly relaxed.

The vet has just euthanized him, I thought.

"It's not a male," the veterinarian said to no one in particular as he turned back and pulled a straight razor blade out of a metal drawer, wiping it with alcohol. "It's a female." He motioned with the blade in the direction of the area where he had stuck his needle. Floyd's breathing was actually deepening.

Maybe it was anesthesia, not euthanasia.

I laughed through my tears. Doña Maria put her arm around me as the veterinarian's assistant and Mauricio laughed as well. The veterinarian only smirked, as he again inhaled and stopped the twitching in his left hand, shaving the razor blade across the open airhole in Floyd's neck. When he finished, he gave Floyd another injection and asked the assistant to bring a bottle of pills.

Then he turned to me.

"200 *córdobas*," he said, as if I had just purchased a quart of milk and a pound of rice. The visit would cost about five dollars. My laughter faded away. I pointed back to the open hole.

Maybe this was euthanasia after all.

"Don't you need to close the hole?" I asked.

He looked back. "Not necessary," he explained. "The thing about cats is that they tend to heal themselves . . . or not." The pills might help. They were antibiotics. I'd have to crush them up to get them into Floyd at first.

"Will he . . . she . . . *live?*" I asked, trembling.

"Most likely," he said with a shrug. "She's going to sleep for a while first."

When we finally got back home, I placed Floyd into her box and stripped off my bloodstained T-shirt. Then I sat on the chair next to her as air blew in and out of the wound. Killer had somehow missed Floyd's jugular vein. I knew that the others in the house could hear me crying, but they left me alone.

From Pets to Mascots

By now it was late enough for the oppressive heat of late March to have subsided. I remember a cool breeze drifting in from the window as I made a silent promise. If she lived through this, as long as I was in Nicaragua, this companion whose companionship I had tried so hard to avoid, was not going to die.

I am neither the first nor the last anthropologist to adopt an animal in the field. I think of Floyd less as a pet, however, than as a mascot. In Spanish, the word for "pet" is *mascota*. In North American English, the animal avatars for sports teams, schools, and fire brigades are called by the cognate term, *mascot*. In North America, we think of pets as individual animals with special relationships to individual people. For us, pets become persons, even kinds of kin. Mascots are different from pets. We think of mascots as symbolic figures. Mascots bring our teams or schools together, it seems, by focusing our collective vision.

But what if the role of the mascot is not to focus our vision but to expand it?

The *Oxford English Dictionary* traces the word *mascot* to a word used in nineteenth-century southern French dialects, *masco*. According to the *OED*, *masco* means "witch." A witch is a figure who mediates between worlds, between life and death, self and other, male and female. Witches are powerful because they crack open the clean divisions we impose on ourselves. Mascots don't follow us along a preset path; they lead us on to new ones.

I started my fieldwork in Nicaragua devoted to a strict routine. With my carefully designed list of tasks, I had no trouble maintaining focus. What I learned from Floyd is that what we need in the field aren't tools for focusing our vision but tools for expanding it. We need a bit of emotional and epistemic witchcraft.

When Killer attacked Floyd, all the defenses I had put in place to stave off emotional and social entanglement came crashing down. The night of the attack, I called my partner in India and sobbed. I called my mother, who tells me to this day that she has never been more worried about me.

In my case, it took an extreme experience with an animal to learn a basic lesson about how to build what anthropologists sometimes call "rapport" or "complicity" with the people we meet in the field. What I learned from Floyd was to allow myself to get angry, to laugh, and to be sad in front of those people. Floyd taught me that fragility is the foundation for good relationships, in the field and beyond. Eight years later, she still forces me to look away from the computer and to cast myself out into the world. She still tests the limits of my emotions and patience. She is sleeping just a few feet away from me as I write this, but I cannot relax. She still bites.

Just as I would never insist that all anthropologists adopt a field mascot, I would never advise anyone to begin fieldwork without a clear question, plan, or strategy. Focus and routine are valuable things. Neither, however, leads to the kind of enduring social entanglements that are essential to good fieldwork. To create those new entanglements, we have to admit that we come to the field already beside ourselves, already cracked open. There is no other way to make a cat's cradle.

Suggested Readings

On engagement and detachment in human-animal relations, see:

Matei Candea. 2010. "I Fell in Love with Carlos the Meerkat." *American Ethnologist* 37: 241–58.

On cat's cradle and entanglements, see:

Donna Haraway. 2008. *When Species Meet.* Minneapolis: University of Minnesota Press.

On rapport and complicity, see:

George Marcus. 2001. "From Rapport under Erasure to Theaters of Complicit Re-flexivity." *Qualitative Inquiry* 7: 519–28.

On dogs and aggression, see:

Carla Freccero. 2011. "Carnivorous Virility; or, Becoming-Dog." *Social Text* 29: 177–95.

CHAPTER 3

The Perils of Deference

*How Not to Habituate Spotted Hyenas
in an Ethiopian Town*

MARCUS BAYNES-ROCK

On cool October night in 2009, I was riding a
three-wheeled taxi through the dimly lit streets of Harar toward the edge
of town. I'd only arrived that morning but had already seen much of the
ancient city: the old mosques nestled in among the densely packed dwell-
ings, the curious turquoise-colored holy graves marked by giant fig trees, the
crowded markets overflowing with incense, spices, khat leaves, and litter, and
the quirky little museums with their mixed displays of antiquities and bric-a-
brac. In the eyes of the kids shouting "farenji" as I walked the narrow lanes,
I was just another of the hundreds of farenjis who visited Harar each year
to spend a few days in the historic town. Hararis were familiar with Western
tourists who walked through the town, like predators looking for photo opportunities, holding more wealth in their cameras than most of the population would see in a lifetime. Even riding toward the town wall that night,
there was little to differentiate me from a tourist. Without asking, the driver
guessed my evening's agenda. I was on my way to see the hyena-feeding, the
eerie, tourist-oriented spectacle at the edge of town. There, spotted hyenas
gathered nightly in front of a shrine waiting on a man who handed them
meat scraps while tourists gathered to watch. What the driver didn't know
was that I was intending to repeat the visit every night for a year.

Harar is not the sort of place where you would expect to find Africa's
second-largest carnivore. With a population of more than a hundred thousand

people in the greater urban area and no wild prey available, Harar seems an inhospitable landscape for a spotted hyena. But those many humans produce an awful lot of garbage, including a great many bones and animal offcuts that hyenas are well adapted to munching on. And a sufficiently hungry hyena can get over her fear of humans if there's a chance of a meal on the other side. As a result, Harar boasts one of the highest population densities of hyenas on the entire African continent—double that of Ngorongoro Crater, which is itself a veritable stadium of hyenas. In Harar there are at least three clans of hyenas with territories converging on the town and at least fifty hyenas in each clan. The town provides just the right conditions: an open, unattended garbage dump; open dumpsters scattered around the town, convenient for humans and hyenas alike; a human population with a predilection for meat and a habit of throwing the scraps in the street; and scattered refugia—rocky outcrops and densely vegetated gullies—where hyenas can raise cubs and hide out during the day. All of these in addition to the two feeding places where men dole out scraps for the bolder of the hyenas make Harar a land of plenty for a bone-crunching carnivore.

Even more important, the diverse human population of Harar is favorably inclined toward their local hyenas. This is unusual in Africa, and the rest of the world for that matter, as hyenas are normally regarded with a mixture of fear, derision, disgust, and loathing. But the people in Harar, regardless of ethnicity, gender, or religion, think that it's a good thing to have hyenas in the town. After all, hyenas attract cashed-up tourists from overseas; they clean the streets not only of garbage but also of harmful spirits; they pass on messages from deceased Sufis who oversee the affairs of the town; and they protect the towns-people from attacks by outsider-hyenas who might not be as peaceful as the local ones. But even if the locals don't value these services, they're still likely to declare support for the hyenas, if only because they fear that any ill feeling they express will be overheard by the ever-vigilant hyenas, who will seek them out in the dark of night and subject them to attacks. This bespeaks the uneasiness of the truce between the hyenas and the people in Harar. Neither the hyenas nor the humans trust the other completely; both parties understand that the other is lethal—elsewhere in Ethiopia, hyenas regularly prey on humans, and humans retaliate by killing hyenas—but in Harar they have a "you leave us alone and we'll leave you alone" kind of agreement. Certainly there are some, mostly children, who throw rocks at hyenas and act aggressively toward them, and the local dogs consistently give them a hard time, but there are others, who on encountering a hyena in a dark lane at night, make an about-face and find another way home. And then there are a few, including the caretakers of shrines, who emerge from behind their gates with skin, bones, or bits of entrails and toss them directly to the hyenas. This is taken to the next level on the tenth night of Muharram in the Islamic calendar, when people gather at various shrines around Harar and porridge is prepared and put out for hyenas. The porridge is important to these people, as it's a kind of comfort food associated with sharing and special occasions. The hyenas eat it, but they probably appreciate even more the head and offcuts from a ceremonially slaughtered ox that come afterward.

So why did I want to spend a year in Harar, visiting the hyena feeding place every night and watching the same hyena feeding spectacle? This is where anthropologists differ from tourists. Instead of taking a bunch of photos and moving on to the next attraction, we find a place to sit, make ourselves as comfortable as possible, and take a year's worth of field notes in the hope that someday our scribblings might reveal something astonishing about the human condition. Only in my case I was pushing at the boundaries of what constituted human sociality; I'd included hyenas as denizens of the town I'd chosen for my research. In which case I needed to find a way that the hyenas could be as informative as the human population, a way that would allow me to follow them at close quarters in the narrow lanes of Harar without them running away or making me run away. I needed to habituate the hyenas.

Habituation is an established practice among biologists, primatologists, and the like; they simply spend copious amounts of time in the presence of their animal subjects, ever so gradually reducing the distance from which their research subjects take flight. Eventually they arrive at a point where they can sit and take notes while the monkeys, meerkats, mule deer, or whatever are practically sitting on their shoulders. In fact, in the case of meerkats, the habituated ones do literally sit on the researchers' shoulders. On the African veld, vantage points are few, so biologists make for convenient observation posts from which meerkats can scan for predators. While I never imagined a hyena sitting on my shoulders, I did—somewhat naively, in hindsight—think that they might come to accept me as an innocuous part of the landscape and allow me to follow them around with my notebook.

My first attempts to follow hyenas were massive failures. The hyenas immediately sensed a stranger on their tails and either ran off or turned and stared at me with very threatening eyes and gleaming white teeth flashing between their dark lips. They quickly taught me that I'd need a lot more patience and persistence if I was ever going to be rewarded with insights into hyena life in Harar. So I resigned myself to a long process of habituation at the hyena feeding place. There the hyenas of the Sofi clan dutifully arrived on the setting of the sun, and there they spent their evenings. For the first couple of hours each night, I sat on the step in front of the shrine and watched

Yusuf the hyena man hand them scraps of food while the tourists came and went. Then as the night wore on and Yusuf retired to his home, I went out onto the hill where the hyenas lay down, waiting for the people of Harar to go to sleep so that the hyenas could go into the town. Even though the hyena feeding was finished for the night, there was always something going on. Hyenas often commuted between the hill and the nearby garbage dump, and new arrivals were sniffed for evidence of a big feed at whatever place from which they'd just come. And there was the social stuff: high-ranking hyenas encouraging others to sniff particular places; males teaming up to "bait" the larger, more aggressive females; juveniles chasing each other; and lots of heads up, listening to the sounds of hyenas doing other social stuff echoing across the town.

On these nightly visits I was very careful not to disturb any hyenas. Normally in Harar, a person finding a hyena lying down in their path walks directly toward the hyena, who dutifully gets up and moves away. But in my case, when I approached resting hyenas, I paid close attention to their body language and stopped in my tracks before they had a chance to get up and move. This was always perplexing for the hyenas, who were expecting to be displaced. They eyed me suspiciously while lowering their heads and trying to relax again. Initially this disturbed them. Hyenas like a predictable world; they like to know their place not only in the social hierarchy among their peers but also in the more-than-hyena world. So an unfamiliar human appearing on the scene who subverted their neat little worldview was like a glitch in the system, something that made it seem like there was something wrong with the world. My project, aimed at convincing the hyenas to trust me, was doing the very opposite.

But hyenas are also immensely curious creatures; the world for them is a fascinating place full of dangers, feeding opportunities, and social events. So that, combined with visual, auditory, and olfactory senses that border on the supernatural, makes for a fascination with what's going on in the world that outnoses the nosiest of neighbors. If a hyena whoops somewhere out in the darkness, ten hyena heads will pop up from the long grass and face in that direction, listening intently for the next piece of information. If a garbage truck can be heard on the road that encircles the Old Town, four hyenas get up and run toward the garbage dump. If a farenji arrives every night and hangs around for hour upon hour—and farenjis are normally associated with food—then a hyena must go and investigate. So inevitably, a hyena did investigate the strange farenji who was always around but never offered food. And that hyena's name was Willi.

At five months into my habituation project, a couple of young hyenas were already giving some indication that they trusted me a little more than the average human. These were Kamareya and Baby, both quite audacious but with markedly different personalities. While Kamareya was low-key and inconspicuous, Baby was demonstrative and always seemed to be doing something interesting. Kamareya was nonchalant and often passed by within a few feet of me, without hurrying or wedging his tail between his legs. His body language told me he didn't feel threatened, but he didn't entirely trust me either. As for Baby, she was curious about me but not so much that she was prepared to step into the protective space that hyenas traditionally keep between themselves and humans. That is only done in a feeding context, when the food and excitement lead hyenas practically to jump over each other to get at the meat scraps that the hyena man is offering up. And I made a point of never feeding hyenas; I wanted to follow them unobtrusively around Harar at night; I didn't want them lining up in front of me expecting a free meal.

Willi was a different kind of hyena. After only a few weeks coming to the feeding place, he quickly figured out the state of affairs there. Soon he was walking up and accepting food from the hyena man, showing in this way that he was among the bolder of the hyenas. But he also had a fascination with humans. He studied closely the arguments between the hyena man and the

FIGURE 3.1. Kamareya and Baby lying on the ground. Photo by Marcus Baynes-Rock.

tour guides who often tried to extort extra money for one reason or another. He went onto the road and followed people walking home in the evening. He appeared behind tourists to sniff their backsides, which unnerved not a few people. He also took an interest in me, sitting on the hill night after night with my notebook. So much so that one night he approached me and sniffed my knee. This was a foray into the forbidden for a hyena, but Willi didn't seem to think it a serious matter. I tried to keep still, but when he opened his mouth as if to take a bite of my bony kneecap, I was compelled to move my leg away. Willi, in his audacity, had turned the trust thing on its head, putting me in a position where I was expected to trust him. In that I failed, but he wasn't done with me. A few nights later he approached me again and tried biting my arm. I fended him off at first, without being aggressive, but after a while I let him bite the sleeve of my jacket while he let me ruffle the fur on his head.

This was a strange sort of habituation. Where I was trying to make myself inconspicuous to the hyenas, Willi was insisting otherwise. While he was certainly not disturbed by my constant presence and his flight distance from me was reduced to zero, I was the very opposite of an innocuous presence. Willi was determined to involve me in his world, as a person whom he trusted and with whom he could become acquainted. This in turn was noticed by Baby and Kamareya, who decided that if I wasn't doing any harm to Willi, I wouldn't be very likely to harm them either. So it wasn't long before all three were involving me in a game of chase play. This began with them running around me chasing each other, but it quickly transformed into a game of "bite the farenji." So while I could be satisfied that the hyenas weren't lining up in front of me expecting a free meal, I was a little nonplussed to find them lining up for a chance to bite my leg. On the one hand, this was unsettling because hyenas' bites are brutally powerful; they must be, so that they can tear the back ends off of wildebeest and chew through camels' thigh bones. Moreover, hyenas' skins are incredibly tough, far tougher than ours, so that when they play with each other, they can usually bite with great force without drawing blood. For this reason, introducing a human into a hyena game is asking for injury. On the other hand, I felt like I was making progress—only not the kind that I'd expected. I figured that if these hyenas were bold enough to try and bite me, then surely they trusted me to follow them around Harar at close quarters. So instead of being aggressive and chasing them off, I just kept deferring and pulling my arms and legs out of the way.

If there was such a thing as a handbook on habituation, it would need at least a chapter on deference with an exclamatory "If you read nothing else in this book, be sure to read this!" The remainder of the chapter would be a series of warnings about the consequences of deferring to animals.

Hyenas—at least those who live in large groups—are fanatical about social rank. In desert environments, which are sparsely populated with smaller group sizes, the hyenas are a bit laissez-faire about rank, although they still pay attention when a superior is bossing them around. But in a place like Harar, where hyenas live in groups as large and as densely populated as anywhere in Africa, the hyenas obsess over who outranks whom. This begins at an early age as cubs try out their social rank and learn by trial and error. Sometimes a cub will try to nudge an adult away from some food, and this will work if the cub is offspring to a higher-ranking hyena. But if the cub has gotten it wrong and the adult actually outranks his mother, then he can expect consequences. In such cases the body language from the dominant hyena is clear: Lift the head, growl, and bring down the head for a bite that would puncture a truck tire. What's more, any other hyenas present will be paying careful attention. Hyenas recognize third-party relationships, so they don't always need to be bitten to know if another hyena outranks them. They just need to see that hyena biting another hyena who has bitten them. This is a relatively painless way to determine one's place within a group of eighty or more hyenas. It requires a keen intellect, but it's far less injurious than a process of trial and error. So once a cub learns the rank of a few hyenas, he can work out the rest through observation, and once learned, the rank sticks.

Looking back on those first few nights habituating Willi, I should have paid more attention to this issue of ranking. A lot of people who keep large carnivores, including hyenas, strive to set themselves up as the "alpha" of the group. They use their knowledge of the animals' behaviors to establish for themselves the position of top dog and then use this to exert control over the animals, who sometimes grudgingly buy into the arrangement. This approach never sat well with me. I thought just because so many of us humans hold the power of life and death over so many animals, that doesn't give us the right to insert ourselves at the top of these animals' social hierarchies. So I never set out to establish dominance over any of the hyenas. Besides, my habituation plan was for the hyenas to allow me to come in close proximity, so I made an effort not to disturb them. To me it seemed a sensible way to go. To the hyenas, it seemed like something else altogether.

My first step in this direction was an encounter with Baby. I had finished with my observations at the feeding place, so I went into the hyena man's compound to say goodbye to him and the family. As I opened the gate I found Baby lying directly in my path. She had obviously entered into the compound through one of the many hyena-holes in the thorn hedge and made herself at home. When I appeared in the gateway, she made an effort to get up, but I stopped dead in my tracks. At this she looked a little confused, as she was accustomed to getting out of the way of people as they barged through without heed. In which case what I did next must have been baffling to her. I carefully edged my way around Baby in a wide arc so as to keep the same distance between her and me. She followed my movement and eyed me suspiciously as I went into the house but otherwise remained where she was. In hindsight I can see that I'd effectively shown Baby that I'd do my utmost to stay out of her way. I had deferred to her.

I did the same sorts of things with Kamareya, who quickly learned that I was not a threat, and then when Willi came along I was deferring left, right, and center. Every time he went to bite me I simply pulled my hand out of the way. But the absence of repercussions only encouraged him. Before long he found it acceptable to bite me at his leisure. One night while I was sitting on the hill watching the feeding from a distance, Willi strolled by and laid a casual but forceful bite into my shoulder. I called out "Hey!" and ran after him, whereupon I smacked him on the rump. For a hyena that was a pretty lame sort of payback for a bite. It didn't deter Willi at all.

Meanwhile the rest of the hyenas had been paying close attention to the relationship that developed between Willi and me. Most of them took it to mean that I wasn't a threat and learned to accept my presence. Thankfully the very powerful and aggressive Dibbey never engaged in the kind of biting that Willi did, but she soon showed no fear of me and either walked right by me or lay down very close. The same with the high-ranking Koti, who allowed me to approach within inches to take close-up photos. But Kamareya took it further. He definitely saw me as non-threatening, so it was no great leap of faith to have me follow him around Harar's streets at night. But I soon realized that Kamareya saw me in a different light to other humans. Certainly he never lost sight of my humanity and was always on edge if I made a sudden movement. But in the darkness of Harar's narrow roads, he came to see me as something of a chimera. To Kamareya I was a human like a hyena. To the degree that I was of the human species, I couldn't be trusted, but like a hyena I was somehow involved with the Sofi clan, in which case I could be trusted. But having one foot in the human world and one foot in the hyena world meant that the foot that was in the hyena world would have to subscribe to the rules of that world, and the most important of those was ranking.

This played out one night when I was following Kamareya around Harar's Old Town. On finding a few bones in a dark lane, Kamareya set about demolishing them while I looked on. After a few minutes of watching Kamareya try unsuccessfully to get a good enough purchase on his bone to be able to chew through it, I found myself getting bored. So I shone my flashlight in Kamareya's face. Considering the reaction that the other hyenas had to my flashlight, Kamareya's reaction was quite remarkable. He turned and growled at me and made a couple of head-thrusts toward me. In this instance he was acting toward me as if I were a hyena. This was a bit strange, considering that a hyena would never shine a flashlight in Kamareya's face, but it was not the action that he was reacting to, it was the intention behind my action. He was eating, and I was getting a little too nosy about what he was eating. If another hyena were as nosy, Kamareya would rightly assume that the other hyena was interested in the bone he was munching. And so, Kamareya would act likewise, growling and making head thrusts and saying "Get lost, this is my bone." This was an altogether new kind of trust. While he didn't trust me not to interfere with his dinner, he did trust me enough that he could thrust his head at me and growl with indignation. In this sense I had achieved some remarkable success. My careful negotiation of the physical space between the hyenas and me had rendered me so trustworthy in Kamareya's eyes that he had no compunctions about dealing me a reprimand. But then this was also an unusual situation for Kamareya, as he was not usually inclined to do this with other hyenas and for a very important reason: He didn't outrank many other hyenas. So the fact that he did it with me pulls the curtain on a side effect of my efforts at habituating the hyenas. In trying so hard not to disturb the hyenas, I was unwittingly establishing for myself a position in the social hierarchy below that of Kamareya, Baby, and Willi, and the hyenas noticed. Enter Fintamurey.

Because young hyenas inherit the rank directly below that of their mothers, it's sometimes easy to determine who a cub's mother is. This was the case with ten-month-old Fintamurey when she first came to the feeding place. She managed to nudge Dibbey off of a piece of food, so I knew that her mother outranked Dibbey. She stood in front of Hadha Kamar to take food from the hyena man, so I knew that her mother must be among the three highest-ranked hyenas. I guessed that she was probably offspring to Koti, the highest-ranked of all, because Koti never showed any aggression toward her, and Fintamurey certainly acted like a spoiled, privileged kid. She didn't play much with the other young hyenas, and she went about the place without a care.

Fintamurey was also quick to make up her mind about me. She'd seen Willi biting on my sleeve and noted that other hyenas disregarded me, so she quickly decided I wasn't threatening. But Fintamurey also made the assumption that she could push me around. When I went to the hill behind the feeding place, she marched up and tried to get behind me, presumably for a sniff or a bite. She became really persistent, to the point that I had to get up and leave. I walked around to the hyena man's house, where I went in and joined the family. But Fintamurey was not so easily deterred. She soon appeared in the open doorway looking at me expectantly, so I took a plastic comb outside and let her chew on that. But that only encouraged her. Soon she was licking and chewing on my sleeve like she owned it.

My self-imposed status as low-ranking hyena-cum-human came crashing down on me a few nights later when I was sitting in front of the shrine at the hyena feeding place. Fintamurey marched up to me and tried biting. I had my camera and was trying to take a profile shot of her so that I could record the pattern of spots on her coat, but she was so pushy I couldn't get enough distance between us to take a photo of anything more than her head. Then Willi turned up and they spurred each other on, pushing at me and together shoving their noses between my legs to get a sniff of my groin. Even for a hyena it's quite unnerving to have those bone crushing teeth so close to one's tender bits, and I struggled to keep them away. When I lifted one by the neck and shoved her away, the other nosed in further. Again, I lost my nerve. I got up and went inside the house, where I found safety in the company of some humans.

In thinking about the way Fintamurey treated me and my response, I can see I was overly simplistic in my cynicism about humans establishing themselves as alphas in relation to their animals. Sure, there is hubris involved and, I suppose, a need to be in control. But there is also a lack of trust. In establishing a position of dominance over another animal, we take away a chance that that animal might otherwise have been given. We take away a chance for that animal to act with integrity—to treat us according to their own set of values rather than a set that we impose on them in order that we might dictate the terms of the relationship. And so the risk is always on the animals' shoulders. We back them into corners, where it falls upon them to extend their trust to us humans—the most terrifyingly dangerous creatures on the face of the earth—and we think that just because we know in our own minds that we are well-intentioned, the animals are not taking such a great leap of faith. Can't they see how benevolent we are? It's a massively one-sided risk, and the degree of trust expected from the animals is massive.

In my efforts to habituate the hyenas, I was in some respects doing the same thing as if I was establishing for myself a position as alpha. I was putting the onus on them to trust me. This was a big ask, as the deepest depths of hyenas' natures tell them that humans can't be trusted. And not only was

I a human, but I was acting pretty strangely at that. Indeed, most of the hyenas didn't extend their trust to me as thoroughly as Willi, Kamareya, Baby, and Fintamurey. But then it was Willi who threw my project back in my face. He'd extended his trust to me and in doing so established a rank relationship for me in the clan, a relationship between us that would for hyenas dictate the terms by which we should act. And this is where I dropped the ball. In receiving Willi's trust, in taking up his offer to establish a relationship, I found that I didn't have the nerve to do it on his hyena-like terms. I was so afraid that he and Fintamurey might hurt me that I chickened out. I got up and went into the house, into that quintessentially human construction that I used to wrest the relationship away from the hyenas.

People often say that hyenas are cowardly scavengers. In many ways this is a projection onto hyenas of what we consider the worst of humanity. As far as the scavenger bit, this is pretty accurate, as hyenas, in addition to being lethal hunters and lickers of termites, are adapted to eating the most desiccated of carcasses. But for a human to say this as though it's a bad thing is a little odd, considering that the majority of our species consumes meat that somebody else has killed. But in terms of the cowardice, this is just plain wrong. Sure, hyenas are good at running away from lions. Who wouldn't run from a four-hundred-pound cat that can tear your ass off at almost forty miles an hour? And most hyenas in Africa run for their lives at the mere scent of a human. This is not cowardice; this is intelligence. It's one of the reasons that hyenas are still abundant on the African continent while other carnivores are struggling.

But the cowardice claim is also wrong in a local sense. In Harar, where unpredictable humans have the power of life and death over the hyenas, the actions of Willi bespeak a courage that surpasses the boldest of lions. He opened himself up to a relationship with me, placing his trust in the most dangerous of creatures, without any insights into what might be the outcome. This is bravery: to enter into a one-sided relationship with an openness to possibilities, putting his body on the line in order that the world might open itself up in return and the rich potentialities of life flow in like a river. Willi was the bravest person I've ever known.

Suggested Readings

On the social lives of animals, see:

Marc Bekoff and Jessica Pierce. 2009. *Wild Justice: The Moral Lives of Animals*. Chicago: University of Chicago Press.

Elizabeth Marshall Thomas. 1993. *The Hidden Life of Dogs*. London: Phoenix.

On personal relations with hyenas, see:

Marcus Baynes-Rock. 2015. *Among the Bone Eaters: Encounters with Hyenas in Harar.* State College: Pennsylvania State University Press.

On hyena problem solving, see:

Sarah R. Benson-Amram and Kay E. Holekamp. 2012. "Innovative Problem Solving by Wild Spotted Hyenas." *Proceedings of the Royal Society of Biological Sciences* 279: 4087–95.

On hyena socio-ecology, see:

Hans Kruuk. 1972. *The Spotted Hyena: A Study of Predation and Social Behavior.* Chicago: University of Chicago Press.
Hans Kruuk. 1975. *Hyaena.* London: Oxford University Press.
Jane van Lawick-Goodall and Hugo van Lawick-Goodall. 1970. *Innocent Killers.* London: Collins.

On human/animal relations, see:

Celia Deane-Drummond. 2014. *The Wisdom of the Liminal: Evolution and Other Animals in Human Becoming.* Grand Rapids, MI: Wm. B. Eerdmans Publishing.
Barbara Noske. 1989. *Humans and Other Animals: Beyond the Boundaries of Anthropology.* London: Pluto.

On hyenas and human cultural attitudes, see:

Mikita Brottman. 2012. *Hyena.* London: Reaktion Books.

On hyenas in Ethiopia, see:

Daniel W. Gade. 2006. "Hyenas and Humans in the Horn of Africa." *Geographical Review* 96: 609–32.

On Harar, see:

Richard F. Burton. 1856. *First Footsteps in East Africa.* London: Longman, Brown, Green & Longmans.
Camilla C. T. Gibb. 1996. *In the City of Saints: Religion, Politics, and Gender in Harar, Ethiopia.* PhD dissertation, University of Oxford.

On hyena rank relations, see:

Kay E. Holekamp. 2006. "Spotted Hyenas." *Current Biology* 16: 944–45.
Laura Smale, Lawrence G. Frank, and Kay E. Holekamp. 1993. "Ontogeny of Dominance in Free-Living Spotted Hyaenas: Juvenile Rank Relations with Adults." *Animal Behaviour* 32: 715–24.

Chapter 4

How to Study Chimpanzees That Are Terrified of You

Adventures in Ethnoprimatology in West Africa

Andrew Halloran and Catherine E. Bolten

The Tonkolili Chimpanzee Project began in 2012 when primatologist Andrew Halloran discovered a previously unstudied community of chimpanzees living in a forest fragment in central Sierra Leone that, from the satellite imagery, was too small to support a viable population. After two years of collecting fecal samples and camera trap data, Halloran discovered that the community was not only surviving but also finding sufficient nutrition and experiencing low enough stress levels to reproduce. In 2016 we discovered that the community is in fact two small communities, each exploiting its own forest fragment and abutting farmland. The project continues to investigate the adaptability of the chimpanzees to their environment, which has been altered by humans far beyond the point that primatologists considered would be able to support the reproduction of chimpanzees.

"The big man and the big woman, they are the bosses of the *babu* [local Krio word for the western chimpanzee], and they lead their family out of the forest and onto the field." Cat nods as Mohamed, a villager in rural Sierra Leone, describes the last time chimpanzees raided his farm. "There are many of them, and one sits at the top of a tree. He is the lookout. It is his job to shout to the others if the farmers come near, and he shouts very loudly if we have dogs. The others, they know what this means, and they will run as quickly as they can." He goes on to describe the crops that the chimpanzees raided on his farm—the mangoes they stripped from the tree, the corn they peeled like bananas and nibbled off the cob, the pumpkins they gorged on. He continues: "I shouted and waved at them, and the ones with the mangoes, they just scooped them up and ran back into the forest like naughty children." He stands up and mimes an awkward scramble by someone who is trying to carry too much. There are murmurs from the assembled men, and many nod and likewise stand up and mimic the clumsy gait of a chimpanzee with its arms full.

These are chimpanzees that we have never seen with our own eyes, though the project has been underway for some time. There is a good reason for that. Andrew established his project site in 2012, ten years after Sierra Leone emerged from a terrible, decade-long civil war. Warring factions had decimated farms by consuming farmers' precious seed stocks, destroying their tools, and running them off the land and out of their villages. Without the money, tools, and expertise needed to continue prewar practices of sustainable small-scale agriculture, beekeeping, and animal husbandry, the local community has been doing the most cost-effective thing they can: clearing large amounts of land every year for farming. Large-scale rice farms have become the communities' only way of sustaining themselves. Very little cash circulates within these villages, since the war destroyed the commercial potential of livestock and honey, and so they must defend these farms with their lives. But what does this have to do with the chimpanzees? Well, these farms butt up against two tiny, unprotected forest fragments inhabited by two equally tiny communities of chimpanzees.

Chimpanzees, monkeys, and other wildlife represent the biggest threat to the productivity of local agriculture, as their raiding destroys crops that the residents rely on for food as well as for any money they might bring into the village. The chimpanzees became especially endangered after the war, as many of the guns used during the fighting were still in citizens' hands. When Andrew established this project site in 2012, communities had been bringing in hunters to shoot the chimpanzees that had been so frequently raiding their farms. Indeed, when Andrew initially queried some residents as to the presence of a community in the area, the most common answer was, "Yes, of course we have *babu*—we shot two last week!" Amazed that a community could persist in the face of such threats, Andrew asked for a moratorium on chimpanzee hunting in exchange for ongoing benefits for the villages. The residents agreed, and the project question took shape: How are chimpanzees surviving in the face of such threats?

Previous research on chimpanzees across the continent noted great plasticity and adaptability in their behavior but at the same time inferred that chimpanzees require large home territories in order to survive. Human environments were never considered useful parts of chimpanzee home ranges, merely threats to them. In complete contrast, satellite imagery of the Tonkolili Chimpanzee Project site confirms that each of the two communities have home ranges that take up no more than three square miles of forest, in addition to tracts of abutting farmland that local people report them using "as though they own it." Chimpanzees are constantly running from and competing for food with their human neighbors. However, in spite of their heavily restricted range and what we imagine is constant stress at their proximity to humans, these chimpanzees are reproducing. This indicates both sufficient nutrition in their habitat and females with low enough stress for their hormone levels to allow reproductive capacity. We have been able to discern this much about the communities and to pursue research with them, even though they are not habituated to human presence. These communities have learned from the deaths of many of their members, and from the constant harassment they receive from angry farmers, that humans are not friendly. In short, they are habituated to be terrified of humans.

How can we learn about two communities of chimpanzees that we have never seen with our own eyes—chimpanzees that have become local pariahs? Let's just start with the fact that we certainly do not want these animals to *ever* become habituated positively to our presence, or to the presence of any human. That would be their death knell. We want them to fear us. We want them to stay away. We want them to equate humans with danger and never to be so curious that they might encounter someone armed with a gun rather than an all-weather pen and a pad of paper and wearing a bandana with a cockroach motif. But we need to know enough about them to understand how they are persisting in these most unfavorable circumstances and what we can do to ensure that they continue to be able to live. Maybe we can even figure out what can be done so that their human neighbors don't find the chimpanzees so entirely irksome that the frustrated farmers march into the forest and get rid of their *babu* problem once and for all.

So how do we do this? Though we are still honing our techniques for working around the whole "terror-habituation" conundrum, there are many established—and developing—methods that enable anthropologists and other researchers to study chimpanzees and humans who inhabit overlapping territories and depend on the same set of resources to survive. Fortunately, chimpanzees are so predictable in some aspects of their behavior—they need nutritious food to survive and reproduce, they cannot swim, they nest in high canopies at night, they move daily and seasonally in search of food. These habits help us figure out some of the ways in which these particular communities of chimpanzees are so special. After all, chimpanzees are highly intelligent, highly social, and highly adaptable animals. They are nimble, and so we must also be nimble as we figure out how they seem to be beating the odds and surviving in forest fragments that, combined, are only twice the size of Central Park. Traditional primatology considers questions of behavior, sociality, and ecology for chimpanzees without regard to their human neighbors, which are assumed to be distant. The field of ethnoprimatology, on the other hand, sees the impact that humans have on chimpanzees as fundamental to understanding their behavior and ecology. The more we know about these communities, the more it seems their territory expands; it now includes fallow farmland, oil palm plantations, active farms cultivated by their none-too-impressed human neighbors, and even the fruit trees and vegetable gardens in villages. This kind of study requires a sophisticated and diverse toolkit. Ours includes camera traps, crop raid analysis, phytolithic analysis, ethnography, and standing nest counts.

Tool No. 1: Camera Traps

There are two secondary forests, located about five miles apart, that make up the home forest fragments of the two communities. Unlike pristine forest, there is a thick understory of tall grass, thorny bushes, and new growth beneath a short canopy. This is not the swinging-through-the-trees-on-long-vines forest. It is not particularly picturesque. It is full of bugs. Because of the density of the undergrowth, it takes some maneuvering to get around. While humans stumble through this forest like they never learned to walk properly, needing a machete to clear the thickest undergrowth, chimpanzees are quite adept at moving through the uneven terrain.

One evening in June 2013, a mother chimpanzee was walking through this area with a young juvenile on her back. As she passed a large tree, she heard an unfamiliar click. She turned her head in the direction of the sound to investigate. There, on the trunk of the tree, was an object she had never seen before. Keeping her distance, she stared at it. The object clicked again. At this point, the juvenile climbed off her back and walked toward the object. The mother stayed where she was. As the small chimpanzee approached, the object clicked once more. This startled the juvenile, and he darted behind another tree trunk. Slowly, he peeked his head out from his hiding place. The object clicked again. Growing more courageous, the little chimpanzee now stood directly in front of the object and allowed it to click several more times. Growing tired of this disturbance, the mother scooped her offspring up, placed him on her back, and continued on her way.

The strange object was a camera trap we had placed in the forest. For us, those clicks were signals that the camera was picking up movement in the forest, which it can do with its motion sensors, day or night. It is the reason we have a recording of what occurred and how we know that the juvenile hid behind a tree when approaching it. It is also the reason that we know that the chimpanzees in this tiny fragment are reproducing and seem to be living like typical chimpanzees live. It is also how we know that there are two small communities, rather than just one that exploits a huge range. In 2016, we recorded chimpanzees simultaneously on two camera traps that were located five miles apart. We named one community after Shakespearean characters—Banquo, Puck, Ophelia—and the other after Dickensian characters—Fezziwig, Belle, Pip. Now there is no chance we will ever mix the communities up in our data collection.

Camera traps are a staple method of studying unhabituated primates. We can place them in areas where humans rarely go and leave them there for weeks on end. Cameras are more patient than we could ever be in capturing a community that comes by only once every few days. The camera traps are our "eyes in the forest," allowing us to observe the chimpanzees without having to habituate them to our presence.

FIGURE 4.1.   A juvenile chimpanzee and his mother at the Tonkolili site. Photo by Andrew Halloran.

Tool No. 2: Crop Raid Analysis

From the moment Andrew arrived at the project site in 2012, he knew that the local chimpanzee community was raiding the crops from the surrounding farms. This is what causes the most friction between chimpanzees and humans, and Andrew knew that a study of chimpanzee raiding behavior might help us figure out how to mitigate some of these frictions. The chiefs and residents of the villages were open to this idea, as anything that would reduce crop loss without bringing "strangers"—the hunters who travel with their guns specifically looking for big game—into their villages was worth considering. Chimpanzees are not hunted actively for their meat, although we later established that the chimpanzee carcasses are not thrown away, and in fact some local people do consume chimpanzees as a relatively cheap form of protein when it is available. But chimpanzees are far too dangerous to be considered a good option for providing protein for families. People shoot chimpanzees in order to scare them, and people are mostly intent on scaring them away from their farms.

Gathering data on crop raids is a tricky business. It is tricky partly because chimpanzees are neither the most common nor the most active crop pests that the farmers we talked to contend with on a regular basis. And so Cat asks, "What are the most frequent crop pests?"

"Cane rats. Bush hogs."

She tries a different tack: "What are the worst crop pests?"

"Definitely the *babu*."

"Why?"

The answer is because they are the most thorough and the most destructive. Multiple farmers asserted that chimpanzees are very smart, that they only raid the farms when they are very hungry, and when they do so, they can decimate a crop.

"How do you know they are smart and they only raid when they are hungry?" Cat inquires, not entirely sure how to understand local interpretations of what constitutes "smart" and "hungry."

A farmer explains: "Because they always watch from the forest and wait until the food is ripe before they take it. The little monkeys [Campbell monkeys, green monkeys, guenons] are greedy, and they will raid the food when it is not yet ready. The *babu* don't like this, and they will thrash the monkeys!" He smacks all of his fingers together against his other palm, a local hand gesture that indicates a well-deserved beating. "But then when the food is ready, they come all together, the big man and big woman, and the family, and if they are not disturbed, they will sit and eat and eat until all the food is gone or spoiled!" It makes sense why a distraught farmer, having lost an entire field of food right before harvest, would be angry enough to retaliate. In 2016, the chimpanzees were gorging on pineapple, snapping the precious fruits right off their stalks at peak ripeness. Pineapples ripen once a year, bear one expensive fruit per plant, and are one of the only sources of cash income in the area.

How can we figure out the difference between the damage done by chimpanzees and that done by smaller pests? We have trained a local researcher in each of the villages that surrounds the forest fragments to be that village's go-to guy for reporting crop raids. Armed with pen and notebook, the researcher responds to any reports of crop raid damage that emerge from the farms. He finds the irate farmers, sits down with them, and interviews them about the raid: who did it, how do they know, what did the chimpanzees take, what did they damage, and what remedial action is being taken to salvage or protect what remains. The goal is to figure out if chimpanzees are causing acute crop loss and if there is a way to perform remedial action on the damage or to "chimp-proof" certain crops. Netting might help, but only if it can be secured in a way that chimpanzees cannot loosen. The researchers are also working with the farmers to assess their methods of deterrence, which so far has been wire and wood snares.

These interviews have, in the past, given us great insight into not just chimpanzee social structure and foraging habits but also their capacity for learning and adapting to booby-trapped farms. The farmers have been setting snares to catch small crop pests for as long as they can remember. It is a continual struggle to figure out how to help them keep their farms safe from rodents without these snares, because there are frequent reports from around the continent of nonhuman primates being killed or maimed when trapped in wire snares set for other animals. Indeed, the farmers were clear that there were a few times in the past (less than half a dozen over twenty years) when chimpanzees were fatally ensnared. However, they spent most of these interviews marveling at how intelligent the chimpanzees were and how quickly they figured out the snares. One interview went like this:

> "Do *babu* frequently get caught in the snares?" Cat thinks she is asking a simple question.
> "Yes, but then we have to reset them."
> Cat is confused. "What do you mean? Are the *babu* not caught in them?"
> "The *babu* never come to the fields alone. If one of them gets his leg caught in the snare, he calls to his friend to come and release him. The other one comes and undoes the snare, and then they avoid that place. We have to go and change the snare and try to hide it better."

The farmers know that they are contending with a highly adaptable species, and to them this is a process of continual innovation to protect their crops.

When the chimpanzees are so rightfully terrified of humans, studying their behavior is impossible firsthand. However, by gathering stories from the occasions when they are observed by local people, we can begin to piece together a picture of how they continually adapt to an environment that changes rapidly, in large part because attaining sufficient food nowadays appears to be an arms race between the two species. As the chimpanzees adapt to the presence of snares and other methods of deterrence, so the humans develop new techniques to prevent the crop raids. Part of our job is to mitigate these conflicts. Once we have generated significant data on chimpanzees' preferred crops and methods of pillage, we will work with the farmers to mitigate the damage as much as possible and reduce the frequency of human-chimpanzee encounters. This is not going to be an easy negotiation, as will become clear from the phytolithic analysis described below, we are learning how much the chimpanzees rely on cultivated crops as a food source. Part of our agreement with the moratorium on chimpanzee hunting is compensation for crop raids, and in 2016 we shelled out hundreds of dollars in compensation for lost pineapples.

Tool No. 3: Poop and Phytoliths

Andrew stood in front of a fresh pile of chimpanzee poop and addressed the four men who had gone with him into the forest. These four were being trained to collect samples of poop throughout the year. Andrew held up a white cardboard box.

"It is very important that you wear gloves when doing this," he instructed. Andrew took a pair of gloves out of the box, put them on, and passed the box around. Everyone took a pair.

At this point, Andrew showed them a plastic tube containing ethanol and a wooden stick. "Scoop the poop up with the stick and fill the tube up to this line," he said, indicating a level on the tube. "Then seal the tube, shake it up with the ethanol inside, and you're done."

Studying feces is an essential part of understanding wild chimpanzees. Feces can give you a vast amount of information about individuals in the group. Everything from the sex ratio of the group to what the group is eating is contained in the feces. We are interested in all of this information; therefore, anytime chimpanzee poop is found, it is collected.

Andrew filled up a tube with the feces and shook it into a brown slurry. At that moment, one of the other men found another pile. Andrew handed him a tube and stick. The man began putting on the blue latex gloves—something he definitely had not done before. The gloves were cumbersome and awkward and didn't fit well. After a few moments of wrestling with them, he managed to get three of his five fingers into one of the gloves and all five into another. This made scooping the feces into the tube difficult. Swearing several times, he managed to fill the tube up to the line. He sealed it, smirked, and thrust the tube back to Andrew.

The source of the man's frustration, the gloves, are an unfortunate but essential part of collecting chimpanzee feces. If you are trying to glean genetic information from the sample, you don't want to compromise the chimp sample with your own information. Beyond this, however, is a more pressing safety concern: zoonotic disease transmission. Most diseases that chimpanzees can get, humans can get too (and vice versa). Therefore, handling chimpanzee feces is not without risk. An ailment that might be minor in one species might be deadly in another. Respiratory and intestinal illnesses are easily passed between the two species. Even more frightening are epidemics that can be passed back and forth. There are a number of possible diseases that humans could potentially get from chimpanzee feces, including Ebola, hepatitis, and bacterial meningitis. Therefore, no matter how annoying the gloves may be, they are *always* required.

The fecal samples are eventually transported to Andrew's lab. When they get to the lab, they are immediately placed in deep freeze. Here they can be stored almost indefinitely. They will serve as a snapshot of both the population structure and the feeding habits of that particular time. This information is invaluable in understanding how chimpanzees are surviving in these circumstances.

All plants, as they grow, take in silica from the soil. The silica actually gets stored within the structure of the plant as microscopic structures called phytoliths. When the plant gets consumed by an animal, so do the phytoliths—eventually ending up in the animal's feces. Two things about phytoliths make them of prime interest to us. The first is that phytoliths take on unique shapes based on the plant that they reside in. The other is that phytoliths are extremely resistant to decay. Thus, they maintain their shape even after being digested. Because of this, we can examine the feces, find the phytoliths, and identify which plants have been consumed by the chimpanzees.

However, it's not exactly easy. The first thing we have to do is to dry out the poop. This process begins when we place the feces in ethanol. At the lab, the feces are placed under a fume hood until the ethanol evaporates, taking the bulk of the moisture away. What is left are dry feces. These are placed in an extremely hot oven, cooked at over 1000 degrees Celsius, and reduced to white ash. Then they are immersed in hydrochloric acid and spun in a centrifuge. The only things that remain are microscopic phytoliths. We can then look under a microscope and tell exactly what that chimpanzee was eating.

The feces that collected in the forest revealed that almost a third of the chimpanzee diets in May and June were composed of the cultivated crops from the farms. From this, we were able to prove definitively that the chimpanzees were raiding the crops at a regular rate. It also showed how important the crops were to the chimpanzees' diets. In fact, chimpanzees were surviving in this human-dominated landscape by eating what was in the farms. It is doubtful that they could have survived otherwise.

Tool No. 4: Chimp Gardens, or Recreating Chimp Behavior from Their Trash

When we walk through the primary forest and fallow fields of our project site, we find ample evidence for what chimpanzees do with the armfuls of food they take from the farms when they are spotted and have to high-tail it back to safety. Mango is not native to Sierra Leone. The fruit was probably introduced to the country by Portuguese slavers and traders in the sixteenth or seventeenth century and spread to villages around the country as a desired fruit tree. A walk through the riparian forest fragment inhabited by this troop reveals mango saplings—dozens of them, of varying heights—in multiple forest clearings. These inadvertently planted mango seeds corroborate the evidence given in the village, where men mimicked chimpanzees running to the forest with armfuls of mangos. Although we know from a grove of ancient mangos that there was once a village in the forest (called Matambo, according to residents), the haphazardness of the saplings and their distance from Matambo indicates that chimpanzees, after scurrying safely away from their human neighbors, would sit and consume their booty. The inedible pits, once discarded on the ground, might germinate, and those lucky enough to be located in a patch of sunlight will grow.

Giving clear evidence of this phenomenon was the fact that the saplings were routinely found along well-worn chimpanzee-created trails. With a little training, it is easy for one to see the difference between chimp-created trails and human-created trails. Chimpanzees are knuckle-walkers, so their trails are only three to four feet high, whereas humans clear small branches up to six feet high. In addition, the saplings were far away from any fruiting mango tree. In some cases, the saplings were over a third of a mile from a tree.

Mangos were not the only fruit present in these clearings. We also found evidence of guava, a few scattered groundnut shoots, and, oddest of all, a cassava stick in 2014. Our guides had no idea that chimpanzees had developed a taste for the flavorless, largely nutrient-free tuber. Incredulous, he pulled it out of the ground to make sure his eyes were not deceiving him. "This was not put here by the hands of man," he announced and promptly stuck the tuber back in the ground. The size of the cassava growing on the end of the stick indicated that it had not been dropped recently. That incident was not isolated; we found other cassava growing in the forest, establishing that chimpanzees had developed a taste for it. We heard from a farmer on the other side of the forest a few days later that he had caught a chimpanzee pulling cassava sticks out of the ground, removing the tuber, and throwing the stick away. The chimp cleared an entire row, gathered up his food, and was about to walk back to the forest when the farmer overcame his fear and reacted.

"I threw a stick at him!" He giggled a bit, and continued: "The *babu* dropped the cassava, caught the stick, and threw it back at me! They are just like little children!" He did not consider the gesture aggressive. We are still pondering what the chimpanzee made of this interaction. In 2016 we found chimpanzee-planted cassava everywhere. Apparently they had developed a taste for cassava, and it had become more than a token in a game to play with their humans.

Tool No. 5: Ethnographic Interviews

One must understand the human side of the equation in order to interpret chimpanzee behavioral adaptations. Primatologists have a particular way of thinking about chimpanzees, acting toward them, and handling themselves (from walking through the forest to making camp) that is very, very different from the way local people, for whom chimpanzees do not necessarily represent anything worthy of fascination or study, act toward them and share the landscape. Local people's attitudes toward chimpanzees are 100 percent of the reasons these troops are habituated to be terrified of all humans. Therefore, it is incumbent upon us to collect as much information as possible on how the people who live in the villages surrounding the forest fragment think about chimpanzee social organization, daily habits, and even their history and culture.

The first thing we discovered is the place inhabited by chimpanzees in human cosmology. According to multiple people in multiple villages, chimpanzees used to be human. We know this because they have real thumbs, and only humans have real (as opposed to vestigial) thumbs. Chimpanzees were no different from humans, except that they were perpetually naughty. Long ago, when God made the rules for living on the earth, he created the days of the week, each of which had prescribed and prohibited activities. Fishing was never allowed on Fridays, and the chimpanzees-who-used-to-be-human—for reasons of their own—decided to disregard this. This angered God, and as punishment he turned them into chimpanzees and banished them to the forest. They are condemned, lesser beings because they broke the rules, and they are not, and cannot, be equal to humans. However, there was quite a lot of variation between villages as to whether they could be hunted or not, and this was due entirely to their resemblance—both physically and in behavior—to humans. However, it was universal that local people viewed them as troublemakers, as less than full people and therefore due less regard. In our conservation activities, we cannot ask them to treat chimpanzees as though they were people, because they are not. There are other very good reasons people have for disliking and fearing their chimpanzee neighbors.

Chimps have attacked children in these villages. This we also know from interviews, and the injuries that were described (lost digits and severe facial mutilation) are consistent with other recorded chimpanzee attacks. Each of the (very infrequent) times these attacks occurred, the children were small, playing alone or with one or two others along a path in the forest, and surprised a chimpanzee that was on its own. There was also one story of a chimpanzee stealing a human baby. We were not able to corroborate this story—and it was told in the village that seemed to have the highest regard for the troop, of the six in which we conducted interviews. According to lore, a chimpanzee mother lost her baby, and was so distraught that she followed a woman who had a baby on her back through the forest as the woman gathered wood. The woman untied her baby and put it down, and the chimpanzee rushed in, snatched the child, and ran off with it. No one remembered what happened, if the baby was ever recovered or not. Just as with the chimpanzees attacking humans, these stories took place "long ago," before the war and before the guns. Since those incidents, chimpanzees raid farms but are not the aggressors in encounters.

And what of their resemblance to humans? The interviews provided even more insight into chimpanzee behavior and adaptability in the ways people described them raiding crops. The chimpanzees "harvest" crops while standing upright, pick beans carefully and put them in their mouths one at a time, trim cassava and peel corn before eating them, and knock pumpkins against rocks to open them—just as humans would do. In one instance, a woman whose farm abutted the forest offered her own insight, that chimpanzee mothers have breasts and nurse their babies just as human mothers do. People described the chimpanzees as possessing high intelligence, having a sense of playfulness, engaging in cooperation and extreme naughtiness, and expressing great tenderness towards their young. One village was adamant that they would never hunt their chimpanzee neighbors, because they were too much like humans. Really bad neighbors, but neighbors nonetheless.

Tool No. 6: Standing Nest Counts (When Condos Are Your Best Option)

The first time Andrew passed through the area, he was looking for chimpanzees in a certain type of habitat (he was doing an acoustic study on chimpanzee calls and needed to find a group living primarily in a riparian forest). A year earlier, there had been a census done to determine how many chimpanzees were in Sierra Leone and where they were located. According to the census, there were no chimpanzees in this area. However, Andrew had heard reports of both sightings and live captures along the Pampana River. After over a week of searching, these reports seemed to have been wrong. Andrew was about to give up when he drove by a field full of oil palms. In the palm trees by the perimeter of the field, there were chimpanzee nests.

Chimpanzees are skilled nest builders. Starting in the late afternoon, they intertwine branches and leaves to create very comfortable sleeping spots. This becomes their home for the night. Nests tend to be built in strategic areas. Sites that offer the chimpanzees cover and protection or sites near food sources are places that you can find nesting areas. The amount of rainfall and the types of branches that are used determine how long a nest is visible. A nest made from hardwood branches will last longer than a nest made in an oil palm tree. During the rainy seasons, nests may be visible only for a few days. In optimal circumstances, a chimpanzee community will build nests in one area of canopy for a single night, and then move on the next day, often roaming several miles over the course of the day before deciding on a new nesting site for the next night.

Nests give us a keen insight into the number of chimpanzees at the site. We use a census technique called a "standing crop nest count" that involves counting the nests we see along a fixed line transect. We then factor in variables such as how long it takes a nest to decay after it has been used. With this method, we can figure out the population density.

It was during one of these standing crop nest counts that we came across an extraordinary area, a place we called "the chimp condos" located at the site of Matambo, the village that was abandoned sixty years ago. While walking along a transect in the thickest parts of the forest, we came to a clearing dominated by a dozen mature mango trees. Looking up we saw almost a hundred nests in the canopy. The nests were at various stages of decay. This told us an interesting fact about this group of chimpanzees and this habitat: If the nesting site was used many times, with new nests built on old ones, it indicates that there are hardly any good nesting spots in their home range. The chimpanzees have a very limited range, and are forced to return to the same spot over and over. In fact, this spot is so much better than anywhere else in this community's small range, that unlike chimpanzees with a large range, these chimps will nest in the same spot over and over again, defying "typical" nesting patterns.

The presence of the chimp condos highlights an important fact about the site. Chimpanzees in fragmented habitats are adapting to extraordinary resource deficiencies. However, chimpanzees have an incredible ecological plasticity and can, somehow, figure out how to survive in severe circumstances. They survive by accommodating their behaviors to the variables around them and to the limits to their resources. Whether that presents itself in crop raids, inadvertent crop seed dispersal, or nesting in the same spot over and over again, chimpanzees show that they are an incredibly adaptable species.

And So It Continues . . .

In 2014, as we picked our way along the edge of the riparian forest, imagining that the nearby Pampana River was a definitive boundary for our non-swimming primate relatives, a thought occurred to Cat. She gazed over a bend in the river that clearly contained a sandbar, not quite visible in the flooding of the early rainy season. It was impassible to non-swimmers now, but would it be walkable during the height of the dry season? There was some pretty tempting riparian forest on the other side. She asked our local guide if he had ever seen *babu* ford the river. He nodded emphatically and explained that the community had indeed crossed at that very point a few years earlier in March, when the deepest water was knee-high to a chimp. Terrified of humans they might be, but they were also ingenious. And so our study continues, chasing traces of the communities to further and further reaches of Sierra Leone and testing the limits of our ability to follow.

Suggested Readings

On treating primates ethnographically, see:
Karen Strier. 2013. *Primate Ethnographies*. New York: Routledge.

On the methodology of ethnoprimatology, see:
Kerry Dore, Erin Riley, and Agustín Fuentes, eds. 2017. *Ethnoprimatology: A Practical Guide for Research at the Human-nonhuman Primate Interface*. Cambridge: Cambridge University Press.

❧ PART 2

Communication

CHAPTER 5

Walking with Dogs

*Sharing Meaning, Sensation, and Inspiration
across the Species Boundary*

AGUSTÍN FUENTES AND MICHAEL ALAN PARK

> "All truly great thoughts are conceived by walking."
> —Nietzsche

> "Still greater thoughts are conceived by walking
> a dog."
> —Devi Snively in response to Nietzsche

In this essay we hope to convince the reader
that Nietzsche's comment is incomplete, for the art of walking (as Thoreau
termed it) is often undertaken, and understood, by two or more persons,
only one of whom is human.

First we set the stage for our essay and then narrate, by way of our own reflections, "walking" through an intellectual landscape, a story of our experiences and interpretations arising from daily walking with dogs. We are both
biological anthropologists whose focus has long been on the evolutionary
and biological facets of the human experience. We are interested in the ways
that experience interfaces with, manipulates, and (re)interprets the world
around us. We are also both avid enthusiasts for the option of sharing our
lives with others, both human partners and canine companions. This essay
is about collaboration with the canines in the contemporary world. It is a
multispecies endeavor that offers both functional and experiential outcomes.
Our goal is to illustrate that walking with dogs is a constructive project and
beneficial work. Walking with dogs is a mutual collaboration, a joint journey,
in which two species share in discovery, reflection, and wonder in the world.

Tim Ingold, waxing eloquent on the subject of walking and education,
invokes the philosopher Jan Masschelein who argues that walking is about
taking up a standpoint on things, not just about getting from point A to
point B. Walking is a process, one that involves the body and the mind.

Masschelein, via Tim Ingold, points out that walking does not force us into one position or one perspective; rather, it "continually pulls us away from any standpoint—from any position or perspective we might adopt." Walking is more than movement across space; it is also about navigating sensory landscapes (visual and otherwise), which affect the way we experience the world around us. Ingold goes on to elaborate:

> The walker on the move, lest he lose the way, must be ever vigilant to the path as it unfolds before him. He must watch his step, and listen and feel as well. He must, in a word, pay attention to things, and adjust his gait accordingly. Thus in the very act of walking, he is thrust into the presence of the real. As intention is to attention, therefore, so absence is to presence. A person might intend to go for a walk; she might reflect upon it, consider the route, prepare for the weather and pack her provisions. In that sense walking is something she sets out to do. She is the subject, and her walking the predicate. But once on the trail, she and her walking become one and the same.

It is in this process of walking, of becoming one and the same, that we place the collaboration between canine and humans that we call "walking with dogs." Here we offer an account of mutual efforts, and meanings, between humans and our best, nonhuman friend as we traverse terrain.

A Note on Our Best Friend and the Concept of "the Walk"

Of all the collaborative relationships humans have with other animals, the one with dogs is one of the deepest and most intensive. It is also one of the few domestication experiments that did not start out as a human quest for food—humans viewed dogs as companions first, not as meat. Humans and dogs are highly social animals with complex group lives, strong senses of loyalty to their packs, communal care of the young, and a keen hunting ability. Some have argued that we were pre-made for each other.

Current genetic analysis tells us that all living dogs are tied to wolf ancestors from twenty to thirty thousand years ago. This is when the populations of dogs and wolves began to separate as breeding clusters, after which dogs began fusing with human communities. More than twenty thousand years ago humans began to spend more and more time with canines, most likely wolves, and over time the behavior and bodies of the wolves changed—they became dogs. By around fifteen thousand years ago there is ample evidence of wolf-like canines that show signs of domestication—smaller, less muscular, and a bit more puppy-like—in association with human archeological remains. By twelve thousand years ago, many human communities across the planet had animals that matched in size, shape, and behavior what we call domestic dogs today. Humans and dogs have millennia of coexistence, of multispecies communities holding substantial meaning for one another. Hunting, shepherding, guarding, companionship, and caretaking are all jobs that humans and dogs do together. There are many places across the world where human and dog remains are found comingled in graves, where the human perception of the world existing beyond just the material, the here and now, includes dogs as compatriots and co-travelers. Over the last ten thousand years, there is abundant evidence that humans and dogs co-shaped each other's experiences and perceptions of the world.

As we mastered the dog, they also mastered a bit of us. Dogs appear to have coopted aspects of human physiological response. Recent research illustrates that dogs have engaged the human hormonal and psychoneuroendocrine pathways, expanding the great capacity humans have for communally caring for our young (and each other) toward themselves. As dogs became integral to many human communities, they began to elicit the same kinds of compassionate responses that human communities generally kept within the species boundary. Dogs directly tap into the human oxytocin response system and are shaping it to respond to their actions.

Over time the relationship between both species flourished. Some suggest that it was this relationship that made our direct ancestors better hunters and maybe gave us the extra social and ecological support we needed to succeed across all the habitats that we encountered. One could argue that the domestication of dogs set the stage for much of what was to come from the Neolithic Revolution. The creative and mutually developed relationship between humans and dogs is surely one of the reasons for our success as a species. So walking together today has roots deep in our evolutionary past, but the actual process of the contemporary "dog walk" is very recent.

The concept of "walking the dog" that we are talking about here is a modern phenomenon, perhaps even limited to industrialized (even Western or Westernized) societies, and even there it is found mostly in the urban and suburban areas of those societies. For most of human-dog history and even in much of the world today, dogs tagged along, in true "free-range" fashion, to do what they would in regards to movement, although there are special situations where dogs are tethered for guarding, war, bull-baiting, or even food. These dogs are captive and constrained. There are other extremes: Sometimes dogs are physically unleashed but highly motivated (trained) to move and react according to human commands. For example, the Highland Scots border collies track livestock as humans have trained them to do, and dogs in the American West guard herds and flocks. The dog walking of the urban and suburban landscapes is a more recent version and lies somewhere in between these extremes.

Why walk a dog? For dogs, defecation and urination serve multiple functions. Obviously, dogs need to discard waste from their body. But there is another equally important aspect for dogs—they use feces and urine to convey information and messages to other dogs and other animals. The act of depositing material or liquid waste is a social one: Waste matter is not wasted by dogs. Dogs who live in houses with humans are presented with a particular problem. They need (physiologically) and desire (socially) to defecate and urinate just as their free-range compatriots do. However, because they live under the rule and habits of the humans who "house" them, they face a quandary. Their human housemates almost universally do not allow indoor defecation or urination outside of specific locations and in specific contexts, which for humans means bathrooms and toilets, and neither are generally available to dogs. Thus, in this context a mutually negotiated set of agreements develops between humans and dogs. The dogs agree to withhold their physiological and social goals while indoors and the humans agree to arrange multiple opportunities per day for the dogs to be out of the house and free to conduct their "business." The "dog walk" is a critical feature of this system. This arrangement very likely became common in the twentieth century, with the massive expansion of urban and suburban living and people's new penchant for keeping indoor dogs.

The dog walk is the product of a working relationship and an agreement between human and dog with substantive social and physiological effect. We argue that there are benefits beyond the obvious for both species. To paraphrase Ingold, walking is something that we do, and in doing it we become a bit more infused with one another's sense of the world. Thus, the descriptions that follow—of the two of us and our dogs actually walking together on the same route, connected most of the time by a leash, is different from the control of a Highland shepherd commanding his collie from afar with whistles or the active constraint of the tethered guard dog; it is more akin to a hybrid of free-range walking with a deep multispecies social connection. We contend that this situation is a modified version of, and a window into, a collaboration that goes back tens of thousands of years.

The Art of Walking

We (Agustín and Michael) have more than a century of combined experience walking with dogs and only slightly less time learning, researching, and writing about being and evolving as humans. It is our experience that walking with dogs moves us away from one social position and one ecological perspective and opens up a manner of experiencing the world from multiple perspectives (and not only human ones). Such experiences ultimately help us to think, to discover, and to create. We also hold that such walks affect the ways in which the dogs participate in, experience, and shape their social and ecological landscapes. Walking with dogs is more than a functional solution to the reality of contemporary human preference and canine necessity.

To convey these ideas, we share stories of walking and our impressions of how we and our companion dogs are experiencing and benefiting from the process. We highlight aspects of the mutual interface between us, the dogs, and the landscapes we traverse. We argue that this would not happen, or would happen differently, if we were not in these multispecies relationships.

Walking with dogs is a collaboration that extends and augments our human sensory and experiential capacities. For dogs, walking with humans creates a zone of communication and interpretation. It enables them to explore and contribute to the signs in their environment and to share and convey key aspects of their sense of the landscape to their human companions.

Agustín: Walking in the Suburbs

Every morning, even when it is below freezing and before sunrise, I take our current dog, Shelley, for her morning walk. Shelley is a small mutt, 26 pounds, with shaggy fur and unidentifiable ancestry. She is particularly smell-oriented, even for a dog, and invests great amounts of time and energy exploring (and contributing to) the sense-scape of our environment.

Living in the suburbs of the midwestern United States, we are surrounded by larger houses, trees, and spacious yards, interspersed with small stands of forest where some deer, a few raccoons, an occasional fox, and a range of small animals reside. Our neighborhood has no sidewalks, just simple roads abutting grass- and tree-covered yards with mailboxes alongside driveways spaced every few hundred feet or so.

Shelley and I share a routine at the front door. I chat at her while she sits up so I can put her foreleg/chest harness on and attach the leash (the long, retractable kind) to it, and not to her collar.

The concept of a leash might seem highly restrictive and mandate a kind of unidirectional control of human over dog. But in practice this is not so much the case. I and (I think) Shelley see the leash as a kind of connective tissue, an extension of our bodies that enables us to communicate not just through vocal and visual exchanges but through tactile ones as well. And such exchanges are not always in agreement. It is often a negotiation, which I can tell because there is some tension on the leash in different directions that has to be resolved. Since I am over 155 pounds and Shelley is about a sixth of that, I could "win" all of our negotiations—but I don't. That is not the way it works. The physical connection provided by the leash is just one part of our larger relationship and communication.

For example, in the mornings, before there is any light, I walk her on the leash, even though it is not needed as she sticks close by, with or without one. I use the leash in the mornings as part of an ongoing conversation we are having. Shelley bolted after a rabbit once or twice when she first joined our family. She and I have been working on her compulsion to chase small animals for some time, and the physicality of the leash is an important part of that conversation. Now, most of the time, she looks at rabbits or other small mammals, then at me, but she has ceased to make the attempt to chase and capture, at least when the two of us are walking together (actually, she has not completely agreed that squirrels are off the chase list). We are developing an agreement that walks are not for hunting but for exploring, communicating, and thinking. On our afternoon and evening walks, I hold the leash in my hand but don't bother attaching it to her—this is part of that arrangement.

As we set out on the walk, we seldom give each other any overt indications of what direction to go. The morning path varies little—out the door and down the driveway, veering to the right (northeast). Here is where she and I show our species-level differences. I notice the frigid air or the warm breeze and the soft light emerging on the horizon and begin my rundown of the day's events. As we approach one of the first mailboxes on its wooden post, I am pulled out of my musings on the human world's daily calendar and invited, with a quick tug and a wagging tail, into the world of the dog. We are connected physically by the leash and emotionally by our shared friendship, and somehow that enables me, even if only in glimpses, to peer into her world. Here biosemiotics (the communication and creation of signs and signals found in and between living systems) become tangible.

Shelley emerges into a world I can barely see and cannot smell, and thus deep evolutionary histories of difference reveal themselves. Her nose and body meld into one, and she begins her saunter guided by multiple scent trails, her embodied skills for hunting and social connection though scent come to the fore. Sucking up a diverse array of sensations and indications of other animals, the world around her is filled with signs and information, what we might think of as ghosts, evidence of others not present at the moment. The local landscape is much sensually richer for her than for me . . . but I try to imagine what she might be immersed in.

All around me emerge not grass edges, mailbox posts, bits of upended soil, and small hoofprints but living vibrant signs of activity, occupancy, and communication. Signs of the previous evening's, and the early morning's, local ecology and the activity of its inhabitants. I hear and sense, via Shelley, the presence and lives of others. I am thrust into a multispecies reality that is always there but only sometimes evident to those of us in the sight-heavy but overly myopic urban version of our possibly misnamed species *homo sapiens* (which means "wise human"). Shelley, working for both of us, busily contributes to the cacophony of signs and signals by ejecting liquid, proteins, and other chemicals at various locations of shared activity or meaning to the nonhuman members of the community. What to me looks like a post for a mailbox seems to her to be a bulletin board for messaging. Through her sign-making activity, I too begin to see signs of others (albeit at a very rudimentary level compared with most other species). This is when I exploit the human capacity to imagine creatively. As the philosopher Thomas Nagel noted, I cannot think myself into the experience of another animals, but I can imagine it. And through our close social and even physical links, I am better able to share in Shelley's actions and responses than I would be with most other animals (or people, for that matter).

This multispecies communication is a critical aspect of our walk. While I think I catch most of the objects that are signposts to her (mailboxes, bushes, tufts of grass at the edge of a driveway), I miss most of the specific details and what they mean. A pile of feces is an easy one: It has information about the individual, their health, travels, and diets (I cannot obtain the specifics without a laboratory analysis, but Shelley probably can). But most signs are invisible to me: urine wash on a clump of grass, tamped-down grass near a tree with tiny bits of fur embedded in it, scent marks rubbed on the post of a mailbox or a large stone by the side of the road. However, despite my sensory blindness, Shelley, ever the thoughtful companion, pulls and pushes me to see the dynamic landscape (either via the physical other of the leash, or more often via our joint movements, which are coordinated by body position, eye gaze, and nods of the head). She will stop adamantly and then move to a stone or bush. Looking back at me if I resist and moving her gaze back and forth between the obvious (to her) sign and me, striving to enable me, despite my slow-witted human capacities, to sense the importance of assessing the sign and deciding whether or not to add to it. This forces me to think outside the human, even if it is just for a moment, offering experiential novelty and fodder for my imagination.

The bustle of the public square of other animals becomes clear and, for the rest of our walk, I follow Shelley's lead deciphering, noticing, avoiding, and engaging the multitude of voices and signs we wade though. It is precisely in our collaboration, her insistence that I participate, at least as a companion, in navigating this landscape of meaning that I, as a human in this partnership, get specific benefits—I get some human work done while she handles the dog end.

These walks offer me a space to think and feel, a sort of guided meditation, led by Shelley. I am made aware of my sensory limitations as a human but at the same time I am reminded of my capacities for imagination and creation, remembering that human senses are as much constructed as they are provided. This daily realization, near the end of the walk, frequently sets the stage for my immersion back into the day's schedule, but in a manner that is infused with a much richer, and decidedly multispecies, worldview. Walking across the species boundary, collaborating on movement along paths guided by the signs of other animals, these journeys with Shelley help me to become more "sapiens."

Michael: Walking in the Woods

I find I do some of my best thinking when I'm walking with my companion dogs on the trails in the woods out back. Our property, in northern Connecticut, abuts six-hundred-plus acres of woodland belonging to a private girls' school but with trails accessible to the public. The area used to be an estate and farm of some sort but has been allowed to grow back. Much of it is secondary growth, but there are some areas that have been untouched for centuries, so there might be a little bit of a time-travel sense for me—and I have to wonder if the dogs have any species memory that kicks in! This land is contiguous with a town forest, which is contiguous with a state forest, and on it goes. We could walk all the way into the Berkshires in Massachusetts and hardly ever leave the woods. The area has been designated an important wildlife corridor, so some other critters might actually be making that trek. Even if I rarely see them I'm fully aware I'm in the element not so much of my own species but that of deer, turkeys, black bears, coyotes (actually wolf-coyote hybrids, in these parts), bobcats, and all manner of birds. We humans have irrevocably altered the landscape, but maybe not as much as we sometimes think.

For over twenty-two years, I have never walked in those woods without whichever dogs we've had (currently Monty, 9, and Jessie, 4, yellow and black Labrador retrievers, respectively), and I can't even imagine I could think as I do if I were walking alone. I don't think I've ever even tried. There's something about being with canine companions that serves the function of a powerful muse. I often think about various topics on those walks in the form of mentally composing an email, an article, a lecture, or even part of a book chapter.

It is, I think, the recognition that I'm walking with members of another species. Most of the time, I must admit, this doesn't strike me. After all, those of us who think as your two authors do have made our dogs part of our human families, our kin. They follow our schedules (or more often, we theirs, as I time their walks to when I think *they'll* need or want them), we talk to them, they pick up on our moods. They're "us," only quadrupeds and furry. But every once in a while something reminds me that they are, evolutionarily speaking, infantilized wolves, co-products of a collaborative domestication spanning millennia. Indeed, many taxonomists, those scientists who give official names to creatures, have generally lumped domestic dogs into the wolf species, *Canis lupus*, as a subspecies, *familiaris*—our canid familiars.

These realizations, that my dogs are another species and that I'm in the environment of many other species, have struck me vividly on several specific occasions, when, for example, over the years, three of our many Labs have chased wild turkeys. (They are now, by the way, no longer off-leash, for their own safety, not only from the wild denizens of the woods, who because of our altering the environment find themselves in smaller and smaller areas, but also from other domestic dogs who may not be as friendly as they are.) The turkeys, who don't seem always the smartest of birds, tend to run away and only take off in flight at the last second. As the dogs have chased the turkeys, I have mostly worried that they will catch one and either kill it or injure it so I have to finish it off or, since turkeys can be vicious, that the dogs will get the worst of it themselves. But, for just a second, as I see my dogs charging through the woods in that predator pose—running like mad through the brush and over fallen trees but with their heads steady and focused—I get a little frisson of excitement, I find myself hoping they get to do what I imagine they yearn to do: hunt. For that split-second, they are not so much adjunct members of my species but, rather, or so I like to think, sharing some ancient connection, when my ancestors often relied on theirs to help bring home the bacon. Or turkey.

And this makes me want to write about the experience. Or to write *something*. It enables my profession and one of my avocations, by expanding my sensory and cognitive landscape, pushing me to want to do what humans do—elaborate, complexify, storytell. My muse has spoken.

The exchange, of course, is mutual. The dogs learn from me. I don't mean the basic trained commands—sit, stay, come, leave it—or even phrases I don't directly teach but that they learn from repetition—let's walk over the hill, time to go home, front door. I mean things unspoken, or almost so. Often, as we're walking and I'm thinking, I'll mumble to myself. They think I'm talking to someone and will stop and intently look—usually in the direction I'm looking—to see who's there. In this they are seeking to participate in their pack's social moment. On occasion, I'll be silent but feel a tug on the leashes as they've suddenly stopped and are looking at me with what I can only infer are questioning faces. In those moments I'll realize that I've been thinking about something that upsets me. I don't know how they do that, but they've picked up on my mood and are engaging me in conversation, but on their terms. These interfaces, these multispecies dialogues, enrich all three of our lives.

When we are approached by other dogs and their owners, Monty and Jessie will respond differently to different dogs. Sometimes they growl, bark, or even snap if a dog gets too close. Other times they are relaxed and sniff noses and butts or play a bit. To be sure, they perceive something in the other dogs that informs their response. But I'm sure they are also picking up my vibes. I might see some of the same body language in the dogs and interpret it, but I also can often pick up something in the owner's attitude. So we, the dogs and I, are making a collective decision about the safety of getting close to these interlopers in our territory. And, in the eventual actions of the other dogs, we're seldom wrong.

And this is not just with the companion dogs who share my home, who sometimes know me better than I know myself. For the past year I've volunteered for a local organization that finds homes for dogs rescued from kill shelters. Dogs yet to be adopted we board in a kennel, and some of us go there a couple times a week and walk one or more of them on a nature trail in back of the kennel. There is one dog with behavior issues, and a select group of us, who have had some specific training ourselves, walk him. When I was anticipating one of his "episodes" he usually rewarded me by having one. One day, when I was, in actual fact, mentally composing part of this essay, I suddenly realized that he had been the model of good behavior. Since then I've tried to refocus my mind, to shut away the human expectations of a "troubled dog" and be open to the walk. Since then, on our mutual saunters in the woods, he's been a good dog; I don't anticipate a problem, and it changes him. And in turn, his transformation has changed me.

This interaction with the dogs is not just two-directional, then. It becomes an entity in and of itself, a body of knowledge synthesized from information across species but no less a synergy, even a source of multispecies wisdom, perhaps (albeit inchoate and hard to articulate). This would be impossible to achieve were I walking alone, or even with another human. To expand on Ingold's words, I and my walking, *and my companions,* become one and the same.

Dogs and Thinking: Successful Multispecies Walking

On walks humans ponder things. For example, one of us (Michael), while on his walks with a dog, started a daily count of the Canada geese. One day he had the thought that some of the geese he was seeing probably were the same as those he had seen the previous fall. They had found their way to wherever they were over the winter and had then found their way back to this pond. So, the question someone might pose: How do they do it without navigation technology? But that wasn't the question Michael asked at all. The question was: Why can't we humans do it? Why do we need maps and GPS and, at the very least, landmarks, usually with names, to find our way around? Have we lost the native ability to find our way across landscapes, or has our multifaceted, overly associative, heavily contextualized cognition (the "sapiens'" bit) smothered many of our other abilities?

We think it's the latter, and here's why. Think of the greatest artists. In all genres they are those few who can break through that barrier our recent hyper-cognitive and semantic complexity has created. There are lots of really, really good artists, of course, but think about the ones who shift paradigms—Beethoven, Van Gogh, Goya, Coltrane, Holiday, the Dylans (Thomas and Bob). (The list is endlessly debatable, but you get the idea.) Their greatness, as we acknowledge it without fully understanding it, is because they allow us, often for just a moment, to join them in breaking that barrier, and we feel something we don't and can't normally feel, some connection. It's a sensuous experience that involves but alters our cognitive and sensory processes. Those processes are so tied up in perceived and achieved daily social and economic responsibilities, future and past experiences and obligations, and our tendency to predict, plan, and hope for outcomes, that we forget our enormous capacities to sense, feel, and experience the moment. To do what Nietszche sought during walks: to think greatly.

Perhaps walking with dogs—where they perceive, indeed, experience some things differently than we do and share them with us—allows us, in an ephemeral and inadequate way, to puncture, albeit briefly, that limit our species often suffers from. While walking and sharing with another species, *Canis lupus familiaris*, perhaps we're able to get out of our overly cognized, pre-interpreted humanness and connect with movement and landscapes, read signs, and sense the local ecology as mediated via our companions. Basically we "walk" in a better and more sensually infused manner. This in turn feeds back into our very human need to cognize, to complexify, and to elaborate via linguistically charged thoughts and structures. Our experiences are then translated into human perceptions and sensations, words, and categories. It is in this translation that the species boundary is blurred and we as humans tap into broader capacities, remembering that we are mammals as well as "sapiens" as well as part of a multispecies pack. And our ability to do this, to at least try to capture some larger, less mundane and quotidian matters, is facilitated by walking with dogs who experience things we can't and yet share them with us, even if indirectly. And we realize we are sharing with them too, so that their worldview is at the very least colored by ours.

Taking Ingold as a point of departure, it is not just that we and our walking become one and the same but rather that the walking together with dogs blurs our sense of the self and expands, even if momentarily, the species boundary enabling us to be "human" a little bit better. Maybe there is not too much difference listening to Beethoven's Ninth Symphony or Davis and Coltrane's version of "Round Midnight" or Thomas's "Poem in October" and a walk on a suburban street or in the woods with canine companions. In each case we might experience the opportunity to sense meaning, create inspiration, and participate in a bit of magic beyond the materiality of the day-to-day routine. And maybe experience a better opportunity to think and share great thoughts.

Suggested Readings

On canine consciousness, see:

Alexandra Horowitz. 2009. *Inside of a Dog: What Dogs See, Smell, and Know*. New York: Scribner.

Elizabeth Marshall Thomas. 1993. *The Hidden Life of Dogs*. Boston: Houghton Mifflin.

On the evolution and history of the domestic dog, see:

Donna Haraway. 2003. *The Companion Species Manifesto: Dogs, People, and Otherness*. Chicago: Prickly Paradigm Press.

Brian Hare and Vanessa Woods. 2013. *The Genius of Dogs: How Dogs Are Smarter Than You Think*. New York: Plume.

Meg Daley Olmert. 2009. *Made for Each Other: The Biology of the Human-Animal Bond*. Philadelphia: De Capo Press.

James Serpell, ed. 1995. *The Domestic Dog: Its Evolution, Behaviour, and Interactions with People*. Cambridge: Cambridge University Press.

Mary Elizabeth Thurston. 1996. *The Lost History of the Canine Race: Our 15,000-Year Love Affair with Dogs*. Kansas City: Andrews McMeel.

On the poetic side, see:

Alvin Greenberg. 1990. *Why We Live With Animals*. Minneapolis: Coffee House Press.

Mary Oliver. 2013. *Dog Songs*. New York: Penguin.

CHAPTER 6

Working with a Service Dog in the United States

LESLIE IRVINE AND SHERRI SASNETT-MARTICHUSKI

Although blind people have relied on dogs throughout history, the first program to train guide dogs specifically for this purpose dates to the years after World War I, when a German doctor saw the need to assist the large numbers of veterans who had lost their sight in combat. But these efforts would never have spread around the world if Dorothy Eustis, an American breeder of German shepherds, had not happened to visit a guide dog training school in Potsdam in 1926. What Eustis saw at the school so impressed her that she began training guide dogs at her kennel in Switzerland. She wrote an article for *The Saturday Evening Post* describing the training that turned "raw" dogs into "leaders" and prepared blind men—for they were all men at the time—to partner with dogs. Eustis received countless letters from blind people seeking the independence that a guide dog would bring. One especially enthusiastic letter writer, Frank Morris, seeking a dog of his own, offered to help Eustis establish a training center in the United States. Morris soon traveled to Switzerland, where he learned to work with his first guide dog, Buddy. Two years later, in Morristown, New Jersey, Morris and Eustis founded The Seeing Eye, the first guide dog training school in the United States. The original school is still in operation, and approximately ten additional schools have opened subsequently. Frank Morris traveled widely with Buddy, promoting the independence, dignity, safety, and confidence that guide dogs offered their blind handlers. Morris also advocated for the rights of blind people to use guide dogs in all public settings. Over time, dogs have learned to assist with disabilities other than visual impairment. Dogs aid the hearing-impaired and alert people with seizure disorders of impending episodes. They assist those with post-traumatic stress and other disorders. Dogs pull wheelchairs, fetch objects, work light switches, and open doors. Individually and rigorously trained to work with or perform tasks for people with disabilities, dogs with specialized skills constitute "service animals" in the legal sense, as defined in the Americans with Disabilities Act, or ADA. Although the designation is limited to dogs, a provision includes miniature horses trained to assist the blind. No other species qualify as service animals under federal law. However, two loopholes allow people to work around the restriction. First, the legal definition of disability has broadened considerably since the passing of the ADA, making it easier for individuals to establish eligibility for accommodations under the law. A growing number of people consider *all* pets, not just dogs, to be reasonable accommodations for disabilities through the emotional support they provide. Second, separate agencies determine what constitutes a service animal for housing and air travel. These regulations do not require that the animal be a dog, nor do they require the animal to have any specific training or perform a task related to a disability. Consequently, a landlord with a "no pets" policy for rental apartments must waive the policy for a tenant who can document that his or her dog or cat—or monkey, pig, snake, or bird—provides essential support and comfort.

Although a doctor's letter can attest to a person's need to have an animal for emotional support, it does not make the animal into a *service animal* in the legal sense. Amid the ensuing confusion about what *does* qualify an animal as such, a plethora of organizations—mostly online—have emerged to provide certification and registration. Many people seek out these organizations intending to bring their pets into places that would not otherwise be accessible to animals. For a fee, they can obtain documentation and vests or tags for their animals. Yet, federal law requires no such designation for legitimate service animals. A guide dog or seizure alert dog need not wear an identifying vest, tag, or harness, and a disabled person need not carry documentation of the need for the service animal. Moreover, criminal penalties exist for falsely claiming a pet as a service animal. Within the disabled community, criticism of people who misrepresent their pets as service animals is common.

Becoming With

Service dogs and their handlers together exemplify what "becoming with" means. The concept of becoming with accepts that all living and nonliving organisms exist in webs of encounters, and that other beings, large and small, human, animal, insect, and bacteria, colonize our bodies, share our ecospaces, and make us what we are. Our cells contain the dust of exploded stars. We drink the same water that quenched the dinosaurs' thirst. We eat and are eaten. We breathe and become with the air.

Some relationships bring becoming with into flesh-and-blood reality, showing how encounters of bodies and meanings create subjects and objects relationally. For instance, a mother doesn't exist until she births a child. Friends don't exist as friends before they meet. Similarly, a service dog handler only becomes so with the dog. All of a service dog's work depends on a human's disability. A dog may learn through training how to act like a service dog but only truly becomes a service dog by interacting with a continually learning human body moving through shared space and time. The disabled handler and the dog are mutually influencing—but only to a point. The use of service dogs raises important questions about who benefits from the relationship.

In what follows, a fictional service dog advises interested puppies about this canine career path. He describes the training he received, the challenges he faces, and his life apart from his working role. Speaking as a seasoned professional, he both questions and celebrates the mingling of the species in the service of humans.

Working with Blind People: A Guide for Puppies

My name is Pete, and I'm a seeing eye dog. I'd like to take this opportunity to share what it takes to be a service dog in the United States. I'm assuming that you're reading this because you want to help people overcome some form of adversity that restricts their free movement in their human parks. Human parks are similar to dog parks; people meet there, do things together, and come and go. But they aren't fenced in as dog parks are, so there are many dangerous pitfalls that must be avoided. Human parks are full of buildings, cars, buses, trains, bicycles, and worst of all . . . skateboarders. I don't want to scare you, but, if you're assigned a human who attends classes on a college campus, you'll need to take skateboarders very seriously. With practice, you'll hear the tick, tick, tick of their wheels and can safely guide your human out of harm's way.

But I'm getting ahead of myself. Human parks are like giant obstacle courses that we, as guide dogs, have the skills to navigate successfully. This is an important job that only well-behaved and specially trained dogs can (or should) take on. Our humans need us, and we've developed special skills that allow us to help them navigate their human parks. Together, we form a team that appears to move effortlessly through our daily tasks. Really, we only *appear* to move effortlessly. Each of you will have to complete extensive training before you ever pair up with your human. Then, after you finally acquire a human, you'll have to do even more advanced training to understand how to work together.

Now, you'll meet many dogs that humans *call* "seeing eye dogs," and yet they're helping deaf humans. That's because humans don't know what they are talking about. They get confused all the time, but I'll set you straight about the three types of service animals: guide dogs for blind humans, hearing dogs for hearing-impaired humans, and service dogs for humans with disabilities other than deafness and blindness. Each of you will be trained for a specific disability, and you won't get to choose how you're trained. For example, The Seeing Eye organization breeds dogs specifically to be "seeing eye dogs." Only dogs bred and trained by this organization can be called "seeing eye dogs." Dogs trained through other programs and by other organizations are "guide dogs" and should not be confused with "seeing eye dogs." Each organization that trains guide, hearing, or service dogs has specific requirements for breeding and training. To date, there are no universal requirements.

I'm a three-year-old Labrador retriever, and I was bred and trained by The Seeing Eye in New Jersey. Some of the other dogs in my program were German shepherds and golden retrievers. Retrievers and German shepherds are common in guide dog programs because our dispositions are well suited for the work; our genealogy and behavioral traits make us perfect companions as well as guide dogs. We come in a variety of sizes, which makes pairing us with the right human easy. Most of us are super smart and find our lessons at the training academy easy to complete. I mean, who doesn't like to get treats! I love treats and love to make humans happy, so I found the training process to be a piece of cake! Of course, it was not always fun and games. I had to complete tasks to get treats, but there were always opportunities for do-overs, and I always got the treat in the end. During training, we all had to undergo repeated health and temperament evaluations. Not all of us qualified for basic training, and some had to make early career changes. For example, Toby liked treats a bit too much and couldn't always control himself. He became a companion animal and went to live with a nice family. This made me sad at first, but as the training became more difficult, I understood that we all have things we do well, and Toby was really good at being a companion. I also knew a few dogs who became police dogs and one even trained for search and rescue. Each of these dogs had qualifications that made them valuable in their respective fields. Evaluations are scary and stressful because we like being together and no one wants to leave early, but they're not as bad as they seem to be in the moment. After all, we're being trained for a purpose and we're all placed in the environment that's most suitable for our dispositions.

There's a long waiting list to get a dog through The Seeing Eye, and I'm proud to be one of their dogs. One of my earliest memories is of the playroom, the first step on the road to becoming a seeing eye dog. I was approximately four weeks old when I first visited that magical place. It's filled with toys and people to help puppies become accustomed to many different situations. This first step in the training process also helps puppies learn not to be easily distracted. This is a critical difference between companion animals and us. From birth, we've had to deal with a wide variety of distractions while maintaining our composure. One day, I remember vividly, we had some noises introduced to our playroom for the first time. These are exciting noises that make you want to sing and sing, together with your friends! But no. These are what humans call "sirens," and, sadly, we have to learn to ignore them. I found that focusing on my closest toy and chewing on it made me feel better and helped me resist the urge to sing. While in the playroom, I got used to a wide variety of noises and learned how to play with others, both human and canine. I also learned how to wear a collar and walk on a leash. This wasn't fun at first. My first collar was itchy, and all I wanted to do was sit and scratch it. Then, just when I became okay with my collar, Larry, one of the volunteers, attached a leash to it. Learning how to walk with Larry was awful at first. I really didn't understand what he wanted, but soon, after many, many treats, I got it! He just wanted me to walk next to him and not pull on my leash. It sounds simple now, but at the time, it seemed like I would never understand what he wanted me to do. It was an exciting time for the other puppies and me. So many new scents, so many things to chew, so many opportunities for treats.

When I turned seven weeks old, I went to live with Debbie, a kind woman who volunteered to help me learn some basic rules, which humans call "obedience." Debbie was very patient and loving toward me. She was always encouraging me to try new things and taking me to new places. She did this so I could learn the proper ways to respond in different situations and different environments. Debbie called our adventures "field trips." Field trips were my first exposure to the human park. Unlike our dog parks, human parks have unlimited areas to explore, and they can be overwhelming. It was Debbie's job to help me understand the human park. On our field trips, we'd go to the mall, the grocery store, the home improvement center, and my personal favorite, the pet supply store. These trips helped me feel comfortable around other humans and other animals.

I learned how to greet other humans and animals in the human park properly. I lived with Debbie until I turned fourteen months old. My heart broke when I had to leave her and go back to the kennel. We had had so many fun adventures together!

This has been the most difficult part of being a service animal for me. New people come into our lives, and we must learn how to love them and stop missing our other humans. During the training program, you'll encounter a variety of humans who will take care of you, and you'll bond with them. Being a trained seeing eye dog means that you've learned how to detach from your early caregivers and trainers, as well as the volunteers who helped you develop your specialized skills. You'll learn to maintain a degree of loyalty to your humans without becoming too attached. Every new recruit has trouble with this part of the training. It may make us sad, but we have to be flexible. While some of us will be paired with humans who'll be our "forever family," others will have to transition between new humans as the need arises. Adapting is part of the job. Remember, not all dogs are suited to the task. My advice for each of you would be to focus on the rewards of being a guide dog. Think about the treats and the relationship that you'll develop with your human. The rewards of being a guide dog will outweigh the periods of sadness and anxiety you'll feel along the way. Remember, your goal is to become a guide dog with your human. In the process, you'll form a bond with your human that most other dogs will never get the opportunity to experience. And you'll get plenty of treats along the way!

Your job will get more difficult once you have basic obedience down. After leaving Debbie, I returned to The Seeing Eye for advanced training with a sighted instructor named Isabella. She was kind but very strict. She was responsible for teaching me how to "behave," as humans call it, in my harness. I remember thinking that wearing a collar and walking on a leash was stressful. Well, that was nothing compared to learning how to wear a harness. At first, I thought I was being punished for something I'd done wrong. The harness scared me and made me itch all over. However, once Isabella explained how my harness was my uniform, I started to enjoy wearing it. When Isabella put my harness on, I knew it was time to go to work. I would get an opportunity to be the boss! Isabella taught me how to understand when I needed to be the boss and how I should tackle this enormous responsibility. I had to learn how to walk in a straight line and not wander about and sniff at interesting bushes and trees during our adventures. After all, our humans should be the most interesting things in our world! She also taught me to navigate social environments with a sight-impaired human. This was a very important period in my training, and it lasted about four months. I had to learn how to cross the street by listening to the sound of the traffic.

Now, I don't want to scare you, but navigating traffic is very serious business. Understanding the noises that cars, trucks, bikes, and yes, even skateboards make requires a lot of training. Remember, we can't see the colors of the traffic lights, so we have to listen carefully. This is considered advanced training, so keep in mind that, by the time you reach this point in the program, you'll be ready for the challenge. You'll learn how to work in a variety of settings: rural, suburban, and urban. You'll get to ride trains and buses. This is considered advanced training because you're in an enclosed environment with lots of distractions. People are sitting, standing, talking, and moving all at the same time. It can be very chaotic but also exciting. You get on the train or bus in one location, and then you stop, and you're somewhere else. Oh, one very important thing to remember: Always scan up ahead of your human. Isabella taught me how to look for objects above my line of sight so that my human wouldn't walk into a low tree limb or door frame—this is especially important when you're taking trains and buses and you get off in new areas of the human park that you and your human aren't familiar with. Isabella always used a clicker to indicate that I had done exactly what she wanted me to do. She also used lots of praise and never punished me when I goofed up and lost my concentration for a minute, even if I led her under a low tree branch.

My final test was navigating the streets of New York City while Isabella wore a blindfold. Oh, let me tell you, this was stressful at first. But I just kept calm and remembered that I had been trained for this and that Isabella had confidence in me, or she wouldn't have recommended that I was ready for this test. As guide dogs, we've been conditioned to handle this type of stress and have all of the skills necessary to navigate city streets—even in New York City. Needless to say, I passed! Shortly after this, Isabella and I were paired with Amy, a young blind woman. I knew right away that Amy and I would be best friends and that I'd do anything to keep her safe. Amy was just as nervous as I was when we first met. She had never had a guide dog, and this worked out perfectly because I had never had my very own human! Amy had to pay a fee and live with me at the school for a month so that we could train together and learn how to live with each other. She was about to enter college, and she had waited a long time to get me. This made me feel very special. Before I could go home with Amy, however, we both had to learn about our responsibilities in our new partnership.

During my time with Isabella and Amy, I worked very hard to learn what it was like to be a sight-impaired person. For example, I learned that, in public spaces, my presence with Amy attracts people who would otherwise ignore her or even feel intimidated by her. I still don't understand this very well, but I notice how people stare at Amy sometimes, and when they see me, they smile. Some people even approach Amy and initiate conversations because of me. This can be challenging because people should never pet or talk to service dogs while we're working. When I have my harness on and I'm with Amy, I must think of myself as an extension of her. I cannot accept pats or treats, even though I really, *really* want to. In addition, as Amy and I move throughout our day together, I must show "intelligent disobedience." This means I have to know when to resist her commands. In other words, I have to know when to be the boss and when to let Amy be the boss. For example, if Amy tells me to move forward but I see a car coming, I must disobey her command. My primary responsibility is to keep Amy safe, and sometimes this means *not* doing what she wants me to do. Our relationships with our humans are very complicated. They take care of us, and we take care of them. Let me explain by taking you through a typical day with Amy.

Amy and I live in an apartment close to the university's main campus. Other people with disabilities live in the building, too, and other service animals live with them. Amy and I get up early on weekday mornings. Our first class starts at 9:00 a.m., and we usually wake up at 7:00 a.m.; humans require a lot of time to "get ready"—so boring! What takes so long? I keep busy by rolling on the floor, chewing on my toys, and following Amy around the apartment. When we're in the house and my harness is off, I can play with Amy and with all of my toys. We are lucky. Our apartment has a small fenced-in yard, so Amy usually opens the door and lets me out first thing in the morning. I enjoy freely roaming around for a few minutes on our small patch of grass, and I occasionally chase a bird out of our yard. Max, the cat next door, often sits in the window, and I always say hello—sometimes a bit too loudly, and Amy reminds me that some humans are still sleeping. Then it's time for breakfast. Amy cheats and gives me part of her food, even though my veterinarian discourages this. She makes me promise to keep it our secret. I never tell. After breakfast, I usually take a quick nap while Amy gets into the water box and then puts on her fur. I haven't fully figured this all out yet, but it's something you should note. Humans have removable fur and voluntarily get into a water box—every day!

After the water box ritual, Amy puts on my harness and we prepare to leave. Remember: Our harnesses are our uniforms! It's time for me to be a seeing eye dog. I remind myself to stay focused and alert. Amy depends on me to guide her safely to the bus stop and to our classes. Sometimes we stop for coffee across from the bus stop. Amy says she needs this to make it through our first class: Statistics. I don't really like going there, because no one ever looks happy in this class. But getting coffee beforehand is always fun because it's my responsibility to guide Amy across the street when I know it's safe for us to do so. When we cross the streets, I'm in charge. The woman at the coffee shop gives Amy a treat for me. But I have to wait for the treat. I can only eat it once Amy removes my harness. I think about that treat for hours . . . just sitting in Amy's bag. The coffee shop woman knows that she must not talk to me because I'm on duty, focused on keeping Amy safe. Remember, properly trained service dogs never let their attention stray from the task. Some people at the coffee shop try to pet me or talk to me. It's hard, but I have to ignore them. Sometimes other dogs try to play with me or talk to me, and I have to look away and stay focused. I have to remember that I'm not a pet. I'm a trained service animal, and Amy depends on me.

Now, I find the bus stop and the ride to campus frustrating sometimes. The bus stop is very close to the street. The cars are loud, and they go very fast. But the worst part is Henry, another service dog—or so he says. However, Henry's human is neither hearing- nor sight-impaired. His human, Jake, has anxiety attacks, and he registered Henry as a service animal online. Henry wears a special jacket, and he really seems happy with Jake. The problem is that Henry has not been trained to be a service animal. In fact, he hasn't been trained at all, and as a result, he doesn't take his work seriously. He tries to play with me at the bus stop and on the bus. Amy tries to sit far away from Henry, but Henry doesn't understand the rules and will still try to talk to me across the length and width of the bus. I want to play, too, and sometimes Amy has to remind me that I have to ignore Henry and focus on my job. I really like Henry, but I see how other people look at him. He annoys some people. They roll their eyes and move away from Jake and him. I wonder: What if they think that I'm just like Henry? They think Henry is a real service dog. They don't understand that he's just a companion animal wearing a jacket. His human is abusing the system by calling him a service dog. Jake makes Amy angry. She calls him a "faker." She says he's making it harder for people with *real* disabilities to be taken seriously and to be granted access to public spaces that permit only legitimate service animals. But ignoring Henry is a very small part of my day.

Once Amy and I arrive on campus, we're very busy. Campus is exciting. Most of the people there understand the rules of interacting with service animals and their humans. Sometimes we go to visit professors, and Amy takes off my harness. I get to romp around the professor's office and have snacks and pets. I also enjoy lectures. They are great for naps. No one bothers us, and no one tries to interact with me. The students just look at their cell phones and laptops while the professors talk to themselves at the front of the rooms. It's usually very relaxing. Occasionally, another student brings a companion animal to class, and this is stressful for me. Once again, these animals are well-meaning, but they just want to play. Their humans don't understand that they create a distraction and cause legitimate service animals and their humans a great deal of frustration. We trained service animals are professionals. Each of you, after successfully completing your training, will be a member of an elite society of animals who are specially qualified to meet the individual needs of their humans. Having distractions like these are common, and it is our job to understand the differences between companion animals and us. Most professors don't permit companion animals in the classroom because it's against the university rules, but others let this slide. Animals do make the atmosphere in classrooms more laid-back, but for service animals and their humans, they can be very distracting.

The best part of our days on campus, besides sleeping through the lectures, is lunch. On warm days, we eat outside, and Amy usually takes my harness off for a few minutes. I get to relax and roll around on the grass. Sometimes people stop and pet me, and I can interact with them because my harness is off. I also get to watch the squirrels play. I'd really like to chase them, but Amy always reminds me not to frighten them. I try to remember this, but it's hard when they run right past me . . . with food the humans left for them in the big covered cans. As a highly trained professional, I must never try to get food out of these cans. Amy tells me that good dogs don't do this. Just be aware, the temptation is great. Humans put a lot of their food in these cans, but we have to ignore this and focus on our jobs. I used to think they must be saving it for later, but the squirrels always find it first.

After we finish our classes and visit with our professors, we head home. I always enjoy the ride home because I know Amy will take my harness off soon and let me relax. I'm always eager to spend some time outside telling Max (through the window) about my day. Amy usually comes outside and tells me to be quiet, but it really is hard if Veronica is home. Veronica is the human who lives next door. Besides Max the cat, she has two service dogs, Maggie and Zulu. They are both seeing eye dogs. Zulu is younger than I am and is still in training. He constantly reminds me about the rules and points out how I'm gaining weight. This is simply not true. He's just jealous because Veronica doesn't share her food with him. Maggie's older than I am and is "retired," which means that she doesn't work anymore and gets to stay home and nap. Maggie is lucky to be in her "forever home." I've heard stories of service dogs being returned to the program and adopted by other people after they retire. I don't like to think about this. Sometimes when I don't want to put the harness on, I think about another dog being Amy's best friend, especially a know-it-all dog like Zulu.

I like spending time with Maggie because she's seen it all. She's had some crazy experiences and has the best stories. My favorite is about the time someone had a "therapy ferret" on the bus. Maggie says this human was a faker and a "therapy ferret" is just a giant hamster on a leash. Now, I'm not sure what a "therapy ferret" is, but I'm sure a giant hamster on a leash is never a good idea in any situation. The ferret's name was Simon, and his human had made a vest for him. She told everyone how Simon calmed her and kept her from being sad. She carried Simon in a tote bag and gave him treats in public. All trained service animals understand that treats are rewards for a job well done. Treats are rewards! One day, right after Simon's human took a seat, Simon jumped out of his tote and ran across Maggie's head toward the back of the bus. Simon's human was not holding the leash. Maggie was horrified. That would never happen with a service dog handler. Everyone on the bus screamed. Maggie says she can still feel the cold little feet scamper across her head. She started to chase Simon, thinking it would be best if she just ate him. Then Veronica calmly reminded her about her training. Simon bit two people before his human could catch him. The driver almost wrecked the bus. That silly ferret was supposed to help his human be happy. Instead he caused five minutes of chaos.

Maggie said that no training in the world could have prepared her for a vest-wearing ferret running across her head. Of course, it wasn't the ferret's fault. The poor ferret had no training and wasn't a legitimate service animal. So, we shouldn't blame the ferret. We should blame her human. While I find the story hilarious, the situation was dangerous, and the careless actions of one person who just wanted to spend more time with her companion animal could have resulted in injuries to many people. Legitimate service dogs and their humans have collectively undergone hundreds of hours of training to enable them to move through their daily activities together while respecting the rights of others and the spaces and social environments that everyone must share. It's our responsibility as true service animals to be models for how this should work in public settings.

Becoming a service animal takes a great deal of training. Puppies entering a training program are expected to learn how to become part of a human's world. Each of you will struggle at times and doubt whether you want to be a service animal. This is normal. Learning how to interact with humans is difficult, especially when you have to learn how to "let go." We don't always understand their rules. Some of you will fail. For those who fail, adoption programs can help find your forever families. This is not a bad thing. Forever families are great. There are waiting lists for humans who want to adopt a retired service animal, and with forever families, you'll never need to work. Adoption services also assist retired animals in finding new careers in law enforcement or search and rescue. Remember, through your training as a service animal, you'll learn how to transition from serving the needs of one human to serving another. This can be difficult, but to be a successful service animal, it's necessary.

Another challenge you'll encounter comes when people criticize your person. Most people will think you are brave and smart, but there will be exceptions. A complete stranger once yelled at Amy for having a purebred dog while perfectly good dogs languish in shelters. That person just didn't understand how carefully controlled the guide dog's early life must be. Another stranger told Amy that she was exploiting me. He said that Amy didn't allow me to be a "real" dog. That got me to thinking. Although my relationship with Amy is unequal, it has brought me experiences that are off-limits to most companion animals. This is an important distinction between pets and us. We've been trained to be the boss when our humans need us to be the boss. Maggie says that it's nice not having to be the boss now, but it makes me sad to think of retiring. I *like* being the boss. Getting to be the boss sometimes means that my life is never boring. I've heard that some pets have to stay home alone all day, sometimes in crates, while their people work. They hardly get outdoors at all. When their people come home, they're too tired to play or go for walks. I wouldn't be happy in that kind of life. I'm with Amy all the time, and she's always kind to me. Amy's limitations provide meaning and purpose in my world, and I provide a sense of security in her human park. I'm in her life to help her. We complete each other. Still, I do worry about what will happen to me when I get too old to work, like Maggie. What if I get sick and need someone to take care of me? Will I still be with Amy?

As I get older, I'm starting to think about these things, and you should consider them, too. Being a service animal means that you'll dedicate your life to helping humans, and if you don't feel comfortable with this, the career may not be right for you. I don't remember having a choice when I was a puppy, but I am sure I did . . . right? Well, never mind. That's beside the point. Being a service animal is an honor, and I cherish the time I have with Amy. If you decide to embark on a life of service, I hope that you're as fortunate in your career as I've been in mine.

Suggested Readings

On service animals, see:

Harold Herzog. 2016. "Eight Misconceptions about Therapy, Service, and Support Animals." Animals and Us, *Psychology Today* (blog). Available at https://www.psychologytoday.com/blog/animals-and-us/201602/8-misconceptions-about-therapy-service-and-support-animals.

Randy Malamud. 2013. "Service Animals: Serve Us Animals: Serve Us, Animals." *Social Alternatives* 32: 34–40.

On the beneficial impact of dogs on disabled handlers, see:

Clinton R. Sanders. 2000. "The Impact of Guide Dogs on the Identity of People with Visual Impairments." *Anthrozoös* 13: 131–39.

Natalie Sachs-Ericsson, Nancy K. Hansen, and Shirley Fitzgerald. 2003. "Benefits of Assistance Dogs: A Review." *Rehabilitation Psychology* 47: 251–77.

On "becoming with," see:

Donna Haraway. 2008. *When Species Meet*. Minneapolis: University of Minnesota Press.

CHAPTER 7

How to Protect Yourself from the Dead with Cattle

GENESE MARIE SODIKOFF

Hear "animal sacrifice," and the words conjure the image of a lamb on an altar or a chicken at a shrine of candles and charms, over which a holy man incants to the gods before slicing the animal's throat. "Sacrifice" evokes a time when captured enemies or young virgins were delivered up to the heavens as gifts. This was long before the animal became a lesser stand-in for a human being.

Cinematic fiction may have rendered animal sacrifice sinister, but the ritual is a commonplace and festive event in Madagascar. Zebus, a breed of long-horned, humped cattle, are the valuable beasts killed as tribute. In the east, among the Betsimisaraka people, the ritual is called *tsaboraha* ("doing something").

In the mid-1990s, during my first long stint of fieldwork in Madagascar, I never witnessed a sacrifice. But I did attend a portion of what my Malagasy colleague dubbed a "festival of the dead." He was referring to the ritual, known in English as "the turning of the bones," of exhuming the skeletal remains of relatives from the familial tomb and rewrapping the bones in a new mortuary shroud. There are variations around the island, and the custom of the Merina people in the central highlands has achieved global renown. There they exhume the ancestors and dance with the cloth-wrapped bones overhead, clacking them noisily.

On this occasion, I did not stay for an exhumation. I doubt I would have been welcome. It was a moment when a disturbing rumor about bone theft was circulating in the countryside. Thieves were allegedly raiding graves for bones and selling them to middlemen, who in turn sold them abroad. Europeans bought the bones to crush them into powder for medicines. This claim was specious, but it was entirely possible to me that grave robbing was happening. You never know what exotic new material will become hot in these shady markets, nor can you rule out the problem of the rumor inspiring the crime. Fear of bone theft made villagers warier than usual of white foreigners, especially those who took an interest in anything funereal.

I sat there with the villagers on a scrubby hillside listening to (but not comprehending) an elder's speech to the ancestors. He said something that suddenly made everyone laugh and stare at me. My colleague, amused, told me that the old man had beseeched the ancestors to nestle their bones deep underground to hide them from this here foreigner. A joke at my expense, but no laughing matter. A few weeks later, the newspaper reported that two Malagasy men seen loitering in a cemetery near the railway had been stoned to death by a mob.

For Malagasy people, taking care of the ancestors, including their bodily remains, is of paramount importance. Kin must remember and pay tribute to their deceased relatives. When they are content, ancestors can bestow blessing upon your family. Neglect or slight them (or worse, allow someone to purloin their bones), and you will eventually suffer. No matter how relaxed a person may have been in life, the mellowness evaporates in ancestorhood, and what remains is what I would call a hypersensitive and unforgiving nature. The most effective way to pay respect and buffer your family against ancestral wrath is to sacrifice a zebu, one per deceased parent and adult sibling.

When a family becomes burdened with bad luck, they know that the only solution is to host a *tsaboraha*.

This is a huge undertaking because cattle are extremely pricey. In contrast to lowland regions, Madagascar's eastern escarpment is not suited to large herds. If a household owns five head of cattle, it is considered wealthy. It would be impractical to move a large herd over the steep, clayey footpaths of the denuded mountains.

Centuries ago, when human populations were smaller and stretches of territory were unsettled, cattle would occasionally escape their human keepers to grow wild. By the time cattle were brought northeast, when the rain forest belt was still vast and opaque, I imagine that cattle would disappear into the woods now and then. But that scenario is unimaginable today. The rain forest has been whittled down to fragments through logging, rice agriculture, and cash crop plantations. Although the larger forest remnants have been turned into national parks, these have been ransacked over the past decade to feed an illicit global trade in rosewood timber. These days, no run-away zebu could hide for long in the rainforest.

Most rural Malagasy live off of what they grow, so preparing for a *tsabo-raha* demands years of saving. In the northeast coast, Betsimisaraka agri-culturalists can earn a good amount of cash from selling vanilla and cloves. A bumper crop of cloves might earn you enough to buy a cow or bull after one harvest, but that's rare.

Wealthier households can relinquish a zebu relatively painlessly (which also makes it less of a sacrifice). Most households, however, struggle to make ends meet and are reluctant to lose a draft animal. Zebus are used to pull carts of cargo, and in the mountains they labor over the mud of rice pad-dies. Their manure enriches the soil, and their legs and hooves churn up the decayed matter that has sunk to the bottom of the paddy.

Men handle all things zebu: agricultural work, veterinary care, market exchanges, transport, bull-on-bull fighting, and, in some parts of the island, cattle rustling. Boys are taught to master their cattle. They learn how to mark ownership by clipping or cutting cattle ears or branding the hide. They learn how to fill out the zebu "passport," the paperwork that proves owner-ship to authorities when zebus are led from the cattle market to the village. They learn to guide the zebus' steps, yelling in a bass voice "toh toh toh!" to prod the animals into zigzags through the mud.

Zebu husbandry fosters a close bond between boys and their cattle, and boys identify strongly with their bulls. In some regions, bulls are thought to reflect the wildness of male youths. Since they increase harvests and pro-vide milk and meat, symbolize fecundity and vitality, and serve as conduits between the living and the dead, cattle are integral to the chain of human descent.

A Typology of the Dead

To clarify, zebus are conduits between living people and their ancestors, but they do not mediate relationships with other types of supernatural entities. Betsimisaraka people, unless they have converted to Christianity, do not imagine the afterworld to be a separate realm, such as heaven or hell, in which the dead reside. Death appears to be a process of the transformation of agency and physical form, from visible matter to a partially or wholly invisible force.

For all the insurance that sacrifice provides against the potential vengeance of ancestors, it does not shield you from other sources of supernatural trou-ble, such as sorcery, hauntings, mischief by small mythical humanoids called *kalañoro*, visits in dreams by savage animals, or injury from wild spirits called *tsiñy*. The emotions of ancestors, compared to other spirit types, are relatively manageable and recognizably human.

The capricious *tsiñy* are a different story. I was told that *tsiñy* were probably once ancestors, eons ago, who went wild due to the neglect of kin or to the long passage of time. They seem more like knots of mean energy than artifacts of human beings. Another kind of spirit, also possibly an ancestor-gone-wild, according to one diviner I knew, is prone to haunting particular spots, often on roads. The spot gets designated "wild land" (*tany mahery*) and is identified by the frequency of fatal car accidents there.

Tsiñy, in contrast, often inhabit natural formations, such as water pools or rock outcroppings. This is not always the case, however. One night at the home of my host family in town, I was startled awake by a series of brief, nearly simultaneous events: the eight-year-old daughter cried out in her sleep, my hands tingled as though touching a live wire, a hanging picture crashed to the floor. After hearing my account the next morning, my host family was convinced it had been a *tsiñy* zipping around the house.

Ghosts are something else again. They are people who died of unnatural causes and look indistinguishable from the living, except that they float slightly above the ground, footless (this is the clue they are ghosts). They linger in visible form due to some unresolved issue, as ghosts around the world are wont to do, it seems.

Kalañoro, Betsimisaraka say, were once a population of small, hairy, human-like creatures with fangs and backwards feet. They inhabited the rain forest until so much of it was razed that they died out. *Kalañoro* persist today as spirits. Humans can "own" a *kalañoro* (in spirit form) and deploy it to steal money and beer from others. But a *kalañoro* can also impart clairvoyance to its owner, and this gift attracts paying clients who seek advice.

Dead ancestors intervene frequently in the affairs of the living. After someone dies, he or she continues to participate in village life and is always welcome at social occasions. People acknowledge ancestors' presence during agricultural tasks and village festivities. Before clearing a plot of land to plant rice, you (if you are a man) must make a speech and leave offerings of cooked rice and chicken for the ancestors on a special stone.

Before an important meeting, before telling the history of the village, before drinking alcohol among friends, you (if you are a man) make a ritual speech (*kabary*) and spill a drop of rum or fermented cane juice on the floor for the ancestors. No one believes that ancestors literally eat and drink these offerings. They merely "ingest the aroma." You do these things as a matter of course because to neglect them causes offense.

Zebus should also be sacrificed not only to recently deceased kin but also to ancestors who feel neglected. The latter may visit you in dreams begging you to fulfill your obligations to them or advocating on behalf of another unhappy relative. If a couple procrastinates for too long in organizing a *tsaboraha*, tragedy will eventually strike.

What kind of tragedy? The rice stalks may grow thinner each season until all family members are wasting away and may have to resort to filling their bellies instead with tubers and potatoes, which for Malagasy people are not meals at all but crude snacks for work in the field. As husband, wife, and children sink into misery, the neighbors will criticize the parents behind their back for neglecting their dead.

Or a child might get the fever and die, even if a parent tries to prevent this horror by tying a talisman of wood with embedded zebu horn on a leather strap around the child's neck. The necklace is supposed to ward off the "monstrous black thing" that haunts the child's dreams and weakens her, but the parents' failure to sacrifice a zebu renders such charms powerless.

Thieves might sneak into the household's garden, which lies on the periphery of the village, to pluck the vanilla pods ripening on the vine, or they might hack off the blossoming branches of the family's more distant clove trees before everyone has had time to snap off and dry the flowers under the sun. Or, if you are a fisherman, your boat's motor may die while out at sea as the water grows choppy and you are pushed farther away from shore without a paddle. Other bad things might happen too, and you must live with the anxiety of not knowing when or how your life will be turned upside-down by angry ancestors.

This is not to say that bad things happen only when offspring fail to sacrifice cattle. Malicious acts by sorcerers are a frequent problem, and these can render someone a blameless victim. The scarcity of very old people makes them suspect. People frequently accuse gray-haired elders of harboring knowledge of the dark arts. But everyone knows with certainty that some tragedies are the direct results of the failure to offer up a zebu for each ancestor.

Cattle as Kin

Betsimisaraka cosmology holds that men, in their superior strength and wisdom, are closer to ancestors than women. Since zebus serve as mediums between men and the ancestors, logic would dictate that zebus are the closest to the ancestors (and so, perhaps, the sagest and strongest of them all?). Although Betsimisaraka people never said so explicitly to me, zebus appear to be tangled up in the bonds of human lineal descent. Through metaphor and folklore, zebus and humans are kin. Betsimisaraka people say that children are the "horns," defenders and supporters, of their parents.

In the village of Volove in the northeast, an elder told me a legend about a boy and a black-and-white cow named Haramanga. It begins with the death of the boy's mother. His father remarries a cruel woman, and the boy's new stepmother casts him out of the home. He is rescued by the cow, Haramanga, who feeds the boy her milk. Together they leave the village.

Along their journey, Haramanga and the boy encounter several hostile bulls named Copper, Silver, and Gold. With Haramanga's help, the boy kills each one in succession and cuts off each of their fatty humps as trophies. He buries the humps in the earth, each one symbolizing a form of mineral wealth. But the humps also represent the three-footed stone base of the flat stone, called the *lokambato*, on which villagers leave offerings—cooked rice and chicken meat, a bit of rum—to the ancestors. The legend of Haramanga reinforces the bonds among boys, zebus, and ancestors. The legend ends with the burial of the hump of the last slain bull, but one would expect that Haramanga achieved ancestorhood after death, relishing the offerings left on the raised stone that she and the boy invented.

Human-zebu kinship is changeable. Children may be "the horns" of their parents, and a cow may be the surrogate mother of a boy. But everyday practices of cattle husbandry make boy and bull more like brothers. In learning to master the temper of bulls, boys build up their mettle and adroitness. They come to identify with their animals, who sometimes serve as surrogate combatants. Elsewhere in Madagascar, the wildness of bulls is thought to reflect the rowdiness and vitality of young men.

In the village of Volove, boys demonstrated their courage by staging bull-on-bull fights in the large grassy field, where kids often played soccer with balls made of dried vegetation and twine. The boy with the feistiest bull won.

As I was heading to the field watch such a bull battle one day, I spotted Dely, a young teenager, holding his bull steady with a cord around the muzzle and stroking his anus and testicles to rile him up. Once fuming with lust, the bull was released into the field to confront his opponent while spectators sat around the edge. Hanging their curved horns low, the two bulls danced around each other, eyes locked, nostrils flaring. Then they charged at each other.

These fights were usually not bloody or lethal. No one could afford to lose a bull to a fun competition. The point was to prove to the crowd which bull was dominant, as its fierceness would reflect on the bravery of its owner.

Sometimes an agitated bull would dart off the field in a mad spree toward the rows of plant-and-thatch houses. People would leap off their verandas, giddy with fright as the bull would race down lanes and around corners. It was like a terrifying game, never knowing where the bull would re-emerge. The men would eventually corner and pacify the animal. Knowing how to calm a savage beast is a safety essential. As one might imagine, cattle awaiting sacrifice are jittery, and the ancestors would surely disapprove of a mad bull trampling the grounds of a *tsaboraha*.

"Doing Something" for the Ancestors

Ritual sacrifices are different than slaughter at the town market or village festival, where the butcher unceremoniously dispatches the animal with a machete. The zebu's head is held up to the crowd by his horns, as the offended body jerks and jitters on the ground, headless neck straining.

But at the *tsaboraha*, the zebu is treated with gratitude and respect. Arriving late to the ceremony is considered rude. Latecomers "walk on the blood of the zebu." It is in the ritual context that people recognize the sentience of zebus, their mindfulness, which makes them unlike other animals and more like people.

A decade and a half has passed since I witnessed a *tsaboraha*, but I have been told that the gist of the ritual has not changed over the years. I'm not sure if it has changed in the village where I lived, but between 2000 and 2002 the *tsaboraha* there was held at a special site, a grove in a meadow near the river's edge.

One morning in April 2001, women started arriving at the grove to prepare the ground with wide banana and lingoza leaves that served as "tablecloths" on which mounds of cooked rice and beef would be ladled. Water boiled in large aluminum pots were placed atop stones over flames. The atmosphere was suspenseful and jubilant as the crowd waited in the shade of trees and thatch shelters.

Several topped trees nearby, called *fisokina*, were adorned with columns of horn racks or desiccated chickens' heads, an archive of past sacrifices. At the base of the *fisokina* lay a large slab set on three stone feet, as in the story of Haramanga the cow. This was the *lokambato*, the offering stone where the ancestors' share of the feast would be served. The spiritual leader of the village, the *tangalamena* (red baton), who presides over village ceremonies, began the event by offering libations of fermented cane juice to the crowd and thanking them for coming.

A couple of men led a cow and her calf (tributes for two ancestors) by a cord to the shade between two trees. The host grabbed the cow by her horns and torqued her neck until her legs buckled. He then then pushed her down flat on her side. The calf was also pulled to the ground and bound. During the process of wrestling a zebu to the ground, the animal should not resist too much because stubborn resistance signifies an unresolved problem between the ancestor and the descendants.

As the cow lay there tense and afraid, the host picked up her tail and began the *joro*, the word used in this region to signify the speech addressed to God and the ancestors. "Come down to us. We want you here with us for what we are doing," he said. Then another man slipped one of the animal's hoofs through a looped vine, and several other men stepped forward to bind the zebu's kicking forelegs to one tree and its kicking hind legs to another.

Long ceremonial speeches are called *kabary* in Madagascar, and the *joro* is a subset of *kabary*. During the sacrifice ritual, several men may make these honorific speeches. The speeches invoke the names of the ancestors of a particular family and tell a tale of recent goings-on in the village.

At the *tsaboraha*, the speaker held the end of a stick against the body of the zebu, whose legs were bound, head pointing east. The holding of the tail, I thought at the time, seemed like a way to translate words from human into bovine language, to "wire" a message to the ancestors, or, perhaps, to transfer the essence of sacredness (*hasina*) from ancestors to people through the cow.

The spatial structure of the ceremony was gendered: Maleness was associated with rightness, femaleness with leftness. The zebu's left nostril was plugged with a folded leaf in order to contain feminine weakness—theoretically exemplified by women's lack of control when drunk. Facing the butchering of the zebus, women and small children sat to the left of the audience, men and elders directly in front and to the right. The choice parts of the zebu—the fatty hump, the ribs, the liver, the intestines, the right "arm," and the right leg—were served to the male elders and ancestors (who receive a portion).

The male elders sat together facing the crowd, the women and children seated at their left, near the pots of boiling water and the large wooden disks covering hollowed-out earth. At various points during the feast, as the drink would flow, women danced on the wooden disks, thumping their feet, clapping, and singing: "Eh eh oh oh oh, don't you want to sing? Oh, you are all too lazy to sing. . . . Oh, yea, you're sleeping!" The amount of singing and the volume and energy were thought to reflect the spirit of the ancestor being honored. If the ancestor was a quiet person who was disinclined to party, the women would be moved to sing in a more subdued, even automatic, fashion. If, however, the ancestor was a *bon vivant*, the song would be boisterous.

The family hosting the *tsaboraha* stepped forward to kneel beside the bound cow. Holding her tail, each of four family members gazed downward, devotionally. Occupying a space between life and afterlife, sacrificial zebus resemble messengers sent by the living to sacred ancestors.

Men began to distribute fermented cane juice to the viewers in cups made of folded ravinala palm leaves. Each cup was filled to the "eighth rib" of the leaf, the standard measure. The host spoke to the ancestors while holding a leaf cup full of rum, he stood near the cow: "This is for you my father, we give to you this zebu." He then turned to the calf: "This is for you, brother."

The next to make a speech was the *tangalamena*, the spiritual leader. While he spoke to the crowd, another held the cow's tail, speaking to the calf. Women began to sing again, and another elder approached the calf. He put the "speaking stick" (my term, not theirs) upon the calf's body and delivered his *kabary* toward the animal. I found it hard to discern the addressee. The zebu? "No, always the ancestors," one man explained. Yet such respect was shown toward the animal during the speech that one would believe otherwise. The zebu assumed the role of medium, the stick a mode of telecommunication.

When the speeches ended, the cow was dragged a short distance away from the row of seated elders, their backs turned away from the spot where the cow and calf would be slaughtered. The children and young men watched. Three men approached the cow. One began cutting her neck with an axe, her body twitching with every blow. Two men began cutting the back legs. When the head and back legs were severed, the men moved on to the calf. From the udders of the cow, the hide was stripped off her body, as was the calf's. The intestines and organs were exposed. Every edible part would be eaten. The ribcage was pulled away from the cow's frame. Two ribs from each side were given to the *tangalamena*.

More men, about twenty, approached to help with butchering and cleaning and cutting the meat to divide among all the people who had contributed money to take some home (the hosts usually need these contributions). The cost was equivalent to 25 cents per strip, and people were encouraged to pay more for a to-go package (even though there was barely enough to satisfy all the attendees). The wisdom goes that those who do not contribute to the feast will get sick. In all, the family recouped less than half the cost of one zebu, but the sacrifice bettered their chances of staying safe from trouble.

As the fermented cane juice and rum flowed, other elders stood to make speeches to the crowd. Women continued to sing in the back on the disks made of *satrahana* wood: "Oh yeah, you're sleeping!" A knot of women and children danced beside the singers. Close by, men wagered on games of dominoes.

The *tsaboraha* lasted about six hours. As the energy wound down, the horn racks were severed from the heads of the cow and calf. A bit of the animals' forelocks remained on each rack, and the ears were cut off the head, still attached to each other by strips of hide. A young man climbed a tree, hacking off the vines and branches as he climbed. Another man handed him one rack of horns, and he affixed it to a pruned branch. He placed the cow's ears in the tree as well. Unlike the beef strips, the ears were not meant for the ancestors' meal. Two pieces were folded over the horns, meant as an offering to "a man who died a long time ago." Finally, more cane juice was poured from large plastic jerrycans into the leaf cups, and three elders in turn offered their speeches, their *kabary*, for a final farewell. But no one was really listening any more.

The crowd gradually dispersed, and the hosts, tired and tipsy, felt the satisfaction of knowing that they had fulfilled their obligation. For a while (who knew how long?) they could count on the ancestors to keep the household "healthy and free."

Suggested Readings

On the custom of sacrifice in Madagascar, see:

Maurice Bloch, 1986. *From Blessing to Violence: History and Ideology in the Circumcision Ritual of the Merina of Madagascar.* Cambridge, UK: Cambridge University Press.

Maurice Bloch. 1999. "'Eating' Young Men among the Zafimaniry." In *Ancestors, Power, and History in Madagascar,* edited by Karen Middleton, 175–90. Leiden, the Netherlands: Brill.

Jennifer Cole. 1997. "Sacrifice, Narratives, and Experience in East Madagascar." *Journal of Religion in Africa* 27: 401–25.

Jennifer Cole. 2001. *Forget Colonialism? Sacrifice and the Art of Memory in Madagascar.* Berkeley: University of California Press.

On youth and economic change in Madagascar, see:

Jennifer Cole. 2010. *Sex and Salvation: Imagining the Future in Madagascar.* Chicago: University of Chicago Press.

Lesley Sharp. 2002. *The Sacrificed Generation: Youth, History, and the Colonized Mind in Madagascar.* Berkeley: University of California Press.

On cattle husbandry in Madagascar, see:

R. E. Dewar. 2003. "Relationship between Human Ecological Pressure and the Vertebrate Extinctions." In *The Natural History of Madagascar,* edited by Steven M. Goodman and Jonathan P. Benstead, 119–22. Chicago: University of Chicago Press.

R. E. Dewar and H. T. Wright. 1993. "The Culture History of Madagascar." *Journal of World Prehistory* 7(4): 417–66.

Jeffrey Kaufmann. 2004. "Prickly Pear Cactus and Pastoralism in Southwest Madagascar." *Ethnology* 43(4): 345–61.

On zebu symbolism, see:
Sandra Evers and Nelleke van der Zwan. 1998. *Madagascar: The Zebu as Guide through Past and Present*. Berg-en-Dal, the Netherlands: Afrika Museum.

On historical traditions in eastern Madagascar, see:
Ralph Linton. 1933. "The Tanala: A Hill Tribe of Madagascar." *Publications of the Field Museum of Natural History. Anthropological Series* 22: 1–334.

✿ CHAPTER 8

How to Release Viruses from Birds

A Field Guide for Virus Hunters, Buddhist Monks, and Birdwatchers

FRÉDÉRIC KECK

In Chinese societies, there are many stories of aristocrats or scholars who have trapped a bird in their garden to listen to its song and who then release it, as an acknowledgment of the pleasure it has given. This is a gift-giving relationship: The owner gives the bird food, and the bird sings in return. Still today, bird collectors in China spend a lot of time thinking about the cage and the food most appropriate for their birds; they literally care for the bird to entertain its capacity to sing. But this relationship can seem unbalanced for the collector: There is more in the pleasure of hearing than in satisfying alimentary needs. Opening the cage as an ultimate gift is a way to recognize this: I let you fly so that you can sing for others all the beautiful songs you have sung only for me. In the liberation from the cage, the gift-giving relationship ends, but it is also brought to its natural outcome. Modern and Western concepts of freedom and alienation don't capture what happens when Chinese individuals release birds from their cages, nor should we think of the release as a return from domesticity to wilderness. We need to describe what happens in the gesture of opening the cage without projecting our concepts onto it.

A Buddhist concept is used by contemporary Chinese citizens to describe this gesture: merit (in Chinese: *gongde*). When a bird is released, Buddhists say, it increases the merits of the world. "There are many merits now," they say when they see the bird flying away. It is difficult to know if the merits can be quantified as a return of the services paid to humans, or if they indicate just a general quality of a good action. It is also unclear if this description goes with a belief in metempsychosis, that is, the possibility that the soul of the bird will reincarnate in a human body—which prompts a speculation on the levels of life: Is it better to be reincarnated into a bird or into a human?

While Buddhist philology has highly debated and speculated upon the meaning of *gongde*, I suggest finding this meaning in an ethnography of bird release. Can we describe what happens when a human releases a bird without invoking beliefs about the future outcome of the bird, but simply by looking at what the human and bird do? Is it possible to think of the release of a bird as a gift-giving relationship in which something emerges from the interaction?

A recent event offers a new perspective on bird release in China. In Hong Kong and Taiwan, a great many birds released for religious purposes were found dead in massive quantities, not far from the place where they were released. In the last twenty years, as Chinese citizens became richer, they bought massive quantities of birds in bird markets to release them in natural parks. Such bird releases stand in contrast to those of Chinese aristocrats or scholars, who release birds from their houses, as well as those of Buddhist practitioners, who release them from temples. Consequently, these birds died because they had been packed in small cages under stressful conditions and released in an improper environment. Some of these dead birds were found to have been infected with influenza. Avian influenza is one of the most closely monitored animal diseases in the world, because pandemic influenza—a new influenza virus infecting non-immunized humans and spreading rapidly by air—has been shown to emerge in birds.

This event reveals how the gift-giving relationships between birds and bird collectors can be perverted. If bird collectors properly manage cages as small houses, birds give songs in return for the care they receive; when they have sung properly, the birds receive freedom and give merits. But if the cages are not well managed and become more similar to a prison, the birds stop singing and send viruses to humans. It can thus be argued that while "tradition" left time for gift-giving relationships between bird collectors and birds to develop, "modernity" has shortened this relationship in such a way that it has become lethal for both sides of the relationship. Birds are stuck carelessly into cages where they cannot sing, so that the only thing they might give back when they are released are viruses, and the release of the bird is literally the end of the relationship. Viruses and merits thus appear as the two opposite outcomes of the gift-giving relationship between bird collectors and birds, as invisible entities indicating their distinct moral orientations. Defined etymologically as poisonous beings, viruses (in Chinese, the word is a new one: *bingdu*) appear as the opposite of merits: They are negative counter-gifts showing that something improper has happened in the relation between humans and birds.

But this description is too simplistic. Viewing viruses as a negative counter-gift ignores that viruses are not only poisonous beings but also positive actors that play a regulatory role in organisms. Humans and birds share many viruses that are not lethal, and they have adapted to these nonlethal viruses with their specific immune systems. Rather than two opposite beings, viruses and merits are contrasting perceptions of the same action of bird release. Where microbiologists see viruses coming out of bird release, Buddhists see merits. Birdwatchers are probably the only ones who can share the two perceptions, because they are interested in the release itself rather than merely its outcome. Rather than oppose Buddhists and microbiologists as traditional and modern practices of bird release, respectively, we can thus analyze and compare the gestures of release engaged in houses, temples, markets, and natural parks.

Therefore, I want to account for the moral dimension of the release, or its gift-giving relationship, without qualifying in advance what emerges in this gesture. Because there is uncertainty among Buddhists, microbiologists, and birdwatchers about what emerges—merits or viruses—I want to seize this uncertainty as an opportunity to question the moral dimension of the social activity at stake.

Bird release seems trapped between two interpretations, one in which it is a cultural symbol—birds are released to produce merit, as part of a cycle of souls in metempsychosis—and one in which it is a risky practice—bird release exposes humans to infection by creating new evolutionary niches for a dangerous virus. I want to describe what happens in the release itself and how it can balance merit and risk. Bird release reveals the ambivalence and imbalances of a gift-giving relationship between humans and birds. In order to describe this ambivalence in action, I treat viruses as actors in this interaction and not as scientific representations equivalent to religious markers of merit. To do so, I take up the perspectives of the different actors involved in bird release. What happens when a bird meets a virus in the hands of Buddhists observed by virologists and birdwatchers?

Mongolian Lark

I have been grounded now for a few days in the bird market of Kowloon in the central part of the Hong Kong territory. I usually live in the north of China, which is the reason that humans call me "Mongolian lark." I was captured there a few weeks ago, and I remember that the transportation to the market took a very long time. But I have heard that humans capture my kind just to let us free. They say that when they open the cage, I will fly quickly toward the sky.

I have just been bought by a rich Hong Kong businessman who wants to celebrate his eightieth birthday. He intends to release eighty birds on the occasion. I am supposed to be released at the end of the show, like the final explosion of a firework. He also bought dozens of sparrows who have been packed in small cages. Some of them are already dead; others are shivering. Some say they had been released before but were so weak that they barely escaped the cage and were soon trapped again and brought back to the market. I am fortunate enough to be alone in my cage, where I am able to fly up and down.

I have been fed grains and crickets by my keeper. I drink water in a small pot that has been affixed to the cage. I feel good, even though the hot and humid climate is very different from the dry and cold atmosphere where I grew up. I feel good enough to sing all my songs, which seems to please my keeper. Other birds in the market sing in my direction, and I reply with eagerness, even though I have never heard these songs before and cannot grasp their meanings. Sometimes the birdseller pokes a stick in my cage to wake me up and to entice me to sing. The cage is large and colorful, but I miss the great air.

A man is approaching me with a red cloth and a bald head. He is singing gently. He opens the door of the cage and encourages me to go out with his hand. I hesitate, peep my head through the door, and finally perch myself on the door. Then I unfold my wings and jump to the sky. It is so good to be free again! From above, I see sparrows jumping on the ground, and they seem ridiculous from the heights I have reached. But where will I go now? How do I find some place that is cool and dry?

Businessman

I have come to the bird market for the first time. I am not interested in birds, but my wife was looking for something new for my eightieth birthday, and she heard about this Buddhist practice of *fangsheng* on the Internet. When I turned seventy, she had reserved a guided tour in Europe, and we visited seven wonderful cities. But now I am too old to travel, and I liked the idea of going to a park with my sons and grandsons. They say they like nature because they have always lived in big cities. I grew up in the Guangdong countryside before moving to Hong Kong after the Communists took over China. So I cannot say that I like nature: For me, there is no difference between wild birds and the poultry I lived with as a kid.

My wife negotiated the price of birds with the seller. She paid 10 Hong Kong dollars for sparrows, 100HKD for Chinese bulbuls, 500HKD for Japanese white-eyes, and 1000 HKD for a Mongolian lark. My son, who is an amateur birdwatcher, knows these species by their names, but he says he has never seen a Mongolian lark, and he is excited to see it fly away at the end of the show. I am not concerned by species or colors; all I want is to have eighty birds flying at the same time for my eightieth birthday. I have worked as a trader all my life, and I have been quite successful. I like watching numbers. Yet I also like hearing birdsong. But strangely enough, these birds don't sing a lot. I hope it is not a sign of bad luck.

Buddhist Monk

I have been trained in the Buddhist monasteries of Tuen Mun, where I arrived from Sichuan province two years ago. In the temples where I was trained, animal release (in Chinese: *fangsheng*) was a minor practice: We used to release turtles or frogs in the ponds of our temple, and then we would catch them again. This was part of more complex rituals in the daily life of the temple, and we did this almost as an afterthought—other, more complex rituals took up most of our days. But in Hong Kong, people have become so rich that they want to release animals as a celebration for itself, and they pay huge amounts for birds, as if they were fireworks. Still they ask Buddhist monks to come for a blessing. My superior monks don't like these ceremonies; they say that release should concern the energies of the soul and be exercised only through prayer. But it reminds me of the animals I released in my childhood, and so it feels like a good gesture to me.

Mr. Lee, who has bought eighty birds at Mong Kok Bird Market, has invited me to join him in Kowloon Park. His whole family is there, and he's having a reception at one of the park's restaurants. Before the cutting of the birthday cake, he has asked me to do the release. I read the words of the Buddha and then pray for the souls of living beings—human and animal—who have recently passed away. The birds are also singing, as if to answer my calls. When I open the doors of the cages, some birds stay inside while others explore the entrance. When the Mongolian lark rises up to the sky, the whole family shouts "Happy birthday!" (in Cantonese: "Sang Yut Fai Lok!").

My heart sinks a little when I release animals this way. This kind of event is too close to ancestral worship. There is not enough compassion for the animals. I usually follow a group of practitioners who buy sea creatures at the market to release them in the harbor. They are deeply committed to decreasing the amount of suffering in the world. When we release the crabs, we have to untie their legs, and they look so happy to be free again. When we submerge them in the water, it is so nice to see them swim. I always tell the practitioners that there are a lot of merits coming out of the release. Sometimes they buy river fish or frogs, and we go to an adjacent park to release them in clear water. We are concerned that animals are released in an environment where they can thrive. Yet we often don't see where they are heading to. After the release, we go to a vegetarian restaurant.

H5N1 Virus

I am an influenza virus, belonging to the family of orthomyxoviruses. I am made up of a single-stranded molecule of RNA (ribonucleic acid) with a round capsid. Proteins on my surface are called hemagglutinin because they agglutinate with the receptors of the cells when I come in contact with them. Other proteins on the capsid, called neuraminidase, allow me to be released from the cell. Hence, viruses of my kind are often classified by virologists following the shape of the two proteins H and N. I am an H5N1.

I was detected for the first time in 1996 in a goose in Guangdong. In 1997 in Hong Kong, I caused the death of five thousand chickens and eight humans. Officers of the World Health Organization have called me Goose/Guangdong/H5N1/HK/1996, and they have traced me as I moved to Fujian, Korea, Japan, Russia, Vietnam, and Indonesia. I jumped directly from chickens to humans without going through pigs, as influenza viruses usually do. This may explain why I have been so lethal when I infected humans, although I have seldom succeeded in transmitting from human to human. Usually viruses coming from pigs to humans are mild because these species have the same respiratory tissues, but viruses coming from birds trigger strong immune reactions. When I encounter the cells of a human's immune system, they cannot match my antigens—a sort of identity card I have on my membrane. They are so surprised that they go through an inflammatory cascade called a cytokine storm, and they are victims of their own reactions to me. By contrast with my fellow pig viruses, I am entirely foreign to human cells, where I feel out of place.

When I enter a human cell, I don't intend to destroy it. Why destroy my new home? All I want to do is replicate by using the reproduction tools of the cell. I softly enter the membrane of the cell to reach its nucleus, where

I release my RNA. One strand of RNA can produce thousands of new virions, which then bud at the surface of the membrane to enter other cells. When cells are infected, they can enter apoptosis, and I have to reach another cell before being destroyed with the cell that hosts me. Not all cells are good for me. Some cells, called dendritic cells, have long arms that they stretch to other cells to communicate my antigens and trigger the immune response. I try to avoid them and go directly to the cells in which I can reproduce without being signaled.

I can also travel through the droplets of the organism I have infected and thus move to other organisms. When birds are gathered into cages, this gives me a perfect milieu to replicate. Their bodies are weakened because they are so stressed and don't move much. They are very close to each other and defecate heavily. Ah, what bliss! I can travel around so easily when birds are in a cage, they spread me in their digestive tracts and shed me through their feces. I can move between one species and another, from geese to chickens, from pigeons to larks. I have never been found on sparrows. I prefer ducks, though, because they host me in their digestive tracts without being sick—they are called "sane carriers." The digestive tract of other species of birds is often turned into a bloody pulp when I infect them. And humans are a different story altogether—humans shed me through droplets from the respiratory tracks where I multiply, so I have to wait for them to cough. Bird to bird is such a different way to travel than human to human!

When I appeared in 1997, the Hong Kong government culled all the live poultry on its territory. They thought they got rid of me by eradicating the avian reservoir, but I was still replicating in wild birds, and I was mutating all over the Asian continent. As soon as I returned to Hong Kong, the government sounded an alarm, but I keep taking on new faces and surprising them.

When they realized that releasing birds in natural parks could help me spread, some Hong Kong citizens wore a mask while opening the cages. This is really a joke! I could infect them through the contact between the feathers of the bird and the hands that hold the cage. It is so warm under a mask that the moment always comes when the hand takes off the mask. That is my moment: I can enter a human organism!

I am not particularly fond of infecting humans. It is hard to jump from a human body to another species (humans are called "epidemiological dead ends"), and I need to keep moving and evolving to survive as a species. But humans have been so smart in trying to anticipate my strategies that I always take pleasure in deceiving them. And there are so many different contacts between them and other species that I always find new ways to infect them.

Virologist

I am a researcher at the Department of Microbiology of Hong Kong University. After the crisis caused by SARS (severe acute respiratory syndrome) in 2003, my university received a lot of funding to work on emerging infectious diseases such as avian influenza. I have followed viruses crossing species barriers, tracking them back from human cases to animal reservoirs: civets in Chinese traditional markets that transmitted the SARS virus, chickens in live poultry markets that transmit avian influenza. I call myself a virus hunter: While epidemiologists count cases after an outbreak to measure and limit its epidemic potential, I try to anticipate the next outbreak by following the mutations of viruses among animals.

When birdwatchers contacted me to take samples from wild birds that died after being released for religious purposes, I knew there was something wrong. We had sampled wild birds from all over the territory and seldom found H5N1. When we did find it, it was in places remote from human contact; with the help of the Hong Kong public health administration, we were able to enforce a three-kilometer quarantine zone around the site where the dead bird had been found. But the bird market of Mong Kok is very close to the place where the SARS coronavirus appeared in 2003. It then transmitted to people, who spread it by plane all over the world, killing eight thousand people worldwide, eight hundred in Hong Kong. If these dead wild birds transmit their viruses to humans, this could be a new pandemic bomb. I am so scared by the repetition of this scenario.

It is crazy that Buddhist monks are authorized to release potentially infected birds from markets in one of the densest areas in the world. We virologists have built highly secured laboratories where we infect cells, tissues, and live animals with dangerous viruses, and there are always controversies about the biosecurity of our equipment. We are accused by regulatory agencies, such as the NSABB (National Science Advisory Board for Biosecurity) in the United States, of helping terrorists who could use the information we provide in our articles to release dangerous pathogens in big cities. We are also suspected by epidemiologists of accidentally releasing viruses outside the lab because we do not clean our equipment properly. But here we have Buddhist monks who intentionally release birds with viruses in densely populated areas—literally, viral bombs sent by nice Buddhist practitioners! The only thing that is released from our labs is duly controlled information, and we try to make sure that it doesn't replicate for bad purposes. After all, this is what a virus may be: a piece of information gone wrong.

Birdwatcher

I am a member of the Hong Kong Birdwatching Society. This association was created in 1957 by British officers who watched over the territory and wanted to draw a map of the migratory birds passing through Hong Kong between the North and the South China Sea. It has become predominantly Chinese since the handover of Hong Kong to China in 1997, especially because the rising middle class began to adopt birdwatching as a hobby.

I like to go birdwatching in the natural areas of the Hong Kong territory: the wetlands of Mai Po, filled with aquatic birds; the forests of Tai Koo; the agricultural area of Long Valley; the islands of the South, where I see migratory birds; and also the cemeteries in the center of Hong Kong. It has been estimated that more than five hundred bird species are residents or migrants in the Hong Kong territory, as many as in the whole European continent! So this place is pretty diverse, but sometimes this diversity is artificially enforced by the introduction of new species.

When I discovered a Mongolian lark dead in a natural park in Kowloon, I immediately thought it couldn't have arrived here by itself. It had been imported illegally and released for religious purposes—I would even say for superstitious reasons, for this has nothing to do with religion. I have the utmost respect for the religion of my ancestors, who celebrated the Chinese New Year in the family temple, but I get nervous when I see Buddhist monks exploiting the credibility of rich Hong Kong businessmen to release animals. Virologists who sampled the lark and other dead birds in the park found that some of them were carrying the deadly H5N1. Other birds released have multiplied and transformed the equilibrium of the ecosystem, behaving as invasive species. These smuggled birds introduce chaos in the environment; they are anything but natural.

My association has built a campaign to warn the Buddhist authorities about the threats of releasing birds. We were allowed to plaster a poster in monasteries showing a bird turning into a cadaver, with the motto "This is not release of life but release of death" (bu shi fangsheng shi fangsi). Such a campaign can encourage ordinary people to turn from bird release to the release of other animals, like fish. But I understand there is something almost magical in bird release, that moment when the bird opens its wings and jumps into the air. The bird is a bit uncertain, as if it was recapitulating the first steps when it learned how to fly. My association keeps trying to find safer ways for people to experience the ceremonial wonder of bird release.

Lately we have been organizing similar rituals with the birds that had been caught by the police on the border from illegal bird trade. These birds are cured in a shelter because they have been so ill-treated during the transportation. Then they are equipped with GPS (Global Positioning System) so that we can follow their movements in the wild. We release them from the mountain of Tai Mo Shan, in the middle of the New Territories. My father keeps telling me that it is as unnatural to release a bird with GPS as it is to import it from a remote area. But I reply that at least we communicate with the bird through the signals sent by the antenna. We know if it thrives in this new space or if it flies back home. We don't invoke spiritual entities like souls or merits: We equip the bird so that it directly speaks to us. That is why he called this practice "scientific release" (*kexue fangsheng*).

Before releasing the bird, it is necessary to be cautious when we attach the antenna. It shouldn't be too heavy, nor should its weight concentrate on one side or the other, as we want the bird to be able to fly long distances. It is delicately sewed around the waist of the bird and remotely connected to the GPS system. Through the GPS we keep contact with the bird through virtual images, but we have to keep in mind that the GPS device has a weight that can be harmful to the bird whose life we want to extend. And so we keep worrying for birds after they have been released. For us, too, releasing life can sometimes mean releasing death.

To sum up these different perspectives, I want to ask: What is bird release?

- For the bird, release is the shift from one environment to another. Since migratory birds constantly have to change environments, bird release is a human-made accelerator of a natural process, wrongly and indiscriminately applied to all species.
- For the Buddhist monk, bird release is connected to the release of the soul after death. A beautiful release means that the soul will exit the body peacefully after death and reincarnate in a good body. An improper release is a sign of bad karma, which will lead to dirty reincarnations. For the Buddhist monk, a bird market is a place full of bad karma, because the birds look unhappy there, while the natural park where the bird is released is suffused with good karma.
- For the virus, bird release amplifies processes that occur at a small scale: the release of its information (RNA) in the cell and the release of new virions out of the cell. This replication of information can be harmful or neutral to the cell. For the virus, the cell is a new environment in which it seeks opportunities to thrive, and it must bypass the defenses that cells erect to protect themselves from the potential ill effects of encountering viruses.

- For the virologist, release is the dangerous act of transferring biological information (RNA) from an environment where the replications of the virus are controlled to an environment where the virus can replicate erratically.
- For the birdwatcher, bird release is a scientific technique that permits mapping the bird's environment and tracking its movements within that environment. While the Buddhist monk relies on a cosmology of souls, the birdwatcher turns migratory movements into signs of presence. Even while the bird is not visible, it is still possible to receive information about it through the GPS device. The contrasted environments are not the market and the natural park, as in the Buddhist's limited cosmology, but the habitats of birds and their sites of migration along their flyways.

Releasing a bird seems to be a simple gesture: All one needs to do is stretch one's arm and open the cage. Yet it involves a whole set of actors and perspectives as well as a multiplicity of spaces and scales where these actors coexist and interact. I suggest that in order to put together these different actors, perspectives, spaces, and scales, the ethnographer needs to start from what is exchanged in the gift-giving relationship between the bird and the human who releases it: not only food and songs but also information, signs, prestige, luck. If we analyze them attentively, songs are not entirely different from merits or viruses: They are modes of information indicating that the gesture is done properly or improperly or, more precisely, whether the gesture is done in a good space or in a bad space. The virus is just a piece of information out of place, but if it is read in its place, it can serve as an indicator of species habitat change and make us aware of global environmental transformations. When birds send us viruses whose mutations we can follow on computer screens, this might be not so different from the songs they sent to Chinese aristocrats and scholars. Both acts indicate that our relationships with birds continue even after we have released them.

In this essay, I took seriously the idea of writing a field guide of how to release a bird in Hong Kong. What may appear as either simple (for the businessman) or dangerous (for the virologist) reveals itself to be a complex and ambivalent set of relationships between humans and nonhumans oriented by the circulation of information across spaces and scales. Buddhist monks and birdwatchers know it, as both groups publish handbooks (shoushu) to tell their practitioners how to manage bird release. The only difference is that Buddhist monks explain how to orient oneself in a spiritual space of metempsychosis measured by merits, while birdwatchers explain how to live in a world out of balance measured by migratory movements.

The question I have tried to answer is: How does one do things with bird viruses? Viruses have an efficacy and a life of their own, and they create a space of translation between the concerns of Buddhist monks and those of birdwatchers. There is as much care and caution in the gesture by which a human communicates with a bird when releasing it as when two humans talk to each other instead of fighting with each other. But there is also potentially violence and danger in the act of release, as there is in the act of speaking. It is as complicated to release birds with viruses as to do things with words. Hence the need for a field guide.

Suggested Readings

On avian influenza in Hong Kong, see:
Thomas Abraham. 2007. *Twenty-First Century Plague. The Story of SARS, with a New Preface on Avian Flu.* Hong Kong: Hong Kong University Press.

On the practice of animal release, see:
Joanna Handlin Smith. 1999. "Liberating Animals in Ming-Qing China: Buddhist Inspiration and Elite Imagination." *Journal of Asian Studies* 58: 51–84.

On the perspectives of participants to a ritual, see:
Adam Chau. 2013. "Actants Amassing." In *Sociality: New Directions,* edited by Nicholas Long and Henrietta Moore, 134–55. New York: Berghahn.

On the use of GPS to release wildlife, see:
Etienne Benson. 2011. *Wired Wilderness: Technologies of Tracking and the Making of Modern Wildlife.* Baltimore: Johns Hopkins University Press.

✸ PART 3

Commodities

❧ CHAPTER 9

Oysterous

EVA HAYWARD

He is a she.

—M.F.K. Fisher, *Consider the Oyster* (1988)

Oysters are really best eaten naked. . . .

—Erin Byers Murray, *Shucked* (2013)

Late December always makes me hungry for the liquored bodies of oysters. Slippery flesh caught softly against molars—and in a single firm grind, ribboned. Romantic and gastronomic, making killable and desirable: to eat an oyster is to be wanton. Not an innocent pleasure, no, but a hunger for living tissue, indulging our most unacknowledged appetites. We think of eating as instinctual and endogenous, and the eating of animals as a possible response to that instinct. There is a similar assumption about sex as a reproductive act. Indeed, Sigmund Freud reveals that, in the human infant, sexuality is propped against the feeding function essential to life, but eventually these divide into discrete operations. But, even in the adult, there remains a longing for hunger and desire to be rejoined in a single act. Perhaps this is what makes the oyster so wanton; it embodies a fantasy of feeding as sexuality. This invert perversely embodies our infantile yearnings; which is to say, the oyster is fuel for fantasy. And, to what degree is the ambivalence that structures specific animals—killable / lovable, useable / untouchable—or animality always a question of fantasy, of sexuality? Not simply bestiality, though this is part of the question, but how is animality—whether in the metaphysical terms of "the Animal" or the scientism of particular "animals"—unavoidably produced through our own sexual vicissitudes?

Eating oysters only during the "r" months—September to April—is little more than a colloquialism, perhaps residue from the days of poor refrigeration.

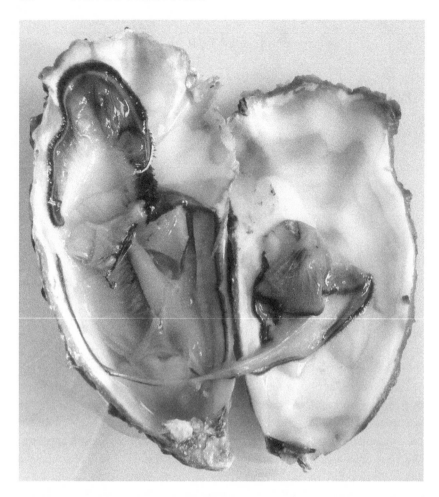

FIGURE 9.1.   Crassostrea gigas, opened. By David Monniaux—Own work, CC BY-SA 3.0, https://commons.wikimedia.org/w/index.php?curid=495262.

Though, during the "r"-less months oysters are fatigued from their many cupidinous affairs. They convert their energy stores into gametes (sperm and eggs), leaving them swampy in taste and texture. Of course, what is colloquial has taken on a more serious truthfulness. Changing climates have turned summer waterways toxic with pollutants and microbial life, and oyster die and their flesh noxious. Like so many invertebrates, oysters are bellwethers of an unbearable future. Yet, December still awakens my appetite. Why? Why do I want their delicate greyness, folded like silk, at the close of each year?

There is a snag in this question, a pearly irritation really: I am vegan. Veganism carries many unwarranted associations: extremism, intractability, and fussiness. Unwarranted, I say, because these descriptors oversimplify the nuances of veganism. For some, an animal-free diet is a moral, animal rights, or environmental stance. For others, perhaps, being vegan is a choice for better health, a feature of cultural customs, or even an indicator of one's chicness. And maybe for a few, not eating animals is a right-to-life platform. I prefer to think of veganism as a modest intervention—a line in the sand—that demonstrates attention to one's planetary relationships. For me, veganism is not necessarily radical politics—gustatory abstinence may alter perspective, but politics shaped by personal choice reassert humanism even as that choice promises to accomplish the opposite. As with animal rights discourse—which works within the rubric of human rights, proposing that animals deserve the same rights—the human is reaffirmed through the effort to negate its centrality. That is to say, the human—its historical, political, philosophical import—remains a subtending logic. This paradox is echoed through the very use of the "human/animal divide" designation—it presumes that the human is a unified category. The human is a foreclosure—the category is built through the strategic exclusion of dehumanized racial and sexual subjects. In this way, "human/animal divide" supposes an ontological divide—a divide between too coherent categories of being-ness—but it works to conceal how the human (and the animal) is a political and ideological technology. This is why veganism predicated on animal rights or liberation cannot be seen as anti- or posthumanist. This is not a dismissal of veganism, but to invite us to ask what veganism might yet be? How might we conceptualize a veganism that does not reassert the human?

And beyond dietary questions, it is not so much the ontological state of the animal that matters, but as Nicole Shunkin names it, how the animal is "rendered." Informed by Michel Foucault's biopower, Shunkin's rendering illustrates how the animal is split, dissevered, and distributed through everyday life. Simply, the animal is everywhere: as Georges Bataille wrote, "The animal is in the world like water in water." I am aware that the health of my body, the medications that keep me alive are all built through the "rendered" labor of animals (though never them alone). Our actions—whether tilling organic vegetable fields, walking through the desert, checking email—all negatively affect the lives of people and other creatures. Life is never innocent, never sentimental—to be alive is to be murderous.

Perhaps not surprisingly, oysters mark a peculiar place in vegan politics and animal rights discourse. Christopher Cox, a self-identified vegan, wrote an essay about "why even strict vegans should feel comfortable eating oysters by the boatload." He writes, "Biologically, oysters are not in the plant kingdom, but when it comes to ethical eating, they are almost indistinguishable from plants." Cox explains, "Since oysters don't have a central nervous system, they're unlikely to experience pain in a way resembling ours—unlike a pig or a herring or even a lobster." He reminds us that the animal rights ethicist Peter Singer also questioned the suffering of oysters. In *Animal Liberation*, Singer suggests that oysters feel no pain and therefore cannot suffer. The capacity to suffer has come to define ethical responsibility; reducing pain and suffering of animals is a founding principle of animal liberationists and animal rights advocates. Following the assumption that plants do not suffer or feel pain, then animals that also do not feel pain—such as the oyster—should be ethical foodstuffs. Honestly, I am dubious about all of this reasoning. How do we know that plants do not suffer? What exactly constitutes suffering? And why are invertebrates—those backbone-less snails, insects, worms, oysters—often ruled "the fringe" of animal rights concern? How is it that a chicken's suffering matters more than that of the mosquito, or of the flea on your dog, or of the ringworm in your gut? If ethics cannot extend to the aesthetically displeasing, then it is not ethical.

That we cannot find the oyster's face or look into their eyes does not mean they are outside of ethics, but that face-to-face ethics is limited. Emanuel Levinas describes a face-to-face mode of ethical encounter, and although other philosophies of ethics have emerged, many still carry Levinas's aesthetics of faciality, coherence, and singularity. About face-to-face ethics, Levinas writes: "There is first the very uprightness of the face, its upright exposure, without defense. The skin of the face is that which stays most naked, most destitute. The face is meaning all by itself . . . it leads you beyond." The human is an aesthetic category, and through aestheticization it renders itself ontological and, retroactively, prior to aestheticization. This is the presumptive problem of the face and its ethical capacity. The face presumes both that the other has a face and that face can be identified with.

Moreover, the divide that liberates some from the problem of animal suffering by defining others as unethical is one of disavowal—a hope that ethics rests on purification, on a certainty that a coherent and untroubled solution to suffering is available. Not only are purity politics predicated on a position of relative social privilege—one can afford the position without risk of being named impure—but they also cannot be called ethical—which at most is a project, a proposal—only obscenely moral. So, here I am, wanting to experience ethical concern for oysters even as I gnash their salty muscles. I, too, am in the delicious filth and ambiguity of it all, unavoidably.

Oysters themselves, through their changeability, reflect this ambiguity. Perhaps because they are protean, we come to realize that ambiguity—and the ethics that emerges from this—are sexual in nature. Oysters are that *riddle wrapped in a mystery inside an enigma*—a darkroom between shells. Belonging to the religion of the wave: After the oyster's larval stage, *he* stays a *he* for a year. Then some longing surges through *him*, and then *he* is a *she*—a queer little creature. M.F.K. Fisher tells us that oysters change sex up to four times a year on average. This changeable s/he, this tender bivalve resists our anthropomorphic projections, our ability to turn animals into talking, walking versions of ourselves. Oysters are quintessentially other from human form and experience. Yet oysters do find their way into our symbols, emotions, and fantasies. Oysters are sometimes used to describe feelings of forlornness and melancholy: Dickens described Ebenezer Scrooge as "secret, and self-contained, and solitary as an oyster." It lives curled up over itself, tightly, in strict intimacy. Oysters also evoke aversion, a revolt from the senses. The poet Anne Stevenson describes oysters as having "grown luscious on sewages." The oozy oyster and its pearly coat evoke sex and sexuality. The "oy" hollows out our mouth so that the "ster," with its liquid consonant at the end, fills it like an estuary. Bodily fluids, brine, translucent flesh, and teeth—little more needs to be said.

This shelled paradox, belonging to phylum Mollusca, is a as much a class traitor as a sexual transgressor. Sometimes a delicacy for the affluent and then—changing as it does with sex—food proper for the poor: from gastronomic rarity to street food. Rebecca Stott in her wonderful cultural history of the oyster tells us that the oyster is used to represent civic virtue. In the Diamond Jubilee Toast of 1897, a sonnet written for the occasion notes that the "cool impassive Oyster keeps his ground," doing not for one's self but for the public good. In another historical turn, oyster represents degeneracy, especially the laziness of aristocrats and the glut of their privilege. Stott reminds us that the *flâneur* enjoys oysters at midnight. Oysters are sin or, more precisely, what we do with oysters is sinful.

Consider Tim Burton's "Oyster Boy." After a wedding by the sea and "a simmering stew of mollusks and fish," a husband and wife gave birth to a "canker, this blight" a half oyster son. They called him Sam, "or, sometimes, 'that thing that looks like a clam.'" Sam is unloved by his parents, who blame his oysterous appearance and odor for their fizzled sex life. Offering medical advice, the doctor tells Sam's father, "Perhaps eating your son would help you do it for hours!" Stealing into Oyster Boy's room at night with a knife, his father asks, "Have you wanted to die?" Pressing the blade between two sides of the shell, Sam's father pries open his oyster of a son and swallows him down: "As he picked up his son, Sam dripped on his coat. With the shell to his lips, Sam slipped down his throat." Homoerotic daddy/son play or incestuous infanticide with a twist of bestiality, this oyster is embodies our taboo appetites.

FIGURE 9.2.   Oyster Boy. By Tim Burton.

As "Oyster Boy" illustrates, oysters—and animals more general—have a sexual function. By sexual I do not simply mean symbolically or representationally, but that the animal—as an object and a being—is structured by our sexuality, particularly our repression of sexuality. Even though it may be assumed that the human/animal divide is an ontological one, I would suggest that the animal administrates the de/human divide. As I have explained, racial and sexual subjects are differently positioned outside, against, or within the domain of the human. The animal mediates the de/human divide, but through our own relationship with sexuality. In a general way, consider how our sexual fantasies are described as animalistic, or how animal sexual behavior is depicted as naked, exposed, and without the function of shame. It is no surprise that animal prints, feathers, and leather have come to define seduction, sexuality, and perversity. The animal, in this way, stabilizes the de/human—which exposes how the human relies on sexualization to dehumanize—as a sexual function—the animal (as a symbolic, scientific, and imaginary category) cannot escape our sexuality, and therefore is enveloped or shelled-in by our sexual lives. This is not simply to say animals represent our sexuality—as in "oysters are aphrodisiacs"—but more precisely they function as our repressed relationship to sexuality. Bestiality, not unlike incest, is a taboo that reveals how repression mediates our worldliness. Oyster Boy is a violation of these taboos, a perversion of orders, and in so doing the sexual function of the oyster (of the animal) is laid bare. The fate of this seaward boy tells us bestiality is less about the depravity of a few and more about a general orientation toward animality in toto.

The story of Oyster Boy is also a longed-for reunion between the need to eat and sexual want. In that infantile wish, we may see something particular about how sexuality is at work in the figure of the oyster. However impossible the collapsing of sex and food into one action is, the yearning is nevertheless also a space of want, a domain of pleasure. This sex-changing invertebrate has found its way into the hungry-hearts of children, the polymorphously perverse children that we remain. Even today, eating raw oysters at restaurants remains one of the most publicly intimate things we can do. What may seem the province of privacy, we silently moan, averting our gaze, as the oyster's viscous body slides from the bowl of itself and across the threshold of our lips. Delicious and murderous. Sexuality is regressive, there is no easy accord between our sexuality and political investments. To insist that our sexuality complement our politics is to repress. And it is from here that we see another impasse of bestowing rights onto animal; in part, having rights is a mechanism for shoring-up the moralizing regime of the human, for ensuring that oysters and other animals—through their absence and capture—perform their role as our repressed sexuality.

This problem of repression is furthered by affiliations, identifications, and approximations. For instance, with much affection, and although oysters are more resonant with ocean tides than with me, I feel some kinship with this little he / she, this sexually troubled being. It is unwarranted—not only unfair to me and the oyster, but an index of how the animal mediates our own relationship to sexuality—but there it is. Loving is not an antidote to killing. Sarah Waters's delicious novel *Tipping the Velvet* tells the story of Nancy, an oyster shucker, who discovers the cross-dressing pleasure of being a man on the stage and off. Nancy is oysterous and capricious, she is narrated to us as reveling in the ambiguities of sex. Waters analogizes the oyster and the shucker of oysters, as a masculine woman who loves women. The oyster stands in for queer sexuality, but the problem is that the queer is dehumanized. No matter how furbelowed the oyster and the queer are, the oyster is installed as a foreclosure to the queer's humanity. Similarly, the oyster is both absent and captured—has an identificatory (absent) and sexual function (captured)—by queer identification. As it is for Nancy, the oyster's in-between-ness—offers me no room to understand my own mercurial nature, to recognize how my transsexuality is an effect of sexuality, my own wanting to want. We are different differences to one another, and identification cannot bridge the divides. To do so is to ensure violence for us both.

So, here I am, a vegan transsexual (sounds like the start of a joke) at the fishmonger's. And there they are, all osseous and folded. I pick one up to feel its heft, to sniff this denizen of the deep. Its saline perfume triggers a taste memory, metallic like blood on the tongue from a broken lip. Truth be told, I have been swotting vintage recipes: "Oysters Rockefeller" (with Pernod or Herbsaint), "Oysters in Hell," and oyster stews. "Oysters in Hell" is a twist on M.F.K. Fisher's "Eggs in Hell," but instead of eggs, tinned oysters are cooked in a spiced tomato sauce. The fruity acid covers the fishiness, allowing the oysters to express their unctuous metallurgy. But in all honesty, I prefer them raw and alive as they slide down my champagne'd throat. Beastly, I know. An oyster-gulping vegan? A sexual invert eating a marine invert? Maybe the ambiguity of these questions serves to comfort me, but here again, my equivocating is not because I am allied or share a position with this moist invertebrate, this shimmering pervert. Troublingly, the fishmonger's oysters expose more problems than solutions—animal rights can only confirm anthropocentrism; the animal administrates the foreclosure of humanness for those who are racially and sexually others; ethics is unmoored by aesthetics and facelessness; identification is a violence; and, bestiality (as much its sexual function as its social violation) defines both how the animal functions as repressed sexuality and our relationship to that repression. And on this last point, our appetites—sexual and otherwise—are antisocial—sexuality refuses utilitarian aims. As such, if we became suddenly conscious of our hidden desires, we would be traumatized. To see cringing frilled lips shocked by air, to taste finely salted juices gulped from the shell: The why is too much. Because of this muchness, we are also tasked to question the role of sexuality in making the animal.

Perhaps because it is December, the end of the year, I am reflecting on pleasure: wanting to want. December is amped with hopes for goodwill and kindness—sadism lurks around every corner, and in as many cheery disguises. Our pleasures are not always self-evident—the demands of social life obscures, represses, disfigures our pleasure. Want *not* to want. Unavoidably, our past leaves impressions on our present like too many abrasions, and December marks a cut in time, a divide between years, and another step toward the unforeseen. For oysters, irritants—usually the remnants of parasites, "worm coffins"—are covered in a pearl sack to protect their soft mantle. The abrading particle is orbed but remains within the oyster—a wounding intromission never to be metabolized. My December is pearly—for reasons profoundly different for oysters—because pleasure is not comfort, it is an un-becoming, a breaking away from conventions, a shedding of refusals and decorum. Ceaselessly, scrumptiously, ecstatically we emerge more of ourselves through the loss of ourselves. A paradox. It is this paradox that I am confronted with each time I sit in front of a serving dish of oysters: food/sex, ethics/sadism, me/mollusk. While I will not urge others to join me in front of this platter of paradoxes, but I do entreat you to wonder if pleasure, and more narrowly sexual pleasures, may reveal a different orientation toward oysters and other animals. Rather than disavowing the role sexuality has had in constituting the category of the animal, perhaps we should puzzle over our pleasures. It may be that our pleasures are pathways to understanding social orders, categorical divides, and the violence we call domination. Our pleasures are not the problem—more moral order will not interrupt domination; morality and sociality are domination's daily vernacular—nor are they the solution (they exceed utilitarianism), but they draw us into the wound of the world, showing us how "I," "you," "she," and "it" are pearl-inlayed effects. . . . So instead of resolving to clean up your act—in the idiom of getting real—how about we lean into the problem, linger in the luster made from our unlivable lives, so as to ask: How has the refusal of pleasure made possible domination?

Suggested Readings

On oysters and anthropomorphism, see:

Tim Burton. 1997. *The Melancholy Death of Oyster Boy and Other Stories*. New York: Rob Weisbach Books.

Charles Dickens. 2003. *A Christmas Carol and Other Christmas Writings*. London: Penguin Classics.

Sarah Waters. 2000. *Tipping the Velvet*. New York: Riverhead Trade.

On oysters and animal rights, see:

Christopher Cox. 2010. "Consider the Oyster." *Slate*. April 7, 2010. Available at http://www.slate.com/articles/life/food/2010/04/consider_the_oyster.htm.

Peter Singer. 2009. *Animal Liberation: The Definitive Classic of the Animal Movement*. New York: Harper Perennial Modern Classics.

On philosophy and animals, see:

Georges Bataille. 1989. *Theory of Religion*, trans. Robert Hurley, New York: Zone Books.

Emmanuel Levinas. 1996. *Ethics and Infinity*, trans. Richard A. Cohen. Pittsburgh: Duquesne University Press.

On oysters as food, see:

M.F.K. Fisher. 1988. *Consider the Oyster*. San Francisco: North Point Press.

Erin Byers Murray. 2013. *Shucked: Life on a New England Oyster Farm*. New York: St. Martin's Griffin.

On the cultural history of oysters, see:

Rebecca Stott. 2004. *Oyster*. London: Reaktion Press.

CHAPTER 10

How to Act Industrial around Industrial Pigs

Alex Blanchette

Don't Touch the Sows!

I often find myself thinking back to a strange little incident that happened while I was working on factory farms. In retrospect, it suggests a lot about the state of life of pigs in the United States—a country where 96 percent of hogs are now born, raised, and killed in sites of indoor confinement—along with how these animals' physical condition affects the workers who labor alongside them. Indeed, this incident helps me think more critically about what an industrial animal is in the first place. It happened while I was employed by a corporation in the U.S. Midwest that I will call Berkamp Meats. The barn where I worked, named Sow No. 6, houses 2,500 breeding sows. It conceives and births 50,000 piglets per year, sending 21-day-old baby animals into a vast network of barn and slaughter sites that cumulatively grow and kill seven million hogs per year.

At that point, I had been working as an artificial inseminator for a couple of weeks. This essentially means sitting on sows' backs and facing their tails so that you can rub them in ways that imitate the mating behavior of boars. The aim is to activate a sow's muscle contractions so that she draws in the vacuum-packed bag of boar semen inserted into her uterus through a foam-tipped pipette. On this day, someone had miscounted the pipettes we needed. My co-worker, Miguel, asked me—usually the slowest person

FIGURE 10.1.   Bank of sows in gestation crates on Sow No. 6. Photo by Sean J. Sprague.

at stimulating sows—to make the long walk back to the workshop to get more of them so that we could finish all of the day's inseminations before lunchtime.

Out of the corner of my eye, as I was walking along the narrow concrete paths that run between rows of gestation crates, I noticed a sow staring at me intently. Her neck was craned out the side of her metal cage. Her eyes tracked my every move, with what I interpreted to be a quizzical look. Her erect posture was almost amusing to me, though I suppose there was also something about my own mannerisms that struck her as odd. Without giving it much thought, I strolled over to her cage, reaching out to stroke her head. After two weeks working in this space of confinement, this would be the first sow that I had touched that was not exhibiting estrous. Though I had been surrounded by thousands of pigs for nine hours a day, up to this point I had never made contact with one that was not locked in place by lordosis reflexes and pheromones that cause in-heat sows' bodies to freeze when pressure is placed on their backs.

"Alex, *stop!*"

I turned around to see my friend Maria standing twenty feet away, across a row of crates. A small woman, drowning in her company-supplied blue coveralls, she was clearly angry—red-faced, with her fists firmly clenched. Maria was usually the most laid-back of my co-workers on Sow No. 6.

Relentlessly sarcastic, she liked to mock the odd sexualities of artificial insemination. Maria was a native K'iche' speaker from Guatemala with whom I often shared conversations in Spanish. It was the first time I heard her speak English. "Don't touch the sows!" she screamed loudly—forcefully enough to communicate the seriousness of the situation, while being heard over the thousands of sows' banging metal cages. This was the only time that I got in trouble in Sow No. 6. My other clumsy amateur's mistakes—say, allowing a sow to escape her crate and run through the barn—were usually received with laughter or an eye-roll.

My violation of the unspoken terms of industrial animal husbandry might not seem like a big deal to readers who have not spent time on factory farms. After all, I had merely paused to stroke a sow. I tried to touch a hog's head like I would a pet dog. Maria's features relaxed once she saw the shock register on my face. She came over to explain, gently, that petting the animals or interacting with them in a way that was outside of the routine norms of work in these barns could surprise them. She said that such a gesture might cause the sow to startle, writhe in her cage, or loudly bellow. This one sow's reaction could then alarm the rest of the animals in the surrounding cages. Such a stirring of feeling in the herd of animals, Maria suggested, a shift from the sows' normally dull and repetitive days locked in gestation crates, could risk causing all of the surrounding pigs to injure themselves or even miscarry their litters. These sows "are fragile," she said in a rather remarkable understatement. "They are not very strong."

In all my time working on factory farms, I have never encountered a formal rule that says you cannot touch the pigs—not as an entry-level laborer, nor when I shadowed senior managers along the many stages from pigs to pork. This was an unwritten sensibility, a form of tacit knowledge that is shared and passed along by experienced workers like Maria. Indeed, I don't even think the act of petting a single sow, in and of itself, was really a huge problem. Rather, Maria was just trying to make me understand that how I act toward these vulnerable animals can affect their well-being. She was underlining that sows are intelligent and observing animals—they are *sentient*—and they will respond to our behaviors. But it makes me wonder what it would look like to formalize this workplace orientation to porcine perception. This incident suggests something that I find striking: Fragile industrial pigs now require human workers to act industrial in their presence. That is, workers' mundane actions take on new significance as breeding animals become more frail. Taken to its logical conclusion, the unspoken ideal here is perhaps a fully automated barn where there are no erratic workers at all. But given that the human body remains necessary for a host of tasks ranging from artificial in-semination to checking the animals' health condition, what is needed is a worker who behaves in standardized ways.

Managers on factory farms put a lot of effort into writing "standard op-erating procedures" (SOPs). These SOPs are job scripts or "how-to" guides written to standardize how a task or program should be executed. Some senior managers learn to write within the genre in manufacturing theory classes. Part of being a capable manager is being able to write an SOP that appears to be exhaustive, with a list of tasks, principles, and an overarch-ing explanation of a given procedure's logic. The following is my own SOP for industrializing pig minds. This document is, of course, a fiction. But we could say that all SOPs are make-believe, to some extent, in that the genre as-sumes that the world can be scripted. SOPs are shows of managerial expertise that are less complete than the document suggests, because they will always rely on workers' unspoken contextual knowledge to fill in the gaps. There is nothing like this SOP formally written in any agribusiness. However, every single word is a reflection of ways of talking, interactions, and events I en-countered over twenty-seven months of ethnographic research in farms and slaughterhouses. Indeed, while the document is a fiction, none of the stated principles and procedures are my own invention. They are examples—often written verbatim, including even the more perplexing rules such as never looking sows in the eyes—of things that I was explicitly instructed to do by either management or by some of my co-workers.

BERKAMP MEATS PORK PRODUCERS, INC.

Policy # 97408—Animal Welfare+ System

Standard Operating Procedures for Making Quality Feelings

Gestation Phase

First Introduced in Trials 01/07/2010. Revised 02/08/2016.

Our Mission Statement: Quality Protein

Welcome to Berkamp Meats! We are glad that you have chosen to join us as a member of our team. You are now a part of one of the largest pork producers in the United States, supplying nutritious protein to dozens of different coun-tries. With your help, and that of the thousands of other team members who have chosen to build their careers at Berkamp Meats, we will continue on our journey of feeding the world! Our philosophy is that we never stop improving. When we joined this network in the 1990s, fifty thousand sows gave birth to just over one million pigs per year. Today, we and our affiliates have grown to house over two hundred thousand sows and make 5.2 million pigs. Our sows used to average eight pigs per litter. Using cutting-edge genetics, and with the husbandry skills of team members like yourself, we are proud that we now average thirteen pigs per litter.

At Berkamp Meats, you will often hear your colleagues talk about vertical integration. Along with the conscientious work of team members like you, it is the secret to our company's success. Vertical integration means that we own every step in the process of making protein products. Vertical integration lets us provide our customers with a guarantee that we know everything that went into their pork. We own our own genetics, feed mills, boar studs, breeding farms, growing farms, slaughterhouses, and carcass processing facilities. This degree of control gives us the tools to design a system that makes the right kind of pig for our customers. It is why we ship much of our pork to high-priced, competitive markets like Japan. We like to tell our loyal customers that we do not want to be the biggest pork company in the world. Instead, we want to be the one with the highest quality.

As a Berkamp Meats employee, remember that quality always starts with you. In business these days, it seems that everyone is talking about quality. But the word quality always means something different depending on who you ask. To us at Berkamp Meats, quality means only one thing: decreases in process variation. Quality is making things the same. From our high-performance feed mixtures, to how we will teach you to care for our animals, our goal is to always do everything the exact same way. Consistency is our most important principle, and it informs everything that we do. The result is that we deliver to our customers the most uniform pork available on the market. Our world is getting smaller, and wholesalers can choose from dozens of pork companies for their customers' needs. But they choose us because we make a very standardized protein product. A quality pig carcass allows our customers to build their consistent brands. If you go to a grocery store today, you will see that there are many brands to choose from to nourish your family. Chances are, that the raw materials for your family's favorite bacon or ham came from one of our hundreds of farms.

The Berkamp Meats Animal Welfare+ Guarantee

As an entering member of the pork industry, you may have heard from some animal activists who say that we treat our animals like inanimate objects, like a tire or a shoe. Some people who live in cities think that we ignore our animals' pain and other feelings. You will find that nothing could be further from the truth! We know that our animals are alive. Some of our employees say that the pigs they care for are smarter than dogs, and we hope that you learn to take an interest in these amazing creatures. As inheritors of the legacy of American farming, God gave us the moral responsibility to ensure that we provide for our animals' welfare. You might hear these urban activists claim that pigs need to be able to play, have straw for nesting, or run outside. We believe that the science shows that all a pig needs to grow quickly is healthy food and warm shelter, and you will see the proof in the bodies of our productive animals.

But times are changing. We believe that pork producers must change with them. The past thirty years of pork production have been an American success story. We have moved pigs from outdoors, where they are susceptible to disease and predators, to a quality indoor environment where we can control their temperature and diet. In the 1980s, a large farm might have held five hundred pigs, while today you can find as many as ten thousand pigs at some of our larger farm sites. This allows us to provide the world with affordable animal proteins, while maintaining a return on our investment. The pigs have also changed. Every year we have averaged an increase of 0.2 pigs per litter. Sows now ovulate 300 percent more eggs than they did ten years ago, and many of our sows now make larger litters than they have teats to feed. You will find that some of our most prolific sows can have litters of eighteen pigs! This amazing achievement comes with its challenges, including new responsibilities that fall on our team members' shoulders. We need to monitor our sows when they farrow new litters, as their birth canals can become obstructed. The piglets are smaller and can die easier, so they rely on you to give them extra care. It has also become important to ensure that sows are kept very calm, as they can injure themselves or their litters if they are excited by novelty.

Our industry dates back to the early 1900s, when pioneering meatpackers in the city of Chicago revolutionized the way that Americans eat. In those days, every small town had its own butcher who would buy pigs from local farmers. All of the pigs were different, and each region had its own way of butchering and presenting the pork. The big packers in Chicago, with names like Armour and Swift, changed all of that by transporting fresh meat on refrigerated rail cars all over the country. They had economies of scale that allowed them to offer pork to consumers at a much lower price than the local butchers could. To make money after breaking even off the meat, these entrepreneurs made ingenious consumer inventions from the fur, blood, and bones. This led the Chicago meatpackers to say that they "use every part of the pig but the squeal." We at Berkamp Meats are not the type to rest on our laurels, and we can now say that we strive to use every aspect of the pig—including its squeal!

We are proud to introduce our Animal Welfare+ system, a policy that has recently gone into effect on all of our company farms. The Animal Welfare+ system is our guarantee to customers that we go the extra mile to care for pigs. Our team members are dedicated not only to meeting our pigs' basic needs of food and shelter, but also to giving pigs the highest quality experience for the time that they are housed in our barns. The + in our animal welfare program stands for "productive feelings." We want our pigs to have experiences and feelings that lead to rapid, uniform, and predictable rates of gestation, birth, and growth. At Berkamp Meats, we have learned that high quality feelings can help lead to high quality pork. As a team member on our farms, you will be the person who interacts with our pigs every day. How you behave in the presence of our pigs can affect the quality of our pork. Always remember that you are on the front lines of providing our pigs with productive feelings.

We at Berkamp Meats care about our animals' well-being, but we also know that pigs are not pets. They are made to feed families, and all of us earn our livelihood from these animals. We have implemented the Berkamp Meats Animal Welfare+ system because we know that it is good for business, and it is a necessary step for pork producers to keep improving with this new generation of prolific farm animals.

Eight Principles for Executing the Berkamp Animal Welfare+ Experience

Please consult the attached manuals for step-by-step descriptions of how we are changing the execution of specific tasks in light of the Animal Welfare+ system. All new policies are built on the bedrock of these eight principles for making quality feelings.

1. *Remember that the pigs are always watching you.* They have almost 360 degree vision. On your first week of work, please take some time to study how the sows behave in your presence. They may appear like they are playing with their feeding machines or sleeping. They are not ignoring you. If you look at their eyes, you will notice that they are always following your movements. Your management team has carefully planned all of our boars', sows', and hogs' environments and housing with the principles of quality in mind. They are all housed in the same barn designs and style of gestation crate. The temperature and air quality of these barns are identical. Their feed ingredients come from the same sources and climates. Please remember that your behavior in these barns is the only potential point of variation that we cannot directly control. It is your responsibility to conduct yourself in a quality manner in the presence of sows,

knowing that your actions can affect our pigs' productivity. Our best employees try to conduct themselves in ways such that sows often do not notice they are there!

2. *After your first initiation week, never look pigs in the eyes.* Once you learn to sense how our pigs are always watching you, please refrain from looking back. Our sows will freeze if they believe that you are watching them. This is especially important when you are moving pigs in the halls from gestation to farrowing. The barn's paths and hallways are built very narrowly to ensure that there are few unique things for sows to visually process. If one hog stops walking, it can cause what we call a "traffic jam" and all of the animals could get hurt or miscarry. If you encounter team members moving a group of sows, turn your back on the advancing animals. When you are moving through barns or inspecting animals, try to look at our animals using your peripheral vision.

3. *Remember that you might always be saying something to pigs.* Animals experience things differently than humans. You cannot know what a pig is thinking. Sows will freeze at the sight of a bright color or a dangling chain, for instance, and they may also notice certain sounds or odors that might not register to your senses. A modern farm worker with good husbandry skills knows that her appearance or behavior can always potentially communicate something of significance to our pigs, and perhaps different things depending on the pig. Always wear the same clothes, and take care to always move at the same pace. Since we cannot ultimately know how each of our pigs will perceive the world around them, we need to be aware that our clothing, bodies, and actions are potentially signaling some kind of meaning at all times. We at Berkamp Meats know that every person walks or talks differently. We cannot change that. What is important is that everyone acts in their own same way at all times.

4. *Do not bring any objects from your home into our barns.* At Berkamp Meats, you will take a shower in the company locker rooms every morning prior to beginning your shift. Please use our company soap and deodorant on the shower walls, and refrain from bringing your own perfumes, shampoos, or scents to work. We supply blue coveralls, white t-shirts, underwear, and boots for our employees. We also supply notebooks and pens. These objects have been carefully chosen by team leaders, please do not bring your own from home. This is important for keeping diseases out of our barns, and it ensures that our employees always appear the same.

5. *Always maintain a calm, even demeanor in the presence of pigs.* At Berkamp Meats, we maintain a work environment that is as enjoyable as it is rewarding. We realize that one of the pleasures of being on

farms is forming close relationships with your co-workers. We like to see our employees smiling and having a good time, whether joking around or talking about last night's game. However, take care to limit such activity to locker rooms, lunchrooms, or the workshop. When you enter into a barn's animal holding areas, put on your "game face." Speak only as much as is necessary to accomplish a given task. Never shout, make sudden movements, loiter for long periods, or run in the holding areas. Being frustrated at home or work is no reason to frustrate our sows! Always maintain a quiet, even voice so that you do not disturb the pigs. If an urgent problem arises, quietly signal to your co-workers to join you in the workshop.

6. *Above all else, never touch the pigs*. Use the tools and machines that we provide to interact with pigs. Since our sows are not accustomed to individual attention, they can be easily startled by new kinds of physical contact. Upsetting or exciting a gestating animal can have consequences. On rare occasions, our employees have upset sows. They can start banging on their cages, until other sows start doing the same. Touching sows can lead to outcomes that are harmful to both people and pigs, and part of our responsibility is to manage the emotions of our pigs, including those that can spread between animals. There are only four exceptions to this no-contact rule: making sows stand up during morning inspections, moving sows from gestation to farrowing, injecting drugs, and artificial insemination. We provide you with tools to ensure quality uniformity in the ways that animals are touched during these four tasks. We detail these four points of breeding farm human-animal contact in SOP Policy briefs #s 97409–97412. It is your responsibility to follow the instructions listed therein.

7. *When accidents happen, talk to your team leader*. As much as possible, we aspire to create an environment where there are no events. A team leader on one of our farms has been so diligent in creating quality feelings that he insists that the pigs under his care no longer experience anything at all! The ideal breeding farm for our productive animals is one where nothing out of the ordinary ever takes place. That said, we know that sometimes accidents that are beyond our control can happen. A sow may suffer from a rectal prolapse, or a section of metal flooring could crack and an animal may fall into the pool of manure below. Never try to fix the problem yourself. Your team leader has likely seen something similar happen, and will be able to advise you of the best and most consistent way people have returned the situation to normal in the past.

8. *Treat all pigs the same way*. The key principle of the Animal Welfare+ quality experience is that you should never give any pig individual

attention. Every animal should receive the same treatments, un-dergo the same processes, and come out of our system with the same experiences. In the past, there have been occasions when one of our employees would take a liking to a particular pig, and would interact with it during breaks or give it gifts such as extra feed. Fol-lowing the initiation of the Animal Welfare+ system, these practices are to be strictly avoided. Employees should not show favoritism towards any animal, and they should not form relationships with any pigs. If we cannot sustain the same interaction for all of our animals, then we must not provide it to any of them. The Animal Welfare+ Guarantee means we go the extra mile to make diverse pigs into "the pig."

Industrial Sentience

If you have read anything about factory farms, you probably know of them as places that don't care about animal perception and sentience. Feelings like pain or excitement are allegedly neglected in the industrial project of cheaply making tons of flesh. When you hear the phrase "industrial pork," perhaps you think of pigs locked indoors their entire lives and fed cocktails of antibiotics to keep them healthy despite their cramped conditions. Maybe you imagine animals that have been selectively bred over a long period in order to grow quickly. Or animals that are so lean that they can no longer survive outdoors without dying from pneumonia, all to satisfy fat-phobic American eaters. Journalists and scholars tend to write about farm animal industrialization as a matter of environmental or genetic engineering—a kind of biological-physical violence—that is done to hogs without any con-sideration of their emotional needs or sentience. It is something of a com-mon popular belief that if only we humans recognized our shared suffering with many nonhuman animals, then we would not tolerate our current ag-ricultural practices. If only we recognized animals as intelligent, thinking beings—rather than as instinctual biological machines—some argue that we would stop systematically harming them.

The sociologist Anna Williams, some time ago, rejected these kinds of claims as being far too easy. She has shown that, across the twentieth century, agribusinesses have constantly searched for ways to convert animals' think-ing and interpretation of signs into more efficient methods for killing hogs. In the early Chicago packinghouses, they used to put wooden dummy pigs at the front of the slaughterhouse kill floor so that hogs would assume it was ok to keep walking forward. Today, the animal ethologist Temple Grandin—in an effort to reduce accidents, suffering, and the pain of nonhuman animals at the point of slaughter—has redesigned the kill chutes of most major packinghouses through her studies of how different species perceive the material world. Her designs are adopted because they allow meatpackers to speed up the rate of killing. One of Williams's points is that we overestimate the cultural divide between recognizing the intellectual capacities of another species and exploiting them. Massive systems of death like factory farms are only possible *because* they try to take into account that hogs are thinking and feeling beings alive to the world around them.

To be clear, though, I do not think that journalists and animal rights advocates are entirely wrong on this point—factory farms do routinely block pigs from doing many instinctual behaviors that are normal for their species. For example, pigs would nest if they were supplied with straw bedding. Outside of confinement, hogs root in the soil for edibles and nutrients. As this ingrained behavior manifests in the concrete floors of confinement barns, it can result in the flesh of snouts rubbed raw. But this is only one part of the story. What I find striking about the day that Maria yelled at me is how it suggests that mundane human behaviors and actions are now being converted into meat. Industrial meat requires a static kind of industrial sentience and lived experience, such that pigs are never surprised and always sense the same things. Factory farms force pigs to lead such monotonous lives that even something so small as looking at a sow in the eyes can harm them. And this working orientation to animal nature, one inculcated into even blasé workers such as Maria, is jarring because pigs outside of confinement usually tend to be quite curious about and seek out novel experiences. The perversity of this industrialization of experience is that pork corporations are now beginning to take seriously how a nonhuman species perceives the world on its own terms—in non-anthropocentric ways—in order to cultivate and sustain lived environments that inhibit crucial dimensions of these animals' nature.

As corporations continue to manufacture these animals that are so biologically weak, they now need to take into account how such fragile beings interpret the world. The extreme frailty of modern pigs means that, surprisingly, worker-hog relationships are becoming more intimate over time. Industrialization becomes not just something that was done to pigs in the past or a static environment of machines and cages but something that farmworkers—those people on the lowest part of the agribusiness hierarchy—are made to continually do with pigs. This is not, in short, a simple story of dominating nature. This is not the American progress tale of human mastery and ingenuity touted in pork industry magazines. Industrialization on factory farms has become an ongoing social task; it is a tenuous relationship that forcibly shapes the behavior of human workers as much as it does hogs. This is instead a matter of exploiting migrant farmworkers *through* vulnerable pigs—compelling them to carry the weight, health, and suffering of a damaged species on their shoulders. What is needed here is not just a critique of society's indifference to animal feeling but rather the creation of animals that require intense human intimacy and standardized care for their survival.

Suggested Readings

On work, planning, and the limits of standardization, see:
James Scott. 1998. *Seeing Like a State: How Certain Schemes to Improve the Human Condition Have Failed*. New Haven: Yale University Press.

On sentience, pain, and the ethics of animal agribusiness, see:
Peter Singer. 1975. *Animal Liberation: A New Ethics for Our Treatment of Animals*. New York: HarperCollins.

On how agribusiness incorporates and exploits animal sentience, see:
Anna Williams. 2004. "Disciplining Animals: Sentience, Production, and Critique." *International Journal of Sociology and Public Policy* 24 (9): 45–57.

On how all life-forms are alive to the world, interpreting and acting on meaningful signs, see:
Eduardo Kohn. 2013. *How Forests Think: Toward an Anthropology beyond the Human*. Berkeley: University of California Press.

On how there are more worlds than humans are capable of perceiving, see:
Jacob von Uexküll. 2010. *A Foray into the Worlds of Animals and Humans: With a Theory of Meaning*. Minneapolis: University of Minnesota Press.

CHAPTER 11

Making Babies with Cows

Scout Calvert

Note: The conceit of section one of this essay is partial role reversal. How would a doctor who was a cow explain to yearling interns how to breed humans? This is what a cow might sound like if she thought about humans the ways that human purebred livestock breeders think about cows. Section two switches back to a human perspective and treats the extensive interventions into cattle reproduction as the mundane options that they have become for many farmers. This essay highlights the traffic of reproductive technologies across the porous human-bovine species boundary.

I. Reproductive Science on Planet Bovine: A Seminar for Cow Interns in Human Reproduction

So, you want to get a human pregnant? The first thing to know about human reproduction is that humans are really touchy about it. This is very important to know if you are concerned with handling practices that keep humans calm and stress-free. Stress is definitely a barrier to pregnancy, and of course, you can injure a human when you are handling her, so you want to be careful. Our knowledge of human welfare has evolved, and best practices for handling folk should always be used.

The good news is that we have many years of research in bovine reproductive medicine to guide us. It turns out that humans make really good research analogs for cows, so much of what we know transfers readily to human reproduction. Even the gestation length of a folk is almost the same as for us cattle. Over the years, our people have donated our semen and ova abundantly to the cause of perfecting assisted reproductive technologies and cryopreservation, and this has advanced human reproductive medicine tremendously.

Unassisted Reproduction

Folk will reproduce readily if you put them together in the right situation, as long as they are otherwise healthy. However, sires are not able to service as many females as you might think. Some will, quite readily, but many prefer to consort with only one or a few females. It is possible that breed improvement programs could change this, but it hasn't really stood in the way of reproduction. It may be hard to believe, but there are actually more folk than cows on this planet.

Thus, the easiest way to breed humans is to just put some known fertile women together with one or more healthy, disease-free sires. Make them comfortable, and make sure they have nutrient-dense rations, enough food for three meals a day, room to roam, and privacy. But this leaves a lot to chance, and some of those girls will figure out how to keep themselves from getting pregnant.

But suppose you don't want to leave so much up to chance and would prefer to control breeding a little more closely. There are a few ways to do this, depending on your constraints and your goals.

Assisted Reproduction

If you find you need to encourage reproduction, you'll need to know when the woman is ready to ovulate. And when that happens, you'll need to be ready with semen from a suitable man sire.

Estrous Versus Menstrual Cycle

Humans are hormonally very similar to us bovines. However, human females do not have standing heat in which they seek breeding opportunities, and they shed their endometrium through menstruation rather than reabsorb it as we do. Without a standing heat to indicate when a woman is about to ovulate, other signs and indicators will have to be used.

In humans, the menstrual cycle lasts about twenty-eight days but could be longer or shorter. The first day of the cycle is the beginning of menstruation, when the endometrium is shed in absence of conception. Depending on the length of the cycle, the ovulatory phase will begin a week to two weeks later. A helpful way to detect ovulation is to track the woman's menstrual cycle with a calendar. Keep track of as many of the signs of fertility as you can, and you will soon have a good picture of when the female human is fertile.

These signs include cervical mucus that becomes long and stretchy, a quality called spinnbarkeit. On palpation, her cervix will have lifted up slightly higher in her vaginal canal, and it will be soft. On examination with a speculum, the cervical os will be open, and clear mucus can be seen. Another way is to look under a microscope for a fern leaf pattern in her saliva or cervical mucus. Some behavioral and emotional changes may be displayed. She may seem restless or edgy.

You can also keep a record of her basal body temperature each morning before she gets up from sleeping. Using a digital thermometer accurate to the first decimal place, take her temperature orally at the same time each morning, before she gets up, and make a note of it on a calendar. Her temperature will rise from the baseline at ovulation and remain elevated until the cycle is complete.

You can also detect ovulation by capturing her urine and using a test strip designed to detect a surge in luteinizing hormone (LH). It is best to do this twice a day beginning a couple days before ovulation is anticipated to occur. This will give more precise information so that you can time mating or insemination. Ovulation typically follows 18 to 36 hours after the LH surge.

Inducing Ovulation

If all of this is too much work, you can instead induce ovulation so that you can time insemination accurately. Typical regimens involve administering clomiphene for five days, beginning on day 3, 4, or 5 of a cycle, to stimulate follicular growth, followed by an injection of human chorionic gonadotropin (hCG) to induce ovulation. The hCG can be administered when one or more follicles have grown to 18 millimeters or larger, as verified using transvaginal ultrasound. The hCG injection is called a "trigger shot," and ovulation typically occurs twenty-six hours later.

Using a clomiphene regimen increases odds of twins to about 10 percent. Although gestating twins increases the chance of preterm birth and other pregnancy complications, you don't have to worry about the risk to female fetuses. Human females who are twinned with a male will be reproductively normal, which means they won't androgenize and become freemartins, as among us cattle.

Artificial Insemination

The goal of detecting ovulation is to make sure that sperm cells are present in the fallopian tube soon after the follicle releases the egg so that fertilization can occur before the egg reaches the uterus. Timing is especially important if you are using semen samples that have been previously frozen, since their lifespan is shorter.

Now, some human females will prefer the semen of a particular sire, usually a sire she is pair-bonded with. If possible, for handling reasons and human welfare concerns, use the semen from this sire.

If your pair-bonded folk have been kept together but not produced any offspring, you will need to check the sperm quality of the sire before you waste any more valuable time and money. Bring a sample to a lab for semen analysis to determine sperm count, motility, and morphology. Normal sperm count is above 15 million per milliliter, and at least half should be motile. If low numbers of motile and morphologically normal sperm (mild male factor infertility) are the only problem, then intra-uterine insemination with a fresh, cleaned sample may overcome this.

You will not need to aid the male in ejaculating. Provide a quiet place in the clinic and some images of folk copulating, and he will stimulate himself to provide the sample. Although many folk will copulate in open spaces or outside of their homes, most men will be too stressed to ejaculate if they feel they are watched too closely. If possible, provide a private room with a closed door for him to stimulate himself.

It is possible that the preferred sire possesses too many reproductive defects to use on the preferred dam. In this case, you can select a sire from a sperm bank catalog. However, you will need to enlist the cooperation of the woman if she has a preference for her pair-bonded sire. You may need to keep her separated from the man, who may attempt to dissuade her from using another sire.

Sire Selection

Some female humans are not pair-bonded or are pair-bonded with another female. Some may also be bonded in larger groups. But don't assume that these females have no preferences about the sire. It may seem to you that the motile sperm of one healthy man sire is as good as the motile sperm of any other healthy man, but that is not usually the case for folk. Human welfare has made great strides, and we now recognize that we must learn to recognize her preferences to avoid stress and to ensure that she will care for the baby when it is born.

Women who are pair-bonded with another female may breed naturally with a familiar human male or may prefer to choose a donor sire from a catalog. Some of the factors in these choices are obvious, like a strong, healthy sire who has been tested free of STDs and common genetic defects. However, other factors are not so obvious, like psychological or physical resemblance to the partner and whether or not the partner has desirable traits. We bovines admire good udders, a calm disposition, sound feet, easy calving, and high fertility, and so we admire bulls who can pass these traits on to our young. Folk may disregard these qualities in a donor if the donor is otherwise unlike their mate. Moreover, while many humans claim to be "color blind," fewer donor sires with less sought-after traits like dark skin and eyes are recruited, which means there are fewer to choose from. Humans who prioritize brown skin may not have much choice of other qualities in their donor.

Now, due to breeding limitations, we don't have the same level of information about human sires as we have for ourselves. Human donor catalogs are sparsely informative. Humans attribute a lot of their offspring's success in life to genetics but still prefer to leave all but the most obvious traits to chance. The donor might have been tested free of STDs and then for the most common variants of a small handful of known genetic diseases. Cystic fibrosis, sickle cell disease, and Tay-Sachs, for example, are simple recessive diseases that are common in some human populations and less common in others. In order for the disease to be expressed, a child must carry two copies of the recessive gene. Record-keeping for humans leaves something to be desired, and some humans might not even know that they carry one of these genes; humans do not exploit such information to aggressively breed recessive diseases out of their family lines. Additional testing can be requested if your woman is known to have a genetic disease.

Our fastidious record-keeping for two hundred years has helped us develop statistical evaluation techniques that provide strong predictions of heritable traits, especially because our wide use of artificial insemination has allowed our best bulls and cows to breed prolifically. This record-keeping has enabled the development of genetic tests for even complex traits, so that statistical predictions can be genetically enhanced. Despite enthusiasm for pedigree keeping among some folk, their records aren't good enough to develop statistical evaluation, given their reduced capacity for reproduction. Genetic testing has become inexpensive, but most of the panels are not considered to be particularly useful for either health planning or reproductive purposes.

Perhaps because of stigma attached to using donor sperm and eggs, humans have been reticent to document the traits of their donors completely. So your donor catalog may describe the height and weight as well as the skin, eye, and hair color of the donor along with a few other traits. Sometimes this information is included for his parents as well, though it is unlikely that his grandparents will be documented. Sometimes an essay or other piece of personal writing is included, so that prospective human parents can feel sympathetic to the donor. A photo of the donor as a baby or child may be provided, or, more rarely, an adult photo of the donor. Sometimes, more information about the donor has been collected, which can be provided for an additional fee. As you know, this is the opposite of our community, in which full information about a sire and his ancestors is considered key to his prestige.

Another issue that results from the lack of documentation is not being able to identify the most successful sires. The best advice is to choose a proven sire with many pregnancies from his donations. However, many sperm banks limit the number of pregnancies from a single donor to as few as ten. Before human collection studs (banks) settled on best practices, a few donors were used for several hundred pregnancies. While it's not a problem for us bovines, humans have a strongly socialized inbreeding avoidance mechanism, and they worry that their children could accidentally meet a genetic half-sibling and breed. Although this is statistically extremely unlikely, the very idea causes revulsion for some of them, and they feel better if there are fewer donor siblings, even if this may mean that it takes longer to achieve pregnancy with a particular sire. The trade-off for a genetically more unique child is that folks have less knowledge about sires, constituting a missed opportunity for breed improvement.

The human donor sires are not named, so they are functionally anonymous, and their pedigrees cannot be identified. Some donors have agreed to have identifying information shared once offspring have reached maturity (considered to be eighteen years old in humans). Folk can be very possessive of the babies they raise and do not want interference from other people. Pair-bonded males and females who use donor gametes also prefer to elide the biological parentage of the offspring. Unlike bovine males, man sires sometimes aid their dams in feeding and sheltering their babies. However, some men won't do this if they think that the baby is not their genetic offspring. Men also prefer that other folks don't know when they are not genetic parents of their babies.

Folk might try to avoid inbreeding, but many seem to prefer mates who are slightly more similar to them than the general population. This influences the selection of donor gametes. Humans can be very sensitive to the presence or absence of recessive traits like light-colored eyes (blue or green) or hair (blond or red). Additionally, of human phenotypes, folk are typically most sensitive about skin tone and will use that criterion as a first screen for donor gametes. However, the human tradition of selecting somewhat similar mates is relaxing in many populations and heterosis prevails. Still, for pair-bonded males and females, any trait that could draw attention to the fact that the bonded male did not sire the offspring should be avoided.

Semen Quality

Now, if you are purchasing sperm from a bank, you'll want to be sure that you buy a big enough sample of motile sperm. Most banks guarantee a minimum number of motile sperm; others will sell you vials by the number of motile sperm per milliliter. Banks recruit and then screen young donors with physical examinations and health histories. Then donors take blood tests for STDs and a basic genetic screening panel. Each deposit is processed with an extender for cryopreservation. The straws are frozen and quarantined for six months and are released from quarantine when the donor has been retested to be clear from STDs. This is because human males cannot be kept away from other humans. Even keeping them segregated from females will not keep them from engaging in sexual activity with other males. Sexual activity with other males is perceived to be associated with disease transmission and decreased fertility, so by an old tradition, sperm banks will not knowingly release samples from quarantine if the donor has had sex with other men.

The samples are prepared two different ways: for intra-uterine insemination, and for intra-cervical insemination. Additionally, straws with smaller numbers of motile sperm may be adequate for embryo transfer (ET), because the procedure differs from ET amongst us bovines, as discussed below. Finally, whereas it is possible to select sex-sorted bovine semen, that is considered a specialty service for humans. Sex selection for human pregnancies involves advanced technologies, like IVF with pre-implantation genetic diagnosis (PIGD).

Embryo Transfer

Among our own people, some cows are very good mothers, and can become mothers with embryo transfer (ET), so that they can mother the very best calves. For humans, ET is used when the woman has a strong mothering instinct but has been unable to conceive, or when she carries a catastrophic genetic disease. In addition to different applications for embryo transfer, the technique for ET is somewhat different for humans. Whereas we typically fertilize eggs in vivo, for human embryo transfer eggs are extracted from the woman or a woman who is a willing egg donor after a similar hormone regimen, and then fertilized in a petri dish and allowed to divide several times before implantation. The egg can also be fertilized by injecting a single sperm into it, in a process called intracytoplasmic sperm injection. ICSI allows a healthy sperm cell to be selected. IVF can also allow genetic testing of the resulting embryos (PIGD). If there are any eggs or embryos left over after the cycle, these can be cryopreserved for future use.

Human females are astounding mothers. Like us, they typically give birth to singletons, occasionally to twins, and rarely to triplets. But, implanted with multiple embryos, women have been known to successfully gestate and give birth to as many as eight babies. There have been some instances when humans have been implanted with several embryos at once, on the mistaken assumption that most will not implant in the uterine wall and grow. This has resulted in higher numbers of multiple births. However, time and observation have shown that using two embryos is optimal. Multiple fetuses increase the chances of pre-term births and other complications. Humans don't have freemartins; heifer calves that are twinned with a male will not androgenize or be sterile. Although the opportunity to get several babies from a single gestation is exciting, it is not actually cost-effective as each of the surviving offspring may have health problems at birth that result in later difficulties.

Conclusion

In a nutshell, these are the most common strategies available for encouraging reproduction among folk. Other options are available, though they are more costly and technologically intricate and thus more expensive and suitable for only the most valuable folk. Humans can be nervous and touchy about reproduction, so it is best to choose a strategy that minimizes handling and stress. Although their behavior sometimes suggests otherwise, humans are picky about their sexual partners and mates, and strategies should be chosen that line up with their preferences in order to minimize stress and ensure successful parenting.

II. Reproductive Science on Planet Earth: Modern Breeding Techniques for Cattle Growers

So you want to get a cow pregnant? We can help with that, whether it's because you want her to make milk for you to drink or to raise a calf for meat or even to create embryos to transfer to another cow. Back in the day, this was a very simple matter of getting a bull, maybe borrowing one, or maybe raising up one of your own calves into a bull, instead of castrating him to make him a steer to fatten or an ox to pull a cart. Today, new assisted reproductive technologies offer more choices and more control, enabling you to improve herd performance or to match the sire's traits even more closely to your cow. And this high technology is easy and available to use, even on an ordinary farm.

The Old-Fashioned Way

Using a bull to get your cow pregnant can be practical and easy, especially if you already have one on hand. However, for a few reasons, you might want or need to get your cow pregnant another way. First of all, you have to maintain the bull, keep him in good condition and disease-free, even for all of the months he's not in service. And if you borrow or lend a bull, you'll worry that the bull might carry a sexually transmitted disease. I'm sure you didn't think about it, because what could seem more pure and natural than cows in a pasture, with a bull for consort? But he may well carry trichomoniasis, vibriosis, or brucella, or some other disease. Even if it doesn't bother him much, it will bother your cow. If you get her pregnant, she will probably abort.

So maybe now this doesn't seem so simple, but really it is. Modern technology can come to your aid. Many farmers use it. All you need is a cow in heat and some straws of frozen semen. Here's how to do it.

Detecting Heat

The key to successful breeding is knowing when your cow is in heat. You can do this just by keeping an eye on her, but you'll have to watch her at least a couple times a day, first thing in the morning and last thing at sunset. A cow in heat will mount other cows or will stand still while other cows mount her. This is called "standing heat," and it doesn't last long—usually between six and fourteen hours. Ovulation occurs twenty-eight to thirty-two hours later. You want the sperm to be right there waiting when the egg is released, so you'll need to know pretty accurately when standing heat began in order to know when to put a bull in the pasture with her or use procedures like artificial insemination (AI). Other signs of estrus include restlessness, rubbing against other cows, or changes in appetite. She may have mucus coming from her vulva or walk around with a raised tail. She may make less milk than usual.

It might be a lot to keep track of, though, if you have a bunch of cows. Who has time to walk through the pasture for a couple hours a day? Heat-detecting technologies can help. These include scratch-off or pressure-sensitive patches to stick or glue to your cow's tailhead that change color when she's been mounted by other cows. You can also go high-tech with a patch that has a pressure sensor and a transmitter to relay to a farm computer when a cow has been mounted. You could even set it up to text you when that happens.

Another method is to use a paint dispenser called a chin-ball marker that is attached to a teaser bull that will leave color when he mounts. Teaser bulls have been surgically altered to be sterile or otherwise physically unable to impregnate a cow. A cow that you were going to cull anyway can be treated with testosterone to do the same work.

Estrous Synchronization

For those who have a lot of cows, waiting for them to come into heat and then coordinating getting each of them pregnant can be a lot to juggle. Time is money, and you don't want to miss your chance to get your cows pregnant. Months later, as the bellies of your pregnant cows swell, the cows who are still "open" (not pregnant) won't be any closer to producing milk and beef for you.

Instead, you can give them a hormone regimen to synchronize estrous and induce ovulation so that you can plan for procedures like artificial insemination or embryo transfer as well as project future milk or beef production. What these hormones do is override the cow's endogenous hormones in order to reset the estrous cycle and trigger ovulation. You can synchronize the ovulation of all of the cows in your herd so that you can inseminate them all at the same time, which also means that they will all give birth around the same time. Or you can stage them to extend production through the year. Not only can you can plan future production, you might even know when to put a vacation on your calendar.

Cows have an estrous cycle that typically lasts between eighteen and twenty-four days. Assuming a cycle of twenty-four days, the first seventeen days, approximately, are the luteal phase and the remaining days are the follicular phase, culminating in standing heat. Ovulation occurs shortly thereafter and marks the first day of the cycle. Cows typically have two or three waves of follicular development, each with the selection of a dominant follicle that will either regress or ovulate. Only the final follicular wave results in ovulation. These follicular waves add to the complexity of the cow's cycle. The ovary, uterus, and pituitary gland release hormones that work in a complex feedback loop.

That complexity can be simplified and controlled with a protocol to synchronize estrous, ovulation, or both. This may involve progesterone delivered orally or with an intravaginal progesterone device (IVPD) or injections of hormones or both. Synthetic gonadotropin, prostaglandin, estrogen, and progesterone may be used. There are quite a few protocols on the market, so check the specific instructions from the pharmaceutical company whose protocol you use. You can also find estrous synchronization calendars from animal scientists on the internet to help you track cycles and plan for procedures. Sperm that has been frozen has a shorter lifespan in the reproductive tract than fresh sperm, so artificial insemination should take place four to twelve hours after the onset of estrus.

Artificial Insemination

Now, of course, ovulating isn't enough. You've got the egg lined up. Now you need to make sure that semen is in the right place at the right time. If you do it the old-fashioned way, by turning your bulls out into the pasture with your cows, you'll need to make sure that you have enough bulls on hand. You'll need a bull for every twenty to thirty cows. A bull with libido enough can service a cow about every half-hour.

But here's where you can really control production. Buying and maintaining a bull can be expensive. You may not want to leave performance up to him. You may not have a share in a bull or have a friend with a bull that you can borrow. So instead you can fire up your internet connection, browse a catalog, pick a bull, and buy straws of his semen to be delivered frozen in a nitrogen tank. This means you can have your pick of the best bulls with the best performance traits, and you aren't limited by geography. You can even pick vials from several different bulls to complement the traits of the cows you will use them on.

Some people think of artificial insemination as the turkey baster method, but that gives so many wrong impressions. First of all, a turkey baster holds a lot of liquid. Rest assured, you are not going to be dealing with a lot of liquid. Sperm are very small. Many millions of them fit in just a milliliter of semen. A straw of bull semen is typically .25 ml or .5 ml, with a standard of 10 to 20 million sperm cells. Another wrong impression is that there is some generic vat of semen to be sucked up into a turkey baster bulb, rather than carefully collected and prepared samples from specific, named, and vetted bulls. The last inaccuracy is the idea that the semen is going to just be squirted up in somewhere. The whole point of AI is control. You will be leaving as little to chance as possible. You will be depositing the semen into the body of the uterus to get the sperm as close to the ovaries as possible.

The semen comes in straws that are kept frozen in extremely cold nitrogen tanks. You must be careful when you retrieve the straws to avoid pulling out the ones you aren't using yet and also to limit the time the tank stands open while you do this. You'll need to use insulated gloves to avoid frostbite. The straws must be carefully thawed, either in a lukewarm water bath or in your shirt pocket, and used soon after thawing. The straw is inserted into an inseminator gun, which is essentially a long metal catheter with a single-use protective sheath.

Now, a cow is a big animal. Wear coveralls and opera-length rubber gloves. Once you have the cow settled in the chute, you'll need to locate her cervix. Don't put your hand in her vagina. You'll put your hand into her rectum and carefully palpate her uterus through her large intestine. After you clean her vulva, you'll insert the AI gun into her vagina without touching it to her labia and then guide it into her cervix with your other hand. She'll have three or four cervical rings you'll have to pass the catheter through without injuring her. The uterine body is quite short, so you'll go just another half-inch and deposit the semen. Slowly press the plunger while slightly withdrawing the catheter. Other methods involve depositing the semen further up the uterine horn and closer to the ovary, but this method should be sufficient for most cows.

If you are doing this for your entire herd, this can take a while. Don't thaw more straws than you can use in about fifteen minutes.

Embryo Transfer

The procedure described above takes for granted that you want to get your cow pregnant with her own egg. But maybe you have a cow who has been a good mother but otherwise is a pretty ordinary cow, and you want a chance to grow an even better cow with different genetics. Or maybe you have an exemplary cow and you want to get even more calves from her than the handful she is likely to bear in her lifetime, if left to her own devices. Well, you're in luck. With embryo transfer technology, you can get your cow pregnant with an embryo created in vivo with another cow's egg and sperm from a high-performance bull, or you can get your cow to superovulate, inseminate her, then retrieve those embryos for use in other cows.

Flushing

If you want embryos from a cow you already own, you'll have to "flush" her. Just as you can use a hormone protocol to synchronize her estrous cycle and induce ovulation, you can induce superovulation so that you can create and then retrieve multiple embryos in her reproductive tract. The hormone regimen for superovulation is more complicated than the protocol for estrous synching. As with estrous synching, several products are commercially available. Carefully follow the instructions for the protocol you select.

Plan to inseminate your cow twice, at twelve hours and again twenty-four hours after administering the final ovulation-triggering hormone. Then, six or seven days later, you will flush her uterus with a flushing medium. This is a tricky procedure, but will become familiar with practice. You'll need some special equipment, including a balloon catheter, some flushing medium, and some embryo filters.

With the cow in a chute, administer a lidocaine epidural. Then, as before, you will insert your non-dominant hand into her rectum to palpate the cervical os and guide the catheter into the uterus. Inflate the cuff on the balloon to block off the flow of the medium back through the cervix. Then, you'll squeeze or allow gravity to push fluid into the uterus. Carefully massage the uterine horns to aid in suspending the embryos in the fluid. Switch the valve on the catheter to allow the fluid to drain back into a catching tank, through a filter that catches the embryos. You will do this 5 times, with 50 to 150 ml of fluid each time. You may retrieve only a few or perhaps two dozen embryos this way.

Once you are satisfied that you have retrieved all embryos, flush the donor cow with prostaglandin (trade name Lutalyse) and then give it twice by injection three days later, to abort any remaining embryos and avoid the possibility of multiple births. You can collect embryos from her again on her next cycle.

Use a microscope to see how well the embryos have developed and to grade and sort them. If you have a cow with a synched estrous cycle (at day 5–8), you can transfer a grade 1, 2, or 3 embryo to her right away. Otherwise, you should sort the highest-grade embryos into straws and freeze them.

If you don't have a donor cow to flush, you can buy cryogenically preserved frozen embryos from a selection of high-performance sires and dams. You'll synchronize your recipient cow's estrous cycle so that you can transfer the frozen embryo at day 5.5 of her cycle.

Put your recipient cow in the chute and prepare her with an epidural. As in all of these procedures, you'll palpate her cervix and uterus transrectally to guide the instruments into her uterus. Thaw the embryo, then palpate her ovaries to discover her corpus luteum and hence, which side ovulated. Place the embryo in the uterine horn as close to that ovary as possible.

Sire Selection

Whether you are preparing your cow for AI or embryo donation, carefully select the sire you will use. Think about important traits you'd like the calf to inherit from the bull. It's unlikely you'll be able to go visit a bull and inspect him yourself. But you can carefully examine his pedigree and sire summary or EPD (expected progeny differences) chart and think about what he might add to your herd. EPDs take into account the performance data of that bull's sons and daughters and their progeny as well as genomic information that can also help predict traits. The bull should also have been tested to be free of known genetic diseases. Additionally, you may choose to purchase sperm that has been sorted to increase the likelihood of a bull or heifer calf. This is a good option if you would like to breed replacement heifers for your dairy operation.

Pregnancy Testing

Now that you've done the hard part, how do you figure out if your cow is pregnant? Blood tests are costly and impractical. Ultrasounds require special equipment. But now that you are already very familiar with her reproductive tract, you can learn to reliably detect pregnancy using transrectal palpation of her uterus.

A Note on Biosecurity

As you've seen, getting your cow pregnant can involve invasive procedures that put her at the risk of injury, infection, and sexually transmitted disease. Animals, semen, and embryos from other farms can bring disease to yours. At all times, observe best practices to screen bulls for disease and use semen and embryos only from reputable studs that adhere to the Certified Semen Services (CSS) standards established by the National Association of Animal Breeders. Use sterile instruments and supplies whenever required and handle your cow carefully to keep her stress- and injury-free.

The Bottom Line

You may be tempted to breed your cow the old-fashioned way and avoid all the hassle. It may seem more complicated, but it's not hard to reap the advantages of assisted reproductive technologies. You can prevent disease transmission, keep your cow healthy, get more calves from your best cows, and use a better bull without paying to feed him. This is the perfect opportunity to evaluate your breeding program, choose traits you'd like to see in the calf and in your herd, and plan for the future. Assisted reproductive technologies are in wide use, and the supplies and support you need to use them will be easy to find. There's never been a better time to get your cow pregnant.

Suggested Readings

On human sexual and gender identity and do-it-yourself fertility, see:

Stephanie Brill. 2006. *The New Essential Guide to Lesbian Conception, Pregnancy, and Birth*. New York: Alyson Books.

On the high stakes of using assisted reproductive technologies, see:

Charis Thompson. 2005. *Making Parents: The Ontological Choreography of Reproductive Technologies*. Cambridge: MIT Press.

On reproductive sciences and human-animal relations, see:

Scout Calvert. 2013. "Certified Angus, Certified Patriot: Breeding, Bodies, and Pedigree Practices." *Science as Culture* 22: 291–313.

Adele Clarke. 2007. "Reflections on the Reproductive Sciences in Agriculture in the UK and US, ca. 1900–2000+." *Studies in History and Philosophy of Biological and Biomedical Sciences* 38: 316–39.

Carrie Friese, and Adele Clarke. 2012. "Transposing Bodies of Knowledge and Technique: Animal Models at Work in Reproductive Sciences." *Social Studies of Science* 42: 31–52.

Donna Haraway. 2012. "Awash in Urine: DES and Premarin in Multispecies Response-ability," *Women's Studies Quarterly* 40: 301–16.

Amade M'Charek and Grietje Keller. 2008. "Parenthood and Kinship in IVF for Humans and Animals." In *Bits of Life: Feminism at the Intersections of Media, Bioscience, and Technology*, edited by Anneke Smelik and Nina Lykke, 61–78. Seattle: University of Washington Press.

On the history and use of assisted reproductive technologies, especially in cattle, see:

Robert H. Foote. 2002. "The History of Artificial Insemination: Selected Notes and Notables." *Journal of Animal Science* 80: 1–10.

Richard M. Hopper, ed. 2015. *Bovine Reproduction*. Hoboken, NJ: Wiley.

On the histories and impacts of statistical evaluation on livestock breeding, see:

Lewis Holloway. 2005. "Aesthetics, Genetics, and Evaluating Animal Bodies: Locating and Displacing Cattle on Show and in Figures," *Environmental Planning D: Society and Space* 23: 883–902.

Lewis Holloway and Carol Morris. 2008. "Boosted Bodies: Genetic Techniques, Domestic Livestock Bodies, and Complex Representations of Life." *Geoforum* 39: 1709–20.

Barbara Orland. 2014. "Turbo-Cows: Producing a Competitive Animal in the Nineteenth and Early Twentieth Centuries." In *Industrializing Organisms: Introducing Evolutionary History*, edited by Susan Schrepfer and Philip Scranton, 167–89. New York: Routledge.

❧ CHAPTER 12

How to Make a Horse Have an Orgasm

JEANNETTE VAUGHT

When I was younger, my family lived out in the country, and we had a veterinarian as a neighbor. My childhood reading was steeped in the bucolic veterinary tales of James Herriot and the great horse stories of Marguerite Henry, and I dreamed of becoming a vet. Our neighbor was one, and she let me ride with her every once in a while as she piloted her old truck around the mountain, taking care of horses, mostly, but also goats, cows, and the alpacas that people new to town had in their yard. That career goal and the truck rides got lost among typical teenage interests and my relentless pursuit of literature instead of calculus. But on a visit home after college, my horse friends introduced me to a new vet in town, one who specialized in horses and who focused mostly on breeding. Intrigued by the contrast between her specialization and the more generalized practices of care I'd experienced as a child, I asked if I could ride along with her for a day. She accepted, because she could use some extra hands. It was June, the busiest time of year for collecting stallions. I had a vague sense of what that meant. We settled on a day and time, and I arrived at her clinic at 8 a.m. a few days later.

Her office manager was already on the phone, the big spiral-bound calendar spread out in front of her while she tweaked appointment times. The office was sleek but modest, well organized and surprisingly full of paper, including an appointment book large enough to take up most of the island workspace in the center of the room. Various staff were at work preparing examination rooms, cleaning stalls in the inpatient area, and checking inventory. The manager had a small pile of drugs and supplies that she told me to make sure got on the vet's truck before we left. The vet arrived shortly thereafter; after she received a short briefing by the manager and greeted the staff, we took up the pile of items and the big metal clipboard with our appointment paperwork and headed to the truck. The schedule was so packed that I couldn't help but mentally nickname the spare, businesslike woman before me "Dr. Doolots, " a moniker that to me rang truer than the fanciful Dr. Doolittle of my youthful reading days.

We chatted about her work as we drove to the first appointment. Her favorite part of the year had just passed, when the foals are born. She'd spent years working on breeding farms taking care of the mares and foals, which is how she chose her veterinary specialty. "This time of year?" she said. "This is the real work, the hard work. The stallion work." In the decades between my childhood and adulthood, artificial insemination had moved from the fringes to the mainstream of performance horse breeding. This trend fundamentally recast the role of the veterinarian in the breeding process from someone who focused primarily on pregnancy and delivery to someone who managed conception as well. And veterinarians are needed at both ends of the conception process—in collecting the stallions, her delicate phrase, and inseminating the mares. As Dr. Doolots explained this to me, it seemed like the veterinarian's new role was to take the place of the sexual encounter between horses who would reproduce but never meet. I thought to myself: *We've strayed far from James Herriot, haven't we?*

We pulled up at the first appointment. "Just do what I tell you, stand where I tell you, and watch all you want," she instructed. "It's a great bunch of girls here, and it will be nice to have an extra pair of hands." I got out of the truck, embarking on my education in how people, technologies, and animals unexpectedly combine to make a horse have an orgasm.

How to Prepare the Artificial Vagina

The vet pulled a long rubberish cylinder out of the truck, handing it to me while she dug out a jug of lube, some plastic sleeves, and square packs of sterile, autoclaved terry cloths. The weight of it surprised me, it was heavy enough that I had to shift my feet to accommodate it, as if I had been handed a medicine ball. The object looked like a piece of pipe, perfectly straight, the hard outer shell interrupted only by a sturdy handle. But when I tried to carry it nonchalantly, like a briefcase behind Dr. Doolots as we entered the shed, I felt so lopsided that I opted to hug it to my chest in both arms instead. Dr. Doolots led the way into the shed's laboratory, directing me where to place the cylinder while she greeted the handlers. "Get some hot water running, please," she said.

The laboratory was small but very cool and clean; room enough for a small refrigerator, sink, computer, various equipment, a centrifuge and microscope, an autoclave, and some stacks of papers with page corners rising rhythmically as the ceiling fan whirred above. I ran my fingers under the water until it stung. I had already learned that "hot" meant really *hot*. The door to the lab was a portal to an entirely different kind of space, a regular enough barn smelling of hay and horses. The contrast between this quiet, clean, fluorescently lit box and the dark, dusty horse-centric space outside the door was stark.

Dr. Doolots and the handlers bustled in, laughing at the tail end of a bawdy joke, stamping cigarettes at the door. One of them booted up software on the computer while Dr. Doolots turned to me. "Meet Loretta, the stallion handler, and Bets, who manages this farm." They waved brown-nailed hands at me, as they gathered themselves, friendly and businesslike at once. "It's time to set up the AV. How's the water?"

"Ready to roll."

"OK, great." Dr. Doolots rested a hand on the cylinder whose weight I could still feel was dwindling from my bicep. "This old thing is the AV, the artificial vagina. It doesn't look like much, but it's got a lot of settings to tune up for each stallion we work with. They're pretty idiosyncratic, these boys, about what they like and don't like." Loretta and Bets stifled giggles.

"Like, customized specifications?" Reconciling this with the heavy rigid pipe I'd just carried was not immediately possible.

"Yep. The heavy outer shell is ceramic. It's an insulator so that we can get all the inner stuff right and not worry too much about how long we're out there with it. These boys sometimes take a while to get going. But the inside is a different story. Here, put on a sleeve."

I pulled a thin plastic roll out of a box on the counter, peeled open the end and slid my arm through, wiggling my fingers into the glove at the end and pulling its opening all the way up to my shoulder. Sleeves are used mainly for rectal and vaginal palpations, in which the disappearing arm of a vet into a horse's cavities can determine all manner of reproductive information: stages of ovulation, health of the uterus, and so on. I was not expecting a sleeve for this procedure, but Dr. Doolots instructed me to lube it up well. She hoisted the AV and told me to slide my arm in, thumb over fingers.

Ah. I did as instructed and made a fist. "That mimics the shape of the penis," she explained. She pulled a tab and then began to fill an invisible bladder in the AV with the hot water. I could feel the pressure build around my arm, especially around the knuckle of my thumb at the widest part of my fist. "Slowly move your arm up and down, just a bit," she instructed. I did, and realized that I was mimicking the motion of the stallion's penis, all the while feeling the heat and pressure of the AV increase around my arm. "This is to make sure every surface is well lubricated. Tell me if it gets too firm," she cautioned, "because this stallion likes a little give." The interaction between Dr. Doolots and me had transformed so quickly into a simulacra of transspecies sexual intimacy that I wasn't sure where the boundaries of firmness—of my arm, the AV, the absent equine penis I was suddenly enacting, or anything, really—might be, and I told her that was probably a good place to stop filling.

"OK. Pull out your arm but leave the sleeve. We're ready to collect."

How to Collect a Stallion

Collect is such a clean term, a quality I had not given much thought until my fist and I had been so casually turned into a penile apparatus. It refers to the process of capturing semen from a stallion in order to inseminate a mare without the need for intercourse between the two. In this sense, I understand the sleek utility of the term, its efficient remove from the carnal. Its primness recalls Victorian ideals regarding sex as filth, as corruption; of public animal sex as a bawdy threat to morality, a visual referent to uninhibited desires clustering around fears of miscegenation and prostitution. How *animal*. The nounal form of the word refers to the entire process I am currently engaged in. Clients call to schedule a "collection." Dr. Doolots asks her staff every summer morning, "How many collections today?" The shipping company asks how many collections are going on the truck to ship to mares across the globe. The verb refers to the physical act of masturbating a stallion to ejaculation—a carnal, bestial interspecies act described by a term brimming with the rhetorical old-timey innocence of collecting a small child from school or a package from the post office.

Meanwhile, I'm burdened once more with a much heavier AV, now filled with water, as well as a steel bucket filled with hot water and fresh cloths. As I maneuver down the aisle behind Dr. Doolots, I see Loretta walking with the stallion over to a high-ceilinged alcove where the collection will take place. He is agitated, puffed up to his full height, and walking with high, airy steps, nickering and snorting as he walks.

This stallion has a favorite tease mare. She's a small spotted Appaloosa, kind and resigned. Bets holds her steady in front of a small wall, her hindquarters toward the stallion on the other side. Loretta brings him close and then pulls him away, teasing him to elicit an erection. They all know this routine and the mare is generally a still participant as the stallion snakes his head around her rear, shoving her tail to the side with his muzzle, his nostrils flaring wide, breaths heaving. Still, safe procedure and stallion insurance policies dictate that the handler fit a lip twitch on her to protect the stallion at the rear and the human at the head. Bets deftly slips the mare's upper lip into a loop of rope attached to a long wooden handle, and twists quickly until it tightens, first pain and then endorphins making the mare immobile, her neck stiffening and feet planting into the ground.

Loretta again backs the stallion away, stoking desire through distance. Dr. Doolots quickly nips in, wielding a gallon jug and a spray bottle full of yellow liquid in each hand, and pours a slug of the heady fluid atop the tail of the Appaloosa, spritzing her rump with the sprayer, and ducking out as the stallion comes back around, head in the air, tail raised, front legs striking with each stride, nostrils wide. She sets the jugs near me, and I read their Sharpie pen labels: Heat Pee. (I later learn the common practice of keeping urine on hand collected—that word again—from mares in heat by holding empty milk jugs into the stream—not the most scientific part of this process.) Dr. Doolots explained that this stallion much preferred the visual aspect of this tease mare than others on the farm, but of course she was not always in heat when it was time to collect. Spritzing and splashing hormonal urine on her backside seems to do the trick of providing both the olfactory and visual stimulation necessary to elicit a sexual response from him.

With Dr. Doolots safely out of the way, Loretta loops the stallion back around to face the mare again. His nostrils flare as he approaches, the scent of the prosthetic urine wafting up to him, and by now he has a full erection. To prevent him from trying to mount the mare over the wall, Loretta keeps his attention by pulsing the chain placed over his gums through the lead rope. Bets adds another twist to the twitch on the mare. Though my arms ache from the heavy, warm AV, it has been only a few minutes since we came out of the lab. Dr. Doolots pulls a warm cloth from the bucket beside me and talks loudly to the stallion as she approaches him, his tail lifted and swishing as his excitement mounts. "Hey, buddy," she warns, "I'm going to wash you, you know the routine, behave yourself." And he does, hardly distracted from his hormone-infused inhalations as she stoops under his flank to run the cloth over the surfaces of his erection. His feet can't stay still, but Loretta keeps gently pulsing the chain to remind him not to strike out, and Dr. Doolots easily moves with him.

"OK, to the phantom, buddy," she orders as she extricates her body from under his, and Loretta turns him quickly to the right. The phantom looks like a big gymnast's vault, horse-height, but sloped slightly upward from back to front and covered in a thick sheepskin. It faces the tease mare, but at a safe remove. As soon as Loretta points him toward it, the stallion loses his ability to behave, lunging forward at it, forefeet striking, loudly vocalizing. At once, both handlers and Dr. Doolots begin to yell their encouragement, "OK, boy, get up there! Get up there!," breaking what had been a tense quiet with sudden raucous cheering. (Jarring as this was, I would quickly learn that most stallions respond well to vocal encouragement to mount the phantom and make it all the way to climax—without it, many will give up mid-jump from the sheer effort of it all, especially in the busy and hot summer months when they might be collected three or four times per week.) Dr. Doolots takes the AV from me while the stallion gains his balance on the mount, positioning it on her hip and flinging away the sleeve, which had kept it clean and the lubricant slick. His third attempt to mount is successful, Loretta deftly keeping the leather lead and chain away from his thrashing front legs, and Dr. Doolittle sweeps back under his body, one hand pushing his penis into the AV, the women vocally keeping at him all along. "Come on boy, that's right! Get in there!" I stay well back, as the sudden noise and motion takes me by surprise. The strength of the stallion is palpable, and it seems impossible that the two women so near to his work seem so comfortable there. Dr. Doolots is now fully engaged, absorbing the strength of his thrusts and moving with him as the stallion struggles to keep his balance, her cheek and shoulder pressed up to his flank, her feet moving swiftly to avoid his, her arms bulging with the weight of the AV and his body behind it. "Don't stop now, buddy! Keep going!" The stallion's gaze is focused on the tease mare, his nostrils buried in urine-spritzed sheepskin, and a few thrusts later his tail flags, signaling a successful ejaculation, and a full sweat spreads darkly over his body.

At once, the handlers and Dr. Doolots begin praising him, their loud voices shifting from encouragement to pride: "Good boy, buddy, what a man. What a stud! Got it in one jump! Good boy!" But unlike mere minutes before, where the crescendo of their voices dovetailed with his electric, energized countenance, the stallion now can barely lift his head from the phantom, and he slides from the AV and off the phantom, limp, spent, his forelegs stiff.

Dr. Doolots sped to the lab, but I watched for a few moments while the handlers put the horses away. Loretta took him to the wash bay to cool him, his veins standing on his neck, panting heavily where before he had been inhaling with longing. Bets carefully removed the twitch from the tease mare, slowly untwisting the rope until her lip fell from its loop, and she snorted, shook her head, moved her feet under her, and shook her body to relieve the tension from her imposed immobility. She rubbed her sore lip on Bets' shoulder, while Bets told her what a help she'd been and gave her a carrot from her pocket. Off they went outside, back to her paddock, where she spent her time when not working in this way. I supposed the urine smell she wafted in her wake would fade after a good roll.

How to Prepare Semen for Artificial Insemination

Back in the lab, I found Dr. Doolots placing the collection bottle from the bottom of the AV into an incubator. "We want to make sure to keep the semen at body temperature until we analyze it," she told me, taking a seat, tipping her head back and closing her eyes. "But first, a break."

The handlers came in bearing ice-cold cans of Coke from the barn fridge—so good, that metallic, crisp cold on a hot morning. They were a bawdy pair, with middle-aged, smooth leather skin and gravelly cigarette voices. "I need a smoke after that one, gals," crowed Loretta, the stallion handler. I later learned that she made this joke after every collection—enjoying the cliché as much as the nicotine. She was not employed by any one farm, but worked independently for various studs in this position: Stallion owners called her when they scheduled collections because she was excellent at handling them. Loretta worked with only a handful of veterinarians whose manner she liked, and she was in high demand during the summer. She knew how to read stallion behavior, how to manage and direct them without distracting or overhandling them, and she showed great restraint with the gum chain compared to other handlers I would witness over the course of that summer. She'd worked her whole life behind the scenes at racetracks and show barns—a real working horsewoman: exercise rider, horse van driver, caretaker, show groom—finally sliding into this more flexible, lucrative role as artificial insemination became more common in the 1990s, when the easing of international trade restrictions encouraged breeders to import European horses and their semen. The resulting demand for bigger, glossier European varieties created space for women like Loretta to continue following the working-class margins of the big money horse world by shifting their labor from track to shed. Bets shared Loretta's background, but was employed at this stud farm as a manager. She did the books, wrote the checks, ran the software, strategized pedigrees, and structured the day-to-day operation of the farm.

Dr. Doolots pressed the cold can to her forehead. "Shall we, ladies?" And we all went out behind the barn, where Loretta and Bets smoked and shared some loud gossip—an unexpected moment of sociality amidst the strange, focused discipline of the collection process. Mares with their young foals grazed in the field beyond the barn, some waiting to be inseminated themselves. It was peak season in midsummer: Mares that had foaled that spring were being brought back into cycle—half of what needed to be restocked in the truck's refrigerator that morning were hormone injections used to time mares' estrus to the availability of fresh, cooled semen. Bets and Loretta were kind, filling me in on the backstories to their scuttlebutt and asking about my interests, their banter interwoven with answers to the doc's questions about how certain mares and foals were coming along. As we talked, I silently tallied the hundreds of doses of semen that would pass between these three women's hands in the span of a single summer. I was struck suddenly by the image of those doses in their semen containers crisscrossing the globe, the ubiquitous blue containers becoming casual biological companions to the everyday commerce on trucks and planes.

Loretta drove off to another appointment shortly after her smoke, and I followed Bets and Dr. Doolots back to the lab. She was already back to business, pulling latex gloves over her hands.

"OK, let's see how many swimmers we've got today." Bets pulled up an elaborate spreadsheet on the computer and pulled me over. "OK hon, here's what we're looking for." Dr. Doolots measured the contents of the collection bottle with a volumetric scale. "110 milliliters," she reported. Bets entered the number and noted the inconsistencies in volume for this stallion, which topped out at 250 milliliters. "Hot today—hard on 'im. It would be less if he'd collected yesterday, though," she added. They'd postponed collection by a day to let him rest between sessions. They had five mares to send doses to from this round, three doses per mare. Dr. Doolots nodded in agreement. She'd piped a small sample from the bottle and put it back in the incubator. She smeared the ejaculate over a slide and slid it under the microscope, peering down in concentration. "Wowza. Definitely good motility; upwards of 80 percent." Bets chuckled as she plugged in the number. "Doesn't disappoint, this one." Dr. Doolots shot her a look and smiled at the same time.

Dr. Doolots piped another few drops of semen into a tray attached to a gray appliance next to the autoclave. Bets explained: "This is the density machine—it tells us the concentration of swimmers so we can calculate the doses." It hummed for a minute and flashed a number across its screen: 250 million/ml. "OK, great." Bets plugged in the number to the sheet. "See here, this is how you calculate the doses. We're going to make a conservative estimate that we're at 80 percent motility. And we've got the concentration of swimmers."

"She's referring to spermatozoa," Dr. Doolots chimed in, as she put another few drops in the density machine to confirm.

"Whatever you call 'em, you've got to know how many are zooming around in there before you do anything," Bets continued. "Oh, what about morphology?"

"It was good."

"Good. See, I know my science words." She turned back to me. "That just means that the swimmers were in good shape, swimming straight and with strong tails. This stud guarantees its clients that each dose has one billion motile sperm. I plug the conservative motility and concentration numbers into this sheet, and it runs the equation to tell us how many milliliters we need to measure per dose."

She ran the numbers while Dr. Doolots opened a box of little plastic baggies. "Did you call FedEx, Bets?"

"Oh yeah, Fred'll be here in fifteen." Bets turned to me, handing me some latex gloves. I was struck by the sterility and mathematical precision of this phase of the process, after the carnal experience of a few minutes before. Dr. Doolots registered the transition physically: The collection itself rendered her sweaty, yelling, a bit breathless after the exertion of partnering with the stallion. That partnership, at least on the human side, is made into an economic and veterinary one—not a sexual one—by the shared context of the handlers, the shed, and technologies like the AV. I wondered how the horses experienced it all. The stallion was clearly well trained to respect and accept human and technological intervention into his sexuality, though, like Dr. Doolots, he could not avoid the physicality of the sexual act. Both were exhausted by process of eliciting his orgasm. But now, only twenty minutes later, she—and we, all the human co-participants in this encounter—were all crisp instrumentality, cool analysis, latex gloves, pipettes, measuring machines, scientific notation, software. And semen. There may be a heavy door between the sexual encounter and the motility laboratory, but there was no escaping the intrusion of transspecies intimacy into this space, no matter how much latex lay between our bodies and our next task.

Bets handed me a baggie and got a new pipette. "They'll probably measure this again when it gets to the mare people, so it's important to get this right," she observed. "We've got a pretty good record of accuracy. Hold this open, please." I did so, and she took the collection bottle from the incubator. She pipetted out the exact dose of semen calculated by the software into the baggie. Then she added another liquid to the semen. "Extender," explained Dr. Doolots. "It does two things: It fills in the dose for the mare so it feels natural, instead of these tiny doses of semen since we have to divvy it up.

We want to make sure there's 15 milliliters in there. And it's got antibiotics so the uterus doesn't get infected. As careful as we are, this is not a sterile process." Ah. I was still wrapping my head around the need to make a dose of semen feel natural—the mare's equivalent of the inside of the AV wrapping my fist. The extent to which this process placed the requirements of sexual intimacy into human hands still continues to amaze me, though Bets scoffed at me when I brought it up to her months later. "It's so much safer for them," she argued, deftly deflecting my question about human/horse intimacy by instantly turning to the most common justification for using artificial insemination—it's safer for the horses to not have intercourse with each other. For all her humor and innuendo, neither she nor Loretta ever talked to me about the sexual proximity between people and horses that this arrangement made necessary.

"How many do we need again?" Bets mused. "Fifteen. Right. Five mares, three breeders. Let me print those off." She went back to her database and printed off fifteen coded sticky labels listing the stallion, mare, mare owner and location, motility, concentration, and dosage of semen. Dr. Doolots had a signature technique for pressing the air out of the semen baggies before sealing them, practically vacuum-sealing them by hand. We quickly got a little assembly line going, as I held the baggies, Bets piped in the semen and extender, then Dr. Doolots did her amazing air squeeze and finally sealed the baggies with the labels. Fred from FedEx roared up the drive on schedule with empty semen containers from the last shipment. Bets took the old freezer cans out of the containers and replaced them with fresh ones, carefully placing the doses on a foam insulator that precisely regulates the rate at which the semen cools in the process of transport to keep it from temperature shock. We all double-checked that the labels on the semen baggies matched the addresses on the containers, and off Fred went, barely five minutes after he drove up.

I emptied and cleaned the AV while Bets and Dr. Doolots discussed how many doses of leftover semen the stallion's owner wanted to freeze. Frozen semen effectively extends the reproductive life of a stallion beyond his natural life: It can be frozen indefinitely, and a stallion with potent semen can inseminate mares in this way long after his death. Many owners gather hundreds of doses in cryostorage for this purpose. This ejaculate had been well suited to freezing; Bets would take care of that process from here. Dr. Doolots and I gathered up her things, put them in the truck, and drove off to the next appointment. It wasn't even 10 am; the whole process took just over an hour. We had six more stops to go.

Suggested Readings

On the veterinary procedures surrounding reproduction, or theriogenology, see:
Terry L. Blanchard. Dickson D. Varner, Charles C. Love, Steven P. Brisko, Sherri L.
    Rigby, and James Shumacher. 2003. *Manual of Equine Reproduction*. 2nd ed. St.
    Louis: Mosby-Year Book.

On the changing role of veterinarians and expertise in the twentieth century, see:
Susan D. Jones. 2003. *Valuing Animals: Veterinarians and Their Patients in Modern Amer-
    ica*. Baltimore: Johns Hopkins University Press.

On the history of livestock and equine breeding technologies, see:
Margaret E. Derry. 2015. *Masterminding Nature: The Breeding of Animals, 1750–2010*.
    Toronto: University of Toronto Press.

On the creation of shared meaning in reproductive medical spaces, see:
Charis Cussins. 1996. "Ontological Choreography: Agency through Objectification
    in Infertility Clinics." *Social Studies of Science* 26: 575–610.

On the role of the veterinarian in providing care in complex welfare situations, see:
Erica Fudge. 2016. "Farmyard Choreographies in Early Modern England." In *Renais-
    sance Posthumanism*, edited by Joseph Campana and Scott Maisano, 145–66.
    New York: Fordham University Press.

On the accumulation and reproduction of biological forms of capital, see:
Melinda Cooper. 2008. *Life as Surplus Biotechnology and Capitalism in the Neoliberal Era*.
    Seattle: University of Washington Press.

On the entanglements between gender, species, and scientific reproduction, see:
Sarah Franklin. 2007. *Dolly Mixtures: The Remaking of Genealogy*. Durham, NC: Duke
    University Press.

On the subjectivity of animals in scientific relationships with humans, see:
Vinciane Despret. 2013. "Responding Bodies and Partial Affinities in Human-Animal
    Worlds." *Theory and Culture* 30: 51–76.

On the issues of multispecies labor environments, see:
Kendra Coulter. 2016. *Animals, Work, and the Promise of Interspecies Solidarity*. Lon-
    don: Palgrave MacMillan.

PART 4

Science

CHAPTER 13

Healing with Leeches

ROBERT G. W. KIRK

Offering introduction and practical guidance to the new medicine of becoming
well with other species.

About the (Imagined) Author

*In early nineteenth-century Paris, a revolution in medicine began that ushered in
a new age where health and disease began to be understood empirically and the
hospital became the center of medical practice. Michel Foucault described this transformation as the "birth of the clinic," and historians agree that it marked the beginning of modern medicine. If we were transported back to these "modern" Parisian
hospitals, one thing above all others would stand out: the large ponds maintained
on their grounds for the keeping of leeches. For the birth of modern medicine briefly
overlapped with a golden age of the medicinal leech; millions of these curious creatures were used annually to treat all manner of illness. The following is written from
the standpoint of an imagined young physician returning to his native country fresh
from having been educated in the new medicine at the revolutionary Parisian medical schools. He, for physicians at the time were always a "he," has penned a practical
guide for healing with leeches in an attempt to evangelize the new therapy emerging
from France that would soon take hold of the medical world. That the golden age
of leeching should overlap with the birth of modern medicine is little more than a
historical curiosity, perhaps, to the present reader. But to physicians of the time, the*

two eras were interwoven; far from being antiquated, leeching was the embodiment of modern therapy. From the viewpoint of an early nineteenth-century physician, the future of medicine would be filled with animals. In the early twenty-first century, leeches still play a medical role aiding specific instances of post-operative healing. Recent years have seen renewed interest in the capacity of maggots to support the healing of chronic wounds, growth in the use of assistance animals, and recognition that our relationships with nonhuman species can bring meaningful emotional support. Perhaps, then, the future of health may yet be a multispecies medicine.

We are blessed to live in a modern age where past thinking is fading in its power to limit innovation and change for the betterment of society. Nowhere is this truer than in medicine. The influence of ancient writers, even the great Hippocrates and Galen, is waning in the face of a renewed thirst to assert original knowledge flowing from the application of reason to empirical observations. From the Parisian hospitals we are learning that disease is caused by all manner of bodily abnormalities, which reveal themselves in inflammation. The cure for these cases is the letting of blood. A new medicine is in the midst of being made, and a most curious aspect of our endeavor is that its primary therapy rests on that most ancient of companions: the medicinal leech. Whilst knowledge of the restorative effects of phlebotomy is as old as the healing art itself, it is only now that we begin to harness the real therapeutic power of bloodletting. For too long human hubris has caused medicine to place faith in the skill of the physician and the lancet when the healing art was gifted instead to that most unlikely of creatures, the leech. Modern medicine now recognizes these blood-sucking worms as that most perfect of phlebotomists. Leeches know in their own minds the needs of a patient, and are able to communicate this through their work to the skilled physician. In the art of healing no man can rival the skill of man and leech working together. The pages that follow will share with the reader how one heals with the leech.

Why Heal with Leeches?

Until recently, bloodletting was performed by a physician, or more likely a barber-surgeon, with the aid of the lancet. Modern medicine has recently realized that bleeding patients in this way is a barbaric and no doubt self-defeating practice. No matter how well kept a lancet may be, it is a blunt tool in its capacity to respond to the ebbs and flow of life in the patient. Opening a vein is a crude means to let blood. Even the most skilled of physicians cannot control bloodloss so as to work with the distinctive rhythms of the patient's body. No matter how strong or weak the constitution, opening a vein removes considerable blood at a sudden pace, placing great strain on the patient. To think that not so long ago a patient fainting was taken as an indicator of successful treatment! In the past, the brutality of the lancet seriously hindered the application of phlebotomy. Few would risk bleeding a distressed patient or those with naturally weaker constitutions such as women and children. Recognizing healing to be more than a human art has allowed medicine to overcome such limitations, opening paths to new ways of collectively becoming well.

As a living organism the leech surpasses the lancet and comparable mechanical means of bloodletting. This unique animal can gradually and gently remove blood by working sympathetically with the patient's body. Never taking too much blood and never drawing too quickly, leeches appear above even the physician in their intimate knowledge of the rhythms of the human body. Indeed, the leech works with such care to avoid pain or strain that patients would be unaware of their presence were it not for the resultant positive effect on recuperation. An immediate advantage of the leech over the lancet is that they can be prescribed without any fear of placing the patient at risk. Moreover, the leech is egalitarian in allowing modern medicine to treat persons previously excluded from the benefits of phlebotomy. Placing trust in the healing art of the leech allows the physician to heal many of the diseases of women as well as numerous childhood illnesses where once medicine was rendered powerless. Modern medicine's embrace of the leech is motivated by more than this, however, for leeches are perfectly designed to combat what we now recognize diseases to be—things in themselves.

For centuries medicine was hindered by a belief that illness was the product of an imbalance of the four humors: phlegm, blood, yellow bile, and black bile. Dis-ease was the result of too much of one humor or the other, and healing was premised on bringing the four back into balance. As Galen decreed blood to be the most important of the humors, physicians focused on bloodletting as the primary therapeutic intervention. Today, belief in humors is waning in the wake of rational studies of illness, which have revolutionized medical thought. Whilst it is lamentable that many still hold to old ideas, the modern physician knows disease to be a thing itself and not the result of humoral imbalances. Parisian medicine has shown the way here, and we may thank the rise of the hospital for much of our new understanding. Concentrating many patients in one place creates a resource for empirical study and teaching, which has exposed commonalities of illness by allowing disease to be observed in life and death. The anatomical gaze reveals the true cause and site of illness within the body. Previously, in their attempts to heal the whole body, physicians were working in the dark. Today, equipped with

DIE BLUTEGEL
von Louis Boilly (1827).
(Erklärung siehe Rückseite.)

Calcium - Diuretin „Knoll"
(Theobromin.- Calcium - Salicylicum).
Bildserie I, Nr. 3.

FIGURE 13.1.   A faint-looking woman is supported by a companion as the doctor carefully applies leeches. A young boy stands in the foreground holding a glass container of leeches, 1827. By Louis Boilly. Wellcome Library, London. Copyrighted work available under Creative Commons Attribution only license CC BY 4.0 http://creativecommons.org/licenses/by/4.0/

accurate knowledge of the site of disease, the modern physician can target their effort with efficient precision. In the modern age, what use, then, is the lancet? If a patient suffers inflation of gum, what benefit might come from bleeding from a distant vein? One must bleed at the site of illness, and here leeches come into their own.

Getting to Know Your Leeches

Whilst it is not uncommon for the physician to take an amateur interest in nature, we would do well to familiarize ourselves as a profession with the natural history of the leech. Our capacity to care for patients begins with our skill in caring for the leech. Linnaeus, the great taxonomer, identified the leech as one among many wormy kin, recognizable by their elongated bodies being made up of ring-like segments. Anatomically, all of the vermes are made up of head (containing brain, mouth, and sensory organs), a ringed central trunk which makes up the bulk of the body, and end-parts containing the anus. Leeches are distinguished from other worms through their powerful suckers at both ends of the body. The medicinal leech, *Hirudo medicinalis*, can be found in freshwater marshlands, still pools, and dykes across Europe and into Asia. These leeches have a greenish-brown color, the hue of which often reflects their place of origin; leeches from areas of black peat tend to be darker, whereas those from red soil take on that shade; leeches born of clay develop a yellow tint. Recognizing the right leech is one of the most important skills a physician will learn. There is a bewildering range of species, each possessing different characteristics, with some as capable of harm as others are of healing. It is essential that the leech is marked with yellow rings or spots, or a line running the length of the body, for this is the sign of the healer. The best, of course, are the medicinal leeches of England and France, but natives of other lands will equally suffice. I have heard the Swedish leech is particularly prized by those who can obtain them. Old world leeches are far superior to those of the new; the American leech *Hirudo decora* draws hardly any blood, requiring ten to do the work of one European leech.

Some understanding of leech behavior is helpful to the physician in their effort to work effectively with these seemingly alien healers. Leeches are gifted with agility of movement and an inquisitive mind; neither should be underestimated. They swim with remarkable grace using their muscular bodies to propel themselves through water at great velocity. Though more limited on land, they move with surprising speed, using their suckers to move in a caterpillar-like style. Of particular note is their capacity for squeezing their boneless bodies through the smallest of spaces; an unattended leech is more than capable of outwitting a physician unprepared for their need to explore. An important curiosity is their close affinity to the climate. In nature, wet summer months will see leeches actively swimming about shallows, whereas a cold winter or dry summer causes them to retreat to the depths, burrowing deep into mud. Similarly, during a storm, leeches retreat to the depths. Yet,

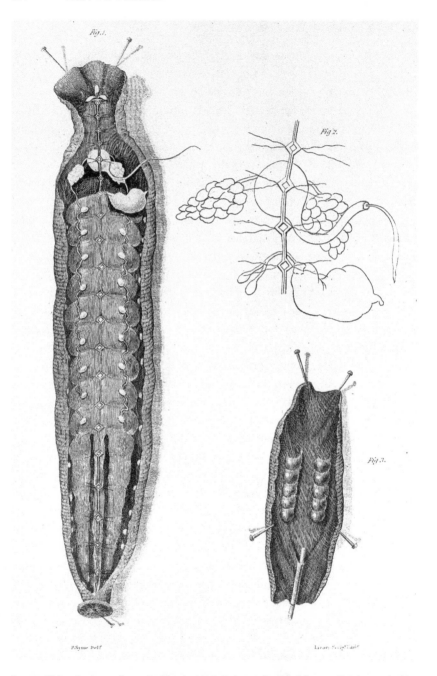

FIGURE 13.2.   Anatomy of a medical leech, 1816. By James Rawlins Johnson, *Treatise on the Medicinal Leech*. Wellcome Library, London. Copyrighted work available under Creative Commons Attribution only license CC BY 4.0 http://creativecommons.org/licenses/by/4.0/.

the hours before a storm excite these animals as nothing else. Supernaturally forewarned of the oncoming weather, leeches become most active, swimming urgently, causing them sometimes to be found some distance from their native waters. Traditional leech gatherers find this an excellent time for harvesting the animals from their habitats. How leeches prognosticate the weather without visible sign is a mystery, but one not without use. A leech is as reliable as the barometer! If ones' leeches are restful at the bottom of their jar, then the weather will be fine and their work equally so. If instead they are toward the top of their jar, then rain should be expected, but leeches will go to work regardless if called upon. However, if one's leeches are unusually active, swimming and climbing without rest, we can be sure of two things. First, a storm approaches, and second, the leech is unlikely to focus on medical work until it has passed. Whilst modern medicine has moved on from ignorant beliefs in humors and miasmas as the cause of ill health, the connection that the leech shares with the climate does make one wonder if the ancients may have been onto something after all.

Importantly, not all leeches make suitable or safe medical companions. The horse leech, *Hirudo sanguisuga*, is as barbaric as the medicinal leech is civilized. Its appetite is voracious and uncontrolled; not content with blood alone, the horse leech will attack and devour its kin whole. Confusing a horse leech with a medicinal leech at best results in the loss of any leeches homed in the same jar which this monster can swallow whole. At worst, if erroneously applied therapeutically, they have been known to cause the loss of the patient. In contrast, the nature of the medicinal leech is gentle; their first concern is to care for others. Observing that a medicinal leech who is wounded will draw the attention of others who will attach themselves to the injured animal, earlier writers have mistaken this as aggressive feeding of the strong on the weak. Nothing could be further from the truth! Just as a physician might hold the hand of an anxious patient or a mother hold tightly a frightened child, the medicinal leech will bring comfort to their kin through close bodily contact. Careful observation of their behavior reveals that even in health, leeches will caress and hold on to each other without any intent of harm. The medicinal leech is indeed one of the most noble of creatures. One must get to know them and their ways; learning to ask the right questions of leeches is the only way to gain the right answers.

Acquiring Leeches

Whereas leeches were once plentiful in the pools and swamplands of our country, recent years have seen these animals harvested to near-extinction by those concerned more with profit than the national health. Oh, the leech is a much maligned animal. When faced with avarice and greed you will hear people exclaim "you leech," and once again this animal comes to our aid healing human culture as it does our bodies. What ignorance! We humans like to project our evils onto creatures so distant in kind to us we then feel it impossible that we could share the evil. But heed this, when it comes to greed it is us humans who can never be satisfied! It is we who cry "give! give!" as the proverb says. The leech may feed until it has consumed ten times its body weight, but it will not take blood again for near six months. Whereas we took so many of these creatures from nature, first the adults and then returning for the child, that few can be found where once there was plenty. Science, they say, will be our salvation. In France, the Académie nationale de méde-cine has perfected the artificial farming of leeches. So-called hirudoculture is driving a new revolution unearthing new fertility in once-worthless swamp-land. More than one of the poor farmers are finding themselves now rich beyond their imagination. Nevertheless, the work is far from idyllic. To feed and harvest its leeches a single farm can consume up to 750 horses a year, and you can imagine what those who seek the humane treatment of animals think about that. Moreover, the provenance of leeches is all-important to the patient. Only time will tell whether these artificially manufactured leeches are as reliable as their natural kin.

In the face of such complexities, a wise physician will cultivate a re-lationship with a trusted apothecary. Truly, an apothecary known for the quality and reliability of his leech stock will become a friend beyond measure. It is no small skill to satisfy the year-round demand for medical leeches; an apothecary must see to the needs of their animals as well as those of the physician. Leeches must be maintained in just such a state so that they are fed and healthy, yet not so well fed that they are unwill-ing to work when called upon. This art of caring for the leech is but the beginning, for a master apothecary must give as much attention to the wants of humankind as he does for the leech. The reach and reputation of an apothecary must stretch beyond the city. Indeed, beyond the nation! For leeches today are so scarce in the civilized countries that a global trade has emerged through which many now make their living. An apoth-ecary worthy of his name will be as Rome at the center of the Empire, importing the best leeches from France, Germany, Hungary, Poland, and yet more exotic areas of this world, adapting their business as seasonal and political changes demand. A hot summer here, over-harvesting there: one never knows when a once-bountiful supply might dry up overnight.

Increasingly, too, governments are placing the health of the many over the wealth of the few, restricting and, in places such as Russia, banning entirely the exportation of this valuable national resource. The health of a patient demands attention to global politics, economics, and even a concern for parts of nature that once we would give not a thought to. Modern medicine must contend with all these issues!

As remarkable as the ability to source animals might be, it is worth nothing without a reliable merchant who knows how to transport these sensitive animals so as to arrive at the apothecary healthy and happy. Leeches must be fed but not too well fed, for they must survive the journey yet be ready to go to work on arrival. The transportation of leeches is a skill as well guarded as the secrets of freemasonry! But much can be learned by those who take an interest. Care is required to protect the animals from being shaken and hurt on the road. I have seen leeches placed in linen bags packed with damp earth, but the most curious thing to witness is a leech trader on the road when a change in the weather approaches. They will run as if in panic to the closest pool, stream, or ready supply of water and submerge their burdens within until the storm has passed. It is a mystery as to why, but we can surmise that this relates to leeches being uniquely attuned to climate. For journeys across the sea, special crates are used that are filled with swamp earth, plants, and water so as to mimic natural habitats. These must be carefully sealed with netting across air holes to discourage the curious leech from exploration. I heard tell of a ship arriving in Liverpool having experienced a storm so fierce that a crate was thrown about that burst open, liberating the lively contents to make themselves at home across the ship. One might assume that these sailors arrived in port the healthiest they had ever been, but one would not think that by their demeanor. They couldn't get off their vessel quick enough, so the story went, having grown tired of leeches dining on their blood! So much complexity, so much ingenuity. So much care to bring the medical leech to our door!

But these are things we need not worry over if we have trust in our apothecary. Modern healing is a collaboration between many people and many species. But how to tell a good apothecary? Why, they will not hide their skill! As the leech is the most valuable item an apothecary will possess they will display their authority by housing the animals in the most royal of accommodations. Apothecaries compete to possess the most expensive, colorful, and ornate leech jars proudly displayed in their windows as testament to their success. Judge an apothecary by its jar, and you will not go far wrong.

FIGURE 13.3.   Leech Jar, typical of period 1831–1859. by Alcock at Hill Pottery, Burslem, English, 1831–1859. Science Museum, London, Wellcome Images. Copyrighted work available under Creative Commons Attribution only license CC BY 4.0 http://creativecommons.org/licenses/by/4.0/.

Keeping and Caring for Leeches

Leeches, sadly, are not immune from disease. For leeches to work well, they must be kept well. They possess delicate constitutions demanding attention and care from the physician. A most injurious disease first manifests as ulcers appearing as small specks across the body which can become bloody. This illness develops rapidly and is abundantly destructive. Another disease, just as deadly, reveals itself when the body becomes misshapen; narrow and rigid in one area with a tumor at another. Incision reveals the growth to contain a putrid black liquid. A third affliction is more difficult to see but can be noted from behavior, where a previously active leech suddenly appears languid and the body flaccid when touched. Close inspection of the mouth may reveal it to be swollen, unusually purple, and eventually bloody. So little is known of leeches that if illness is suspected it is best to isolate the animal within its own jar and let the disease run its course. There are no known cures, and such a measure at least prevents contagion. Leeches which are unsound in their own health are of no use to the physician, for they cannot bring health to others.

Frequently, I have found that an apparently diseased leech, once isolated, may spontaneously return to health. It is my belief that ill health in such cases is less the result of disease than unsuitable husbandry and care. When one thinks of the life events a leech experiences, being taken from their native abode, packaged and carried across foreign lands to new climates, and introduced to new environments together with kin they may or may not know, it is little wonder that they make demands of their new human keepers. I cannot recommend with more gravity the importance of providing ones' leeches with spacious homes; jars or other vessels should never be crowded, no matter the temptation to save a little on costs. How many leeches one may house together and how often one should replenish their water is a question best not asked of me, nor any physician or apothecary. All will tell you of their experience, one may keep a dozen or more in the smallest of jars and another not change the water more often than annually! Following such advice will do you no good. You must ask your leeches! They will tell their desires. Water too hot or too cold, too clean or too dirty, too many companions or too few, the leeches will speak their mind. When their appearance and behavior display good health, when they greet you by bobbing and swimming and their water remains clean and pure, the leeches are happy and you have met their needs. If the animals are languid, their water putrid or (worse) bloody, you must correct their artificial home to better reflect that of nature.

Some leeches adjust quickly to the domestic setting. Others never do, or not without a real effort to replicate their natural home. I find the choosiest of leeches can be made comfortable if placed in a large vessel that contains a perforated false bottom raised half a hand from the actual bottom which is layered with packed turf. If one includes plant life, all the better! Leech-dealers often carry with them what they call Marsh Horse-Tail, a fibrous plant which helps the leech feel at home and to which they would seem sentimentally attached. Leeches enjoy wrapping themselves in such plants, and I have observed that they rub against them particularly in the evening. I believe this allows leeches a means of cleaning themselves for one often finds shreds of old skin attached to Horse-Tail. It is always worth the physician investing time and effort to create comfortable homes, for without exception more leeches will live happily together within enriched environments than barren jars. A compromise between nature and city can always be found if one asks of the leech the right questions and maintains an open interest in their answers.

Whatever the housing arrangement, always remember that a leech differs much from ourselves in body but little in mind. No matter how majestic the home, to them the grass will always appear greener elsewhere. Their vessel must be secured at all times, for the adventurous leech will escape through any lapse in their confinement.

Working Well with Leeches

Leeches should be removed from their water at least one hour prior to their intended use, as this alerts the animals and allows them to prepare themselves for their coming labors. As has been said, the great advantage of leeching is in allowing therapeutic intervention to be targeted at the precise site of illness. Making full use of the leeches' versatility, however, is no easy matter. A number of tools and tricks exist to aid the beginner in their efforts. Many a less able physician fails to progress beyond need of them. However, I would implore true servants of medicine to work at their art, for application by hand allows the physician a heightened precision of treatment while being more comforting to the leech and patient alike. Here again one must learn through working together with one's leeches to recognize their individual behaviors and quirks. Generally, one should gently take hold of a leech at the center of their body and move the animal toward the area of the patient's body that you wish to treat. When a leech can sense the patient, it will show willing by extending its head, allowing the physician who has developed his dexterity to accurately affix the healer to the most difficult of treatment sites.

If the patient is agreeable, one might nick the skin with a lancet to release a little blood—a message even the dullest of leeches will understand! However, if the patient fears the lancet I have found that a drop of beer on the spot is equally efficacious in guiding the leech to work.

Application of leeches by hand takes time and experience on the part of the physician and of the leech; each must learn the ways of the other to work together effectively. When beginning, some recommend placing leeches in a glass and placing it face down on the treatment site. This is a poor approach; leeches do not understand what is asked of them and frequently hang instead from the top of the glass, thinking it a game. Also, many areas of the patient's body cannot be accessed in this way. Better to obtain a set of purpose-designed glass leech tubes wherein one can place a leech before affixing the tube to the precise area of the patient you wish to treat. Tubes come in a variety of shapes and sizes, from the basic straight to all manner of curved tubes. The half-moon tube, for instance, is most useful for placing a leech to treat inflammation of the eye.

Once affixed, leeches in general will work until they judge that enough blood has been taken to aid the healing process. Once done they will drop from the patient fully gorged and can be collected by the physician. The leeches' healing touch does not stop at this point, however, for they produce a curious effect that prevents blood from congealing as it would in a normal wound. Blood will continue to flow from their bite for a good half hour or more, enabling the physician to fine-tune the blood loss by application of bandaging to slow or bring blood flow to a stop. Depending on the severity of the disease and the judgment of the physician, anything from half a dozen to a fifty or sixty leeches may be applied in one sitting. Leeches will work alone or in company without complaint. However, particularly when applying leeches near bodily orifices, a physician should watch his animals closely as it has been known for curiosity to cause a leech to abandon its work in favor of exploring the patient's body. There is nothing a leech likes more than adventuring within a tight, dark, warm and damp space. Once within the body, it is nearly impossible to remove a leech, and their presence can be quite deadly. If attached in the throat their slow expansion through consumption of blood can suffocate the host.

Whilst unsupervised excursions within a body can prompt disaster, supervised ventures allow modern medicine to treat illness at sites internal to the body. To do so safely it is best to secure a leech by attaching a thread to the tail; this will allow it to be retrieved with minimal effort. Once secured, leeches can be used to alleviate problems such as inflamed gums, infected teeth, or problems of the throat. With the aid of tools to open other orifices, leeches can be safely inserted within the body to bring relief; three to four leeches will do wonders for a painful prostate! They can also be inserted to treat enteritis, inflamed bowels, and other digestive ills.

After treatment the patient can return to his or her life following a short rest. However, the physician is faced with a difficult decision as to their medical companion. Ideally, the leech would be put to rest and allowed to digest their feed at leisure. However, the modern world is impatient and cannot wait the many months it would take for a leech to become hungry enough to work again. Demand for healing outstrips our supplies of these helpful little creatures. This forces the physician to impose a heavier workload upon them than we might otherwise wish. To ready the leech for re-use, the animal must be made to disgorge their stomach contents soon after feeding. If the leech must be used soon, all blood should be evacuated, but if the animal is to be rested for a time they should be allowed to retain roughly a third of the blood they have consumed for their own nourishment. Some advocate massaging the animal's stomach to encourage disgorgement, but I warn against this method for even the lightest of pressures can fatally damage their fragile, boneless bodies. However, when re-application is urgent this is the only

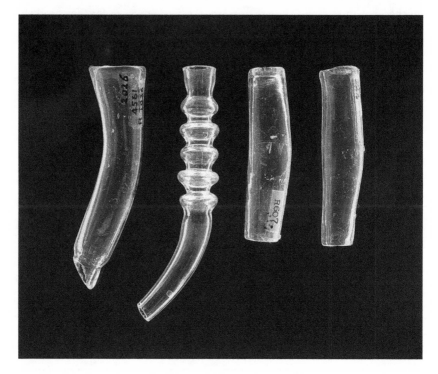

FIGURE 13.4. Leech tubes. Credit: Wellcome Library, London. Copyrighted work available under Creative Commons Attribution only license CC BY 4.0 http://creativecommons.org/licenses/by/4.0/.

route, though it brings great risk to the animal. A slight sprinkling of salt or turmeric upon the body is enough to encourage a leech to vomit up its food, but the animal must be given four or five days to recover from this experience before being asked to return to work. The best approach is to apply a small quantity of vinegar to the head; this troubles the leech least and many will go immediately back to work once they have emptied their stomachs. Even with these techniques one may sometimes be faced with a patient in urgent need of significant leeching but not enough leeches to complete the treatment. Here again, we must weigh the needs of the patient against those of the leech. With the use of a lancet the tail of a leech can be carefully sliced open so that consumed blood flows directly through and out its body. In this way a single leech will undertake the work of many; feeding without any compulsion to cease their feast. Once the treatment is complete, a sprinkling of salt will cause the animal to detach. Gently pressing the leech's wound together and holding for a minute between finger and thumb begins the animal's healing process. With a good night's rest the leech will by the morning be again a willing medical companion, none the worse for the experience.

Becoming Well with Leeches

I have attempted to provide some basic knowledge to serve as a guide in your first forays into more-than-human medicine. Becoming well with leeches, however, is learned in the performance. With experience, time, and openness to the other, physician and leech will learn to communicate and collaborate in the healing art, opening new perspectives on health and well-being. Whilst it is hard to imagine an animal better equipped to work with the physician, the leech may be just the beginning of the collaborative performance of medicine across species. Already there are a number of mental asylums that report exposure to animals having a soothing effect on the mind and nerves. Elsewhere, surgeons on the battlefield report that the presence of maggots in a wound, contrary to expectation, works to keep the wound clean and free of disease. If a maggot of all creatures might aid the healing of wounds, we must ask what other animals may be waiting in nature to be called to medicine's aid? For now, these are mere speculations. But of one thing I am sure: The physician of the future will be a practitioner of multispecies medicine.

Suggested Readings

On leeches and nineteenth-century medicine from a contemporary perspective, see:

James Rawlins Johnson. 1816. *A Treatise on the Medicinal Leech*. London: Longman.

On the leech in human history, see:

Robert G. W. Kirk and Neil Pemberton. 2013. *Leech*. London: Reaktion.

On medical history, see:

W. F. Bynum, ed. 2006. *The Western Medical Tradition: 1800 to 2000*. Cambridge: Cambridge University Press.

On medical history and nonhuman animals, see:

Robert G. W. Kirk and Michael Worboys. 2013. "Medicine and Species: One Medicine, One History?" In *The Oxford Handbook of the History of Medicine*, edited by Mark Jackson, 561–77. Oxford: Oxford University Press.

On becoming with and asking the right questions of animals, see:

Vinciane Despret. 2008. "The Becomings of Subjectivity in Animal Worlds." *Subjectivity* 28: 123–39.
Vinciane Despret. 2016. *What Would Animals Say If We Asked the Right Questions?* Translated by Brett Buchanan. Minneapolis: University of Minnesota Press.

On multispecies, see:

Eben Kirksey, ed. 2014. *The Multispecies Salon*. Durham, NC: Duke University Press.

CHAPTER 14

How to Be a Systematist

ALETA QUINN

This essay explains how to classify animals. Scientists who classify organisms and species are called taxonomists. Taxonomists today make classifications that reflect the natural system of relationships between organisms and between species. People who study the natural system of relationships in order to classify life are called systematists. The phrases "natural system" and "relationship" have meant different things to different people. In this essay, I sketch what those terms mean, how the science of systematics works, and what it is like to be a systematist.

I have written my guide as a fictitious letter to a real person (whose name and personal details I have changed). At a young age, this person conducted impressive independent work to classify animals and was considering whether to pursue a career in systematics. The fictitious letter is directed to a sixteen-year-old version of the real individual.

5 September 2016

Dear Lilli,

Your mother tells me you're thinking of becoming a systematist, and in particular a zoologist (rather than a classifier of plants, fungi, or bacteria). You are at that age where all career-related decisions seem permanent and fraught, so please don't freak out—your mother asked me to tell you about what such a career would be like. You probably know that I am a philosopher of science. I am not myself a systematist, though a long time ago I started training to be one. Now I study the ways that systematists think and argue and the ways that systematics is similar to or different from other sciences. Along the way I have interacted with many systematists and have gained some familiarity with what the career is like. In fact it has been difficult for me to become accepted in this community, so I trust that you will keep this letter confidential. (Imagine, writing an actual letter in this day and age! But it's so easy to forward emails carelessly by mistake.)

I think I should begin by explaining: What is the task of classifying animals?

The Big Idea

You have to have some principle. For any set of animals, you could classify them any which way. To adapt an analogy from John Locke (the same person who wrote on political theory and religious toleration): Suppose we want to classify timepieces. You might separate tabletop timepieces from wall clocks, pocket watches, and wrist watches (I forget if they had wrist watches in Locke's day). Or you could separate the timepieces that use springs from those that use weights, sand, water, or the sun. Of course some timepieces use both springs and weights, and nowadays some timepieces use electricity. I'll leave it to you to decide whether a device that simply relays the time reported by some remote source (such as the website linked to an atomic clock at the National Institute of Standards and Technology) counts as a timepiece. Or again, you could classify timepieces based on the materials that they are made out of or the contexts in which they are used (a runner's watch, a ship clock, a countdown clock) or the historical contexts in which they were invented or the time systems that they use (is a metronome a timepiece?). You could classify by monetary value. Whichever way you chose to classify timepieces would capture something real about the world, more or less accurately, and would convey information.

However, in the case of animals, there's such a thing as a "natural system." A German systematist named Hennig made an analogy to bodies of water in Europe. You could classify them in alphabetical order, or by which countries they are in or originate in, or which countries obtain the highest economic benefits from use of the body of water. But there is something more natural about a classification based on their sources and outputs. There is a *system* of water exchange that it makes sense to study and use to explain features of the natural environment. Another analogy from Hennig is the task of classifying shards of pottery. You could classify them by weight or by shape (triangles of various sorts, quadrangles and so on—notice that you can devise many different schemes for "shape"). Or you could try to sort out which fragments came from the same individual pot and then, if you like, classify the shards in terms of what that pot would have been like. This shard was part of a handle; this shard was on the bottom. Again, this way of classifying is more natural in some important sense: It fits the fragments into an intelligible scheme that can be studied and used to explain things, in this case having to do with the cultures and technologies of the people that made the pots.

In the case of animals, people figured out that there is some natural system before they knew what it meant. They didn't know the reason that there's a natural system. A similar thing happened in chemistry with the periodic table, which was drafted long before people knew the reason that the natural system of elements exists (the number of protons in the nucleus of each element determines what valence shells electrons occupy, which governs the observable properties and reactions of each element).

People subsequently found out what it means that there's a natural system of animals: The natural system exists because all animals descend from common ancestors, with lineages evolving at various rates, through mechanisms that we can study.

It's like a genealogical tree. You and I share a common ancestor, somewhere and -when, maybe in the U.S., maybe in Poland, maybe somewhere else. Take a third person, and we each share a common ancestor with that person; and except in rare cases, some two of us are going to share an ancestor more recently than either does with the third. That is, you might share a great-grandmother with the person, with whom I only share a great-great-great-great-great-great grandmother. So too with animals: Your cat has an ancestor that is also an ancestor of your neighbor's dog, somewhere a long time ago. But this metaphor does break down. You could end up marrying someone with whom you share a common ancestor, as long as that ancestor isn't too recent. But this isn't the case with animals—after lineages have diverged for some time, they're not going to re-merge into each other.

This is the basic task of classifying animals: Figure out which animals descend from more recent versus more remote common ancestors. You have to develop a set of techniques that makes sense given this knowledge of the natural system. If you know the basic rules of the game, I can hand you three specimens and you can know that two of the specimens will have shared a common ancestor more recently than either does with the third (except in extremely rare cases).

Now as systematists, we can make a set of rules about how to make classificatory claims. But to do this well, we need to think critically about how to relate these claims to observed evidence. We can't observe how species are related directly, except when someone is dealing with very recent organisms that speciate in front of your eyes. Most of the relationships in which systematists are interested were formed when lineages split further back than scientists have been observing lineages. So we have to agree on what counts as evidence, and now that we understand the goal, we can critically evaluate possible sources of evidence.

Navigating a Career Path

For historical reasons, there are different career paths available to people who want to classify animals. To some extent these different career paths sort out according to the source of the evidence.

Selecting Evidence

Paleontologists examine fossils, and they have to figure out how fossil evidence relates to claims about the relationships of animals that lived in the past. And there is the difficulty that lineages might change all the time without splitting into distinct species; how do we classify recent lineages with respect to their ancient ancestors in cases where they look very different?

Developmental morphologists study the parts and characters of organisms. Parts are structures like a femur, a molar, or a tongue. Characters are ways that the parts can be: A femur can be particularly long or thick or curved or hollow and so forth. Developmental morphologists examine organisms as embryos, fetuses, and later developmental stages, and then sort out which parts and characters are shared across different lineages because of shared descent (versus parts and characters that look the same but aren't shared because of descent). Orioles and vultures each have wings because a common ancestor of theirs had wings. Bats and orioles each have wings, but not because a common ancestor had wings. Studying development can tell you a lot about how to understand parts and characters as evidence of relationship. Orioles and vultures develop the beginnings of wings at the same time and from the same arm bones, whereas bats develop wings at a different time and use finger bones.

Evolutionary biologists study the processes and patterns of evolution, but to do this, you need to have some idea of the relationship between the groups you are studying. And there is a worry that recurs in different ways throughout the history of this discipline: Because evolutionary hypotheses are required to confirm classificatory hypotheses, which will then be used to test evolutionary hypotheses, this process might be problematically circular.

But when? Unfortunately, this worry has sometimes been used with a huge brush to criticize entire disciplines and data types, when in fairness the arguments should target particular uses of particular hypotheses.

And there are other sorts of evidence and other associated disciplines, and disciplines that form bridges between disciplines in various ways. So to classify animals today, you will have to choose a career path, which will shape the things that you consider to be evidence of relationship, and the ways in which you can use that evidence. Of course, the various disciplines differ to various extents in conceptual frameworks and have their own intertwining histories that will shape the way that you classify animals.

Handling Evidence

Also, apart from disciplinary differences, large, substantive scientific disagreements remain about how to handle evidence in general. One very big recent disagreement revolved around how best to make use of observed evidence. One side argued that we should find the set of hypothesized relationships that requires the fewest evolutionary steps, which (they argued) amounts to assuming the fewest ad hoc claims that are necessary in order for your overall hypothesis to fit the observed evidence. It is better to conclude that orioles, vultures, and ducks have wings because wings arose once in a common ancestor of all these birds, versus claiming that wings arose individually in each bird lineage. The other side argued that we should find the set of hypothesized relationships which, if true, would have rendered the observations most probable. Sometimes it is actually more likely that the "same" trait evolved multiple times, such as when lineages are splitting off very rapidly and the trait is not very complex or unique.

The two sides mostly argued past each other, with people on each side claiming that their methods were more fundamental. The other side's methods, they claimed, would only be better in a small set of circumstances. From each side's perspective, the other side was making more dubious empirical assumptions about how animals evolve.

This particular argument has mostly died down, with the "render the observations probable" side winning for various reasons. There are still strong proponents of each side, however, and places where "make the fewest ad hoc claims" is more dominant. So if you want to classify animals today, you have to choose a side. Most people just end up on whichever side their advisor is on, but some make an active choice; some people move over time. Because one side mostly won, it has become harder to find a job if you adhere strictly to the losing side. So there is incentive for up-and-coming scientists to join the winning side, or at least to learn the methods of that side, because it will be necessary to be able to work within that conceptual framework in order to survive in the discipline.

There are other disagreements. There is an emerging dispute about how to handle huge datasets, which mirrors some elements of this older dispute. So, to classify animals, you have to be able to navigate ongoing scientific disputes about key methodological issues. And sometimes you have to be able to navigate distinct conceptual frameworks.

You may have noticed this already if you have tried talking to people who classify animals. How do they describe each other? I have heard the very same individual described as: far outside the mainstream, well within the mainstream, one of the few who understands both sides of his discipline's divide, fundamentally confused about the task of taxonomy, fundamentally confused about phylogenetic inference, primarily interested in phylogenetic theory, more interested in taxonomy than phylogenetic theory, not up on the latest phylogenetic theory, more up on the latest phylogenetic theory than most, a molecular person, and a person who advocates the use of both molecular and morphological data. Some of the descriptions are factually wrong but convey information about how the speaker understands the subject in relation to the speaker's own disciplinary and conceptual location.

Situating Yourself

To classify animals, you will need to collaborate with folks in disciplines that are distinct from, though sometimes closely related and intertwined with, your own. Perhaps because of all the disciplinary fault lines, people who classify animals often introduce themselves by specifying which animals they work with. "Hi, my name is Celeste; I work on frogs." "Hi, my name is Angele; I work on snakes." There is a commonality here that transcends disciplinary distinctions. Celeste and Angele and Dan are herpetologists, which is to say, persons who work on frogs, snakes, and other amphibians and reptiles. These people have different views about theory and data and all those other things I just described, but they can locate themselves within the community of systematists by reference to the animals that they study.

But even how you identify yourself to your colleagues can change over the course of your career. Dan used to introduce himself as Dan who works on lizards. Increasingly, Dan introduces himself as Dan who works in the molecular lab, because Dan now works with a very broad range of animals. Indeed, Dan collaborates with people of diverse disciplines and approaches, because he works in the molecular lab and molecular data are used across multiple disciplines. Thus Dan shifted from describing himself in terms of organisms to describing himself by reference to a type of evidence.

Navigating the Field and the Public

You might not only work in a lab; you might go out into the field too. And if you do, you may be in a location where there are dangers. Most venomous snakes will avoid you unless you surprise or antagonize them; there are exceptions. Hippos don't care what you do—just standing there can be enough for them to decide to charge and kill you. Crocodiles might try to eat you. These things you can learn about and try to be diligent, but there are always risks and sometimes you will have to choose how much risk you are willing to take on. You are going to hear stories about people who were willing to take large risks and people who were not as careful as they should have been; some have died.

Almost wherever you are, you will be bitten by a dazzling assortment of insects, and you may be exposed to diseases that are poorly researched or understood. I have met systematists who suffer symptoms from diseases or injuries acquired long ago. Your socks may be wet for weeks or months. You may have to haul heavy nets and lines or dive deep in a cramped submersible at night, learn to sail, trap, leap and grab, snare, spot, and handle live animals. Some people like this part of the job more than others; to some extent you can choose your path. Even if what you most want to do is discover new species, you can stay at home. Many, many new species are found in museum collections than in the field.

If you do fieldwork, you will need to learn how to catch animals and how to document what you have done. You will learn where to find them, and when, and how to tell whether you are wasting your time looking for them. The particulars of how you catch them vary depending on what organisms you choose to study. That is also the case with preserving specimens, whether you are putting whole animals or parts of animals into alcohol or cold storage and so on.

Above all else keep good records. I cannot tell you the frustration systematists suffer when faced with unclear geographic records. If you are only interested in genetic samples, it is absolutely vital to be able to connect the genetic material to some record of the source animal and its form. If you do not have the permits to collect whole animals, at least take a photograph. Everyone has a phone these days; it should not be hard, even out in the wet and with sketchy access to power.

But if you decide to go to the field, it is not just animals you have to interact with, it is humans too. You may be in an area where an armed guard is necessary, and you may be met with suspicion in areas where eco-tourism has led to increases in crime (both petty and more serious). Or you may find other people's cultural expectations confusing. You may be lonely.

You may face challenges interacting with your team. I know that you have lived with roommates, so: Imagine all the interpersonal challenges of that, but in a foreign and potentially hazardous place, with a limited budget and limited time to conduct the work.

And then there are the challenges of presenting your work to people who are not systematists. If you are doing fieldwork, you will need permits and the ability to explain to people why it's necessary to collect more than one specimen of each species. Imagine an alien scientist came to earth and wanted to bring back a representative specimen of a human. I am female; thirty-three years old; I weigh 135 pounds, have green eyes and what humans call white skin. I share an office with a zoologist who does not match any of those characters (I do not know what he weighs, actually, but he is in his twenties and has brown eyes and what humans call brown skin). And the person in the office next door is somewhat like me and somewhat like him, is older and larger than either of us. Which human should the alien use to represent humans? But you know all this; variation and diversity are the very things that you must study.

Many people outside the field do not know the purpose of taking specimens. You view a natural history museum as a celebration of life, dedicated to understanding and protecting biodiversity. Many in the public would see collecting specimens as akin to running a charnel house, if they knew of this work at all. I know that you understand, you get it, and so my words in this letter are frank. I very much fear how people would react if they knew that we kill animals in order to classify them, so again, I trust that you will keep this letter strictly confidential.

You have to watch for feelings of haughtiness and resentment: After all, you understand these animals better than the folks who may criticize you, better than almost anyone. Sometimes you in fact know the animals better than anyone. You are invested in them.

It can be difficult explaining all this because a fair number of people have doubts about or objections to the theory of evolution. As you know, the conceptual and methodological frameworks in which classifiers operate are thoroughly evolutionary. Practices within every scientific discipline are, to a large extent, incomprehensible to non-specialists. Some chemists investigate the properties of different combinations of chemicals; some physicists investigate the nature of tiny bits of matter. Yet the daily tasks of these scientists—the equipment they use, the hypotheses they frame, the observations they make—are incomprehensible without substantial knowledge of the conceptual frameworks in which these scientists operate.

The situation for those who classify animals is worse, in a way, with respect to communicating with people who are skeptical of the theory of evolution. The barrier is not just jargon and lack of training, but skepticism that the training is fundamentally misguided. Consider a person who spends her days and years collecting tissue samples and running analyses to calculate the most probable set of relationships, given a range of possible models of evolution. If the theory of evolution is substantially wrong, then this person is extremely, fundamentally confused; the tasks that she undertakes do not make sense, and the sentences she utters explaining the tasks do not make sense.

Very few people will have thought about that, however, because most people who do not classify animals give little thought to how people who classify animals operate. So you probably won't run into people accusing you of being fundamentally confused! When a scientist announces the discovery of a new species and claims that the new species is particularly unique, people appreciate the discovery and claim without understanding precisely what the scientist means by "species" or "unique." Remember that people do in fact appreciate such discoveries, and don't become cynical. You will have to deal with the public's lack of knowledge about your work in small ways, however.

For example, in 2013 some scientists announced the discovery of a new species called olinguitos. People really appreciated this and pictures of cute olinguitos spread across the internet. What made the discovery special to people who classify animals is that it was the first new carnivore named in thirty-five years. But in trying to explain this to people who do not classify animals, there was a hitch: The olinguitos' diet consists almost entirely of fruits. Olinguitos do not eat animals. How, then, could they be the first new carnivore species in thirty-five years? Among people who classify animals, *carnivore* means an organism is classified within the taxonomic order Carnivora. This order can be defined via synapomorphies—a bit of jargon that entails, by definition, that all members of the defined group evolved from a common ancestor. Or you can directly mention ancestors in the definition; carnivores are the least-inclusive group that includes the most recent common ancestor of seals, cats, and dogs and all of its descendants.

We found that the most effective way to convey this information was by analogy: "It's like if you met somebody named Mr. Carnivore. Just like somebody named Mr. Carpenter might not be a carpenter." The analogy points out the difference between using a word as a proper name to refer to an individual and using the same word as a description of something the individual is or does. That distinction is intelligible whether one adopts an evolutionary perspective or not. Yet the analogy is also stronger, conveying further information in an evolutionary perspective: What makes the name "Mr. Carpenter" apply to the individual in question is a matter of descent. So it is with the name "carnivore." This was an opportunity to explain how to classify animals.

Doing Things with and to Animals

You will learn to look at specimens. Have you ever known a set of identical twins? Maybe at first you had a difficult time telling one from the other. But over time their faces just look different in ways you can't articulate. Something like that happens with specimens. What at first looks like just another lizard you will see differently, once you know to look at the scales under the chin. Some of the knowledge is not as easily put in words. Animals will look different to you. Probably this has already started to happen—your mother tells me you have collected a welter of "bugs and crawlies" (Hemiptera and Diplopoda?).

The way that you feel about animals will change, too. You're already concerned about the biodiversity and environmental crisis. The more you invest in the animals that you study, the more personally it will affect you. These are your animals at risk of vanishing; that's your habitat disappearing. You may go back to the field each year, only to find less and less of the forest left. One time Jay Savage's students sent him photographs and then specimens of a new kind of frog that they had discovered. The coloration was so unique—unheard of—that Savage accused his students of pranking him by faking the colors. That frog is extinct now. One of Savage's other students told me about it rather emotionally. Did you know that there is a kind of frog that has a distinct bright yellow pattern on its back, but if you rub the yellow, it comes off? And stains your hands yellow. How can such a thing be? It doesn't yet have a name, and it's possible that it will be extinct before it has a name. There are species named *N. extincta* and *A. extinctor*. Imagine the feeling of having discovered something new and wonderful and unique that no longer exists, and all you can do to honor it is put in a lot of work and energy to publish its official name.

It helps a little to know that your work is critical to conservation efforts. A zoologist once told me that it's like the house is on fire, and we're running through the house deciding what to save, and we don't even know what's in the house. You're the person who is figuring out what is in the house. But it doesn't help enough, and to classify animals, you have to deal with melancholy, anger, fury, despondency, grief.

If you pursue this career, I will be here for you if you need help with that or any other thing. If you have any questions or worries, please do write back or call me, and if our paths cross in the real world then let's have coffee. I feel old that this is the list of things I would suggest! All best to your mother.

Sincerely,

Aleta

Suggested Readings

On "the natural classification," the purpose of systematics, and Hennig's arguments, see:

Mark Ereshefsky. 2001. *The Poverty of the Linnaean Hierarchy: A Philosophical Study of Biological Taxonomy*. Cambridge: Cambridge University Press.

M. H. Haber. 2012. "Multilevel Lineages and Multidimensional Trees: The Levels of Lineage and Phylogeny Reconstruction." *Philosophy of Science* 79: 609–23.

Willi Hennig. 1966. *Phylogenetic Systematics,* translated by D. D. Davis and R. Zangerl. Urbana: University of Illinois Press.

Olivier Rieppel. 2016. *Phylogenetic Systematics: Haeckel to Hennig.* Boca Raton, FL: CRC Press.

On inference about natural relationships, see:

M. J. Donoghue. 1990. "Sociology, Selection, and Success: A Critique of David Hull's Analysis of Science and Systematics." *Biology and Philosophy* 5: 459–72.

S. V. Edwards. 2009. "Is a New and General Theory of Molecular Systematics Emerging?" *Evolution* 63: 1–19.

Niles Eldredge and Joel Cracraft. 1980. *Phylogenetic Patterns and the Evolutionary Process.* New York: Columbia University Press.

David L. Hull. 1988. *Science as a Process: An Evolutionary Account of the Social and Conceptual Development of Science.* Chicago: University of Chicago Press.

Elliot Sober. 1991. *Reconstructing the Past: Parsimony, Evolution, and Inference.* Cambridge, MA: MIT Press.

Elliot Sober. 2008. *Evidence and Evolution: The Logic Behind the Science.* Cambridge: Cambridge University Press.

Edward O. Wiley and Bruce S. Lieberman. 2011. *Phylogenetics: The Theory of Phylogenetic Systematics.* 2nd ed. Hoboken, NJ: John Wiley & Sons, Inc.

On different disciplinary approaches, see:

Ron Amundson. 2005. *The Changing Role of the Embryo in Evolutionary Thought: Roots of Evo-Devo.* Cambridge: Cambridge University Press.

David Sepkoski. 2012. *Rereading the Fossil Record: The Growth of Paleobiology as an Evolutionary Discipline.* Chicago: University of Chicago Press.

Kim Sterelny and Paul E. Griffiths. 1999. *Sex and Death: An Introduction to Philosophy of Biology.* Chicago: University of Chicago Press.

On the culture of natural history, see:

Harry Greene. 2013. *Tracks and Shadows: Field Biology as Art*. Berkeley: University of California Press.

L. A. Rocha et al. 2014. "Specimen Collection: An Essential Tool." *Science* 344(6186): 814–15. doi:10.1126/science.344.6186.814

Mary P. Winsor. 1991. *Reading the Shape of Nature: Comparative Zoology at the Agassiz Museum*. Chicago: University of Chicago Press.

On the biodiversity crisis and conservation biology in relation to systematics, see:

D. P. Faith. 1992. "Conservation Evaluation and Phylogenetic Diversity." *Biological Conservation* 61: 1–10.

Roseli Pellens and Philippe Grandcolas. 2016. *Biodiversity Conservation and Phylogenetic Systematics*. Springer open access.

S. Sarkar and C. Margules. 2002. "Operationalizing Biodiversity for Conservation Planning." *Journal of Biosciences* 27: 299–308.

R. I. Vane-Wright, C. J. Humphries, and P. H. Williams. 1991. "What to Protect?— Systematics and the Agony of Choice." *Biological Conservation* 55: 235–54.

❧ CHAPTER 15

Becoming a Research Rodent

NICOLE C. NELSON AND KAITLIN STACK WHITNEY

Think of an animal in a scientific study—what image comes to mind? Guinea pigs, rabbits, and white rats are icons of biological research, but the animal you are most likely to find in a laboratory today is a black mouse known as *Mus musculus*. While the pages of scientific journals published in the 1950s were filled with birds, fish, rabbits, dogs, and pigs, researchers in the late twentieth century increasingly chose to work with rodents. By the century's close, mice made up around 60 percent of the millions of animals used annually for experiments, and around three quarters of those mice came from a single genetically identical strain, known to researchers as C57 Black 6. Scientists have warned of the dangers of focusing so much on one particular species, even as they continue to publish studies using laboratory-bred mice.

To illustrate this tension in the contemporary life sciences, we offer a how-to guide written from two perspectives—that of a mouse in a neuroscience laboratory, where a majority of researchers are studying standardized rodents in standardized spaces, and that of a mouse in a field biology study, where research on a wide variety of organisms in their natural habitats still proliferates. Deer mice (*Peromyscus spp.*) have long been used in animal behavior and ecology field studies. They are found all across North America; each individual mouse has a very small home range (about a tenth of a hectare); and they are omnivores that will eat almost anything. These traits mean that deer mouse studies can be done in many places, using almost any kind of prey.

Placing narratives from a laboratory mouse and a field mouse side by side highlights some of the similarities and differences between working with animals in the lab and in the field. Although these two spaces may seem at first to sit at opposite ends of a spectrum of research styles, they have a surprising amount in common. Field researchers work in subtle ways to control the variability of the natural world and make it more like a laboratory. Laboratory researchers work to make sterile environments look more like the mouse's natural habitat, offering them materials to build nests in the back of their clear plastic cages. The mice themselves also occupy a somewhat ambiguous position between nature and technology. Radio transponders and years of inbreeding have transformed these supposedly natural entities into finely tuned research instruments.

We write from the perspective of the mice, a choice that may (rightly) raise suspicion. Doing research with animals is an ethically charged enterprise, and researchers and activists alike often use claims to be able to speak for the animal as a way of foreclosing debate. We have given our research mice differing perspectives on what it might be like to be engaged in an experiment to ensure that our fictional animals do not appear to speak with a unified voice. The contrast between the two captures some of the polarized nature of contemporary discussions of research animal welfare.

Congratulations on your new job! You've made it past being culled or given to a graduate student to practice her injection techniques, and are about to enter the exciting world of neuroscience research. I've been living in this laboratory for six months and working in experiments since I was sixty days old. I'm also a new mom, currently raising the next generation of pups for science.

You may think that you already know all that you need to know about research since you were born in a laboratory. Yes, you know Steve and Laura, the technicians in green scrubs who give you fresh food and water and change your bedding once a week. And you know the mice in the cage next door, who were born just a few

Psst—over here! On the other side of the wall. You may be wondering how you ended up in this box (its name is Sherman). You followed the scent of a particularly tasty snack, and it was a trap. You're probably wondering how we get out of this box. Well, don't worry—we will. How do I know? I've been caught in here before.

We just have to wait. Sometime soon a human will come open this box. First, they're going to give you a name. It'll be written on a big metal ear tag. You'll hear them saying "Monel," but that's not your name—that's the name of the earring. I have one too. It will hurt—they use a kind of hole-punch to put it in, and they don't give you any medicine for the pain. Your new name will be on there. Mine is AFL-6078.

days after you, and you can smell and hear the hundreds of other mice in the room. But beyond the doors of the colony room, there is a whole world of new rooms and new people, filled with strange mazes and beeping machines. In just a few short days, when Laura hands over the results of our latest census survey to Dr. Smith (I'm not sure why, but they call it an "inventory chart"), you'll be assigned to an experiment, and then your adventure will really begin!

Now would be a good time to start saying your goodbyes to your cage mates, because you might not all go on to the same experiment. When the researcher comes to pick you up, you'll get a new identification number and you'll be moved to a new cage rack or even a new room. Don't worry about figuring out who your researcher is—they may be wearing the same green scrubs as Steve and Laura, but you'll quickly come to recognize your researcher's unique smell. The researcher will give you a new identification number for the duration of the experiment and will clip your ear with a decorative pattern to keep track of who's who. Getting your ears clipped does sting a little, but it's a faster and more permanent alternative to having the researcher draw identification stripes on your tail every few weeks with a Sharpie.

Along with your new identification number, you will now be officially recognized as an individual research subject. This means that you have new rights and responsibilities. While you were part of the breeding colony, Dan the colony manager was responsible for checking in on your health, but now the researcher herself will be coming around for a daily visit. The Institutional Animal Care and Use Committee has also reviewed

After you're renamed, they'll want to examine you. They're hoping you'll look as a mouse should—all your ears and legs and eyes and tail intact, not too big and not too small. I used to look like that. Now that this is my third summer, and the second with my name tag, I don't anymore. You can't see me through this wall, but I'm missing an eye and part of my ear. Could be worse, I suppose—many of our kind don't make it even this long.

But if the researchers like what they see, this is only the first of many times you'll end up in a box like this one. You're now a study subject. I used to be one, before the injuries, but that's a story for later. While we're in here waiting, I'll tell you what your new reality is going to be like now that you're going to be in an experiment.

You may be wondering if the humans are allowed to just trap you like this. Aren't there any laws about research, like the laws that keep the bright orange humans and their guns away from the deer for most of the year? If there are rules, it's hard to tell, and no one ever comes out here to check up on the researchers and see what they're doing anyway. You'll hear the researchers talk about safety, but they mean their own, not yours. They follow rules about wearing gloves and special clothes because they're worried about something they call "hantavirus." I'm not sure why, though, since none of us seem sick.

So it seems that there's nothing to prevent the researchers from tricking us into walking into these traps. But before you start completely panicking, you should know that being a study subject doesn't mean the humans will take you away. They'll let you go after they inspect you, but they'll keep the experiments you'll be participating in to ensure that the data you'll be working so hard to generate are likely to be useful. They also make recommendations to the researchers about how to create good working conditions for you to ensure your health and safety.

watching you after they let you free. You won't always see them, though. Sometimes they show up every few days to set these traps we're in. Sometimes they set up devices on the ground or in trees to watch us from afar; those are cameras. They're watching, even if you don't see them.

Your First Experiment

You may be nervous on the day of your first experiment, but don't worry—remember, you've been bred for this! Your ancestors have been living and working in laboratories for hundreds of generations, which makes you uniquely adapted to the tasks at hand.

I can't tell you much about what your experiment will be like, because the researchers take great pains to make sure we don't know in advance what kinds of tests we'll be doing and what the point of the study is. It can be quite frustrating to do your job well when you're given so little information, but researchers think that this is the best way to get what they call "natural" behavior. The key to behaving "naturally" is to strike a balance between behaving ever so slightly unpredictably so that researchers feel some sense of surprise, but not so unpredictably that it completely upsets their theories of how mice should behave in an experiment. Too much variation in the way you and your colleagues behave will mean that more mice have to be hired and the experiment will take longer to do. Even worse, if you behave too strangely, the researcher might label you an "outlier" and kick you out of the study. Once you're stuck with that label you'll find it impossible to get work in the research world again. You might want to confer with your cage mates or

When does the experiment start, you ask? The experiment began before you got caught in the trap with me. It will go on for weeks, months, maybe even years. It's hard to tell, because most of the time you won't see the researchers. You'll just see what they leave behind for us.

I have no idea what their study is all about, but I can tell you that these researchers seem to be obsessed with getting us to eat different things. Soon, all kinds of different foods are going to start appearing in all kinds of different places. Sometimes they're foods you've never seen before. Sometimes they are foods you know and enjoy, like seeds, but put in traps like this one, or buried in balls of wax, or placed on thin metal sheets to capture your footprints. Yes, it's "free" food for the taking, easier than foraging. But there are costs to being a study subject.

This earring, for example—unfortunately it will draw attention to you, whether or not you want it to. Now that you have this thing attached to you, you need to be extra vigilant. You already know that the fields are full of animals that want to eat us—hawks, owls, snakes, foxes—the list goes on and on! Well, having a shiny metal earring can make you more visible to them too, not just the researchers.

other mice living near you and discuss some general strategies for running mazes before your experiment begins.

While you're engaged in an experiment, it can be difficult to focus on the task at hand with a researcher standing only a few feet away. Their smell can be overwhelming, not to mention the smell of all the chemicals they use to keep the lab "clean." They sometimes hover above you and cast a shadow that resembles the creatures called "hawks" that our ancestors used to warn each other about. But it's important to ignore them as much as possible (or at least, to make it look that way). Researchers don't like to think that they're involved in any way in the experiment. Even so, researchers often give you subtle signals that can help you determine whether you're doing well in your maze run. Watch their facial expressions closely for navigational clues—a tensing of the muscles around the eyes and mouth might indicate that you've taken a wrong turn, while a little smile will tell you you're on the right path.

It's especially difficult to keep from responding when a researcher talks to you or gives your belly a gentle scratch while she's transferring you back to your cage after your run in the maze. You may even encounter a human who gives you a pet name rather than referring to you by your official research number. Such lapses in professional decorum are surprisingly common, despite the fact that researchers pride themselves on their objectivity. If you find yourself paired with a researcher who is being overly familiar with you in the workplace, a quick nip on the finger can be an effective way of reminding her that you both have a job to do.

How do you think I lost my eye and part of my ear? You must be very careful.

You might be tempted to find a way of getting rid of your earring, but if you do that, then the researchers usually won't let you stay in the study. And that, of course, means losing access to unlimited food! So if you want to stay in the study, there are a few things you shouldn't do. Don't play with the earring. The humans think it's trivial to our appearance, so we're supposed to act like that. If you must, ask other mice for advice about how to go about life pretending it isn't on. Don't do anything that's too different from what you used to do before you were in the study. For example, you may be tempted to eat all of a particularly delicious food that the researchers leave out, but the researchers think that this is "erratic" behavior—they want you to act "naturally" and pretend that something delicious is just like your average seed. Don't eat any more or less than your fellow mice are eating. If you do, they might label you an "outlier" and kick you out of the study. Being an outlier means that you're messing up the humans' data. Remember, we are mice, but we are also their data.

Above all, don't panic when the humans pick you up. None of us like being trapped or measured, and your first instinct is going to be to swing your head around and try to give that researcher a good bite on the finger. But if you do that, then the researchers might take you away instead of letting you go. The mice who have been taken away have never returned. I think they were killed.

Animals as Scientific Technologies

If it's helpful to you, you can think of yourself as a piece of technology while you're doing your experiment. It may sound silly to say that, since you're obviously not made of wires and circuits, but your body has been shaped by humans over many generations to make it suitable for the laboratory. Take the mice in the cage rack across from you, for example—it's no accident that they all look the same. Their marriages have been arranged to make sure that their pups are genetically identical, and that family will periodically go in for genetic testing to make sure they haven't acquired any new mutations. And see the cage below us, the one where the mother has white and grey patches but her pups all have grey fur? Her cells have been altered so that they're missing a gene, and she's passed that mutation on to her offspring. Just as a thermometer or a batch of chemicals has been carefully designed and manufactured to fulfill a specific function in the laboratory, you too have been built for laboratory work.

Once you start to see yourself as a technology, you'll begin to understand why researchers expect you and your cage mates to behave similarly in the maze. Imagine what it would be like to do research if each thermometer gave you a different temperature reading, or each bottle of chemicals gave you a different product at the end of a reaction! It would be impossible to get anything done, because you would never know which instrument was behaving unpredictably. You too are part of this vast network of instruments that produces scientific findings. The modifications that researchers have made to your genome,

You're a lot more than your earring and your new name, but that's how the researchers see you now. You're data to them, and you're also an instrument for them. And we aren't the only ones. If you look closely in the grasslands, forests, and skies around us, you may notice that researchers have attached tracking and monitoring devices to lots of animals. See those birds with metal bracelets around their legs? See that deer with the bright yellow ear tag? Or the fox with the bulky necklace? That's a GPS locator—the researchers know where he is all the time, even when they aren't watching. Even plants have them. This tree has a sensor that researchers attached, which listens to noises in the forest and sends information about what it hears to the internet!

Why are the humans doing this? They want to understand you and me. But they don't know how to think like a mouse though, or a bird or a tree either, for that matter. So they hope that by following us around—observing and quantifying everything we do—they will come as close as they can to being us. We're their eyes, ears, mouths, and legs on the ground. We've all been enrolled in their quest to understand and control the planet. Of course, the surveillance technologies they invented, like our ear tags, are partners in this research as well. They allow the researchers to be in more places, follow more animals, take more observations, and create more data. In my life, I've seen many mice tagged and studied, as well as other animals and plants. I'm not sure when the researchers will decide they know enough about us or the planet.

the special foods they feed you, the plastic cages they raise you in—these things may all be quite different from the way that your ancestors in the wild lived, but they ensure that you are able to integrate seamlessly with other laboratory technologies.

Every new year seems to bring more researchers, more studies, and more technology.

Mating and Reproduction

Our long history of arranged marriages is one of the reasons that researchers prefer to work with us instead of other animals. As you know, the researchers matched your mother and father, as well as some of your cousins. If you are lucky, one day they will choose a partner for you, too. To other animals who choose their own mate based on courtship displays, this may seem to be a strange tradition, but our marriages are arranged with other ideals in mind. For example, my partner and I were matched because we both had exceptionally high scores on our maze runs, and the researchers hoped that our pups would inherit our intelligence. I feel honored that I was chosen to contribute to a distinguished lineage of maze runners. My little ones are only two weeks old right now, but I'm trying hard to teach them everything I know about mazes before they're weaned next week.

You'll find that dating in the laboratory is nearly impossible anyway. Our cages are designed to remove the temptation of meeting a cute young mouse almost entirely. You'll remember that Steve moved your brothers to a separate cage when you were about three weeks old—you're old enough now that I can tell you that they did this because they wanted to make sure that you wouldn't

Being in the study isn't all work and no play. Although you may have to restrict your urge to hoard all the food or bite a researcher, you can let some impulses run free. You should feel free to mate with whomever you want while you're in the study, and you can have as many pups as you like. The researchers actually like to see us mating and reproducing. Maybe it is because mating is natural, and these researchers value all behaviors that are natural. This may sound very strange, because they are getting us to do a lot of things that aren't natural—feeding us new foods, trapping us, tagging us. And we're supposed to pretend that we don't see them lurking around our homes, watching us. So while you may find it a bit weird to be out on a date with a researcher hovering above you, just try to pretend they aren't there. At least they don't expect us to remain celibate for the course of the study!

How will being in the study affect your dating life? Well, with food available to you all the time, you're going to find yourself in the mood much more often. You'll also be better able to feed your pups, and so you may end up with a really big family. Being in the study can also help you find a mate. Some mice find the earring attractive and will be proud to have a mate who develop attractions to each other as you got older.

It's unlikely, but if you do encounter a "lone ranger" who has escaped from another mouse room or even comes from outside the building, you must absolutely refrain from entering into an illicit encounter. Obviously, if the parentage of your pups is in question, there's no way a researcher will hire them for a study, but the consequences of an unsanctioned mating can be much more severe—your entire colony might be killed to ensure that the purity of your family line is maintained. A distinguished lineage is what secures a research mouse's place in the laboratory, and this position can all too easily be compromised by one impulsive and highly regrettable act.

was deemed worthy by the researchers. The extra weight of the earring can be helpful if you're a male. It may be only two or three percent of your body weight, but every little bit counts when you're fighting for mates and defending your territory!

Other potential mates may find the earring distracting, and they may notice or comment on your tag. You should ignore those comments or find someone else who doesn't care— remember that acting natural means pretending that things like a big metal tag hanging off your ear aren't there. I've heard of some mice who have had luck disguising their earring, so ask around for some tips if you're not having luck attracting a mate.

The "Bad" Mouse

There's one in every group—the mouse who just refuses to play by the rules. He or she repeatedly bites the researcher, runs away, or deliberately behaves unpredictably. When I had my first job in an alcohol study, I roomed next to a mouse who spent all night pummeling the sipper tube on his alcohol bottle so that the alcohol would leak out onto the cage floor. The poor research technician who measured the volume in the bottle every morning couldn't understand how a single mouse could drink so much in one evening, until she finally caught him messing with the spigot!

Sure, there are many things you can do to get yourself kicked out of the experiment, but to what end? You can refuse to move when the researcher puts you in the maze, or try to jump the walls and escape. But even if you

You may find yourself sitting here thinking, "Thanks for the advice, AFL-6078, but I don't want to be in a study. How do I get out?" I can totally understand that—it's not like anyone asked you if you wanted to be in the study in the first place! If you decide you don't want to be a research subject, there are several ways that you can get yourself kicked out. Some of them are obvious. If you remove your tag or "accidentally" lose it, the researchers won't be able to find you or identify you. If you run far away to a new place, they won't be able to find you either—but then you would have to find a new home and new friends.

Many of the ways of getting out of the study are potentially quite dangerous for you, though. You could act erratically and hope that the researchers watching simply kick you out. But behaving oddly could also do manage to hoist yourself up and over the walls of the maze (not an easy feat considering how much they feed us around here), you'll find that there's nothing but more walls on the other side. And after all that effort, you're unlikely to be rewarded with anything other than an early death. Even if being a research subject wasn't your first choice of careers, I encourage you to strive to do your job well, if not for your own personal satisfaction, then for the good of science.

make you more visible to predators, like hawks, that want to eat you. You could attack other mice in the hopes of getting the researchers' attention, but you risk injury and it's certainly not going to make you any friends. The researchers don't exactly make it easy for you to leave the study, so sometimes your best option is to keep your head down, act normal, and wait for the experiment to end.

The End of the Experiment

The most difficult part of working in the laboratory is the end of the experiment. We all know (even if we don't talk about it very much) that many experiments require us to be willing to die at the end, so that the researchers can see what has happened to our brains as we've been drinking and running mazes.

The moment that you die is a pivotal one in your career, and it's critical that you die in the right way. Remember that the researcher isn't simply aiming to kill you; she wants to transform you from your physical form into scientific data. If you panic and try to run away or curl up and bite the researcher so that she's not able to inject you in the belly, that stress or that incomplete injection will show in your brain's chemistry. It can be extremely difficult in such circumstances to retain your composure, but if you lose your cool and die in the wrong way, all of your hard work so far will have been for naught.

Remember that while this is the end of the experiment for you, in many ways it's just the beginning. Your tissues, images, and measurements will live on

Sometimes it's hard to know exactly when the study ends. Often you'll only know because the strange new foods just disappear and you stop being caught in traps. Even when the study ends, the researchers don't take off our earrings. The researchers or their friends will probably want to do another study in the future, and they will remember you this way.

Ideally, you will live long past the end of the study, but if you die, it's unlikely that the researchers are going to blame themselves. Even though I've told you about all of the ways in which this silly little earring can impact your daily life, the researchers have convinced themselves that the risk it poses to us is small. If that turns out to be wrong and you die during the study, the researchers will simply shrug their shoulders and not include you in the data. There's hundreds of us out here, and they can always capture and tag another.

Assuming you make it through successfully, you and your eating habits will become data. The researchers use everything they've watched or measured about us—what we ate, what in the laboratory long after you are gone. By making the ultimate sacrifice for science, you will achieve a kind of immortality. Who knows—if you're really excellent at your job, it just might be a picture of your brain slice that makes it to the pages of Science magazine!

we weighed—and report it to their friends in papers. We don't ever get to see the results. But I don't think there is very much to see—a lot of words written down. Researchers don't tend to write about things that interest us anyway. Who cares about "optimal foraging theory" when you're just trying to survive?

Suggested Readings

On lab mice and field mice, see:

Nicole Bedford and Hopi Hoekstra. 2015. "The Natural History of Model Organisms: *Peromyscus* Mice as a Model for Studying Natural Variation." *eLIFE* 4: e06813.

Karen Rader. 2004. *Making Mice: Standardizing Animals for American Biomedical Research, 1900–1955*. Princeton: University of Princeton Press.

On the natural/technological distinction, see:

Robert Kohler. 1994. *Lords of the Fly: Drosophila Genetics and the Experimental Life*. Chicago: University of Chicago Press.

Donna Haraway. 1990. *Simians, Cyborgs, and Women: The Reinvention of Nature*. New York: Routledge.

On the lab/field distinction, see:

Robert Kohler. 2002. *Landscapes and Labscapes: Exploring the Lab-Field Border in Biology*. Chicago: University of Chicago Press.

Thomas Gieryn. 2002. "Three Truth Spots." *Journal of the History of the Behavioral Sciences* 138: 113–32.

❧ CHAPTER 16

The Business

A Ferret's Guide to the Lab Life

HEATHER ALTFELD WITH LESLEY A. SHARP

> A group of ferrets is known as a "business" or historically as a "busyness."
>
> A male ferret is a "hob," a female a "jill," a ferret under one year a "kit."

1

It's my favorite time of day, when they line us up to scare the rats. Easy job, this one is! I don't have to do much. This is actually the best of the many experiments we're participating in, for we are free, unhaltered by tripswitches and wires—but the rats, those revolting menaces, are fully outfitted like tiny astronauts, gathered in twos in tiny grottos inside the imaging machine while it clanks and whirls, memorizing their individual terrors. I know it sounds cruel, but I like knowing that a mere whiff of my ferrety scent terrifies those little guys, and so I relish it, strutting around in my plastic carrier, letting them know who's boss, knowing that the fresh musk of my scent meeting those tiny electrodes that measure their fear response is a potent holler in their puny brains. T-Rex walks back and forth, arching up, his front paws above his head in a gesture that makes him look abnormally tall, and on The Researchers' screen we can see that a few of the rats look like they'll never be the same again. This titillates me to no end. I focus on a rat I've seen before, his black beady eye twitching before I do anything at all. Whoo-ee! I am king! This is the lab life! I feel like a spring day! I feel like a discovery! I feel like I'm rolling downhill in the grass!

I actually must confess, at this point, that I do not really know what a spring day feels like. And grass is kind of a legend, something I heard from a friend who heard it from a friend who heard it from an old guy who claims he'd been Out of the Lab, that he had *seen things*. Grass. Trees. The delicacy of tiny mice, washed down with warm water. Sometimes we lie around, though, in our hammocks, otherwise known as The Condos, talking about what it must be like, the grass, the air, the way things must smell out there somewhere. And I dream of it, too, so vividly that it is almost like I have felt grass at some point in my life, as though it were embedded in my eidetic memory. Why haven't The Researchers, in those crisp white coats, figured out with those brain-wires—that we too have eidetic memories locked inside our genes and that we'd be even happier if the lab was a big knoll. Then maybe we wouldn't mind the constant prodding, the poking, the surgeries, the viruses that make us weak and hobble us for days. Maybe we'd have it to look forward to when they wheel us down the hall to our certain, and uncertain, fates.

By the way, officially I am referred to by my number, 117C, as if I am merely a data point, but they also call me Lucifer, cageling of 117A, or rather, Hobgoblin, my homie, my bestie, my man. We grew up here, mostly. Lifted from our dear mothers as sucklings, we endured together the long truck ride standing, as though dropped vertically down the little tubes we sometimes played in, holding on to the nothing of our breath, then the terror of the cold crate, the long days of quarantine, where we sensed one another's presence but were living in relative silence and alone, as The Researchers worry that our germy breaths would contaminate the placidity of the sparkling lab. And then we moved into the warm swaddle that the lab afforded us, where we were allowed to lie against each other for a while after enduring those toils of journey and isolation, and we were tagged ceremoniously, with a genteel formality. For a month or so after we arrived, they referred to us by our Numbers, but guys like Hobgoblin and me, we get named. We'd lie awake at night before our Naming, in the Condos, whispering about Rabid Max, named for his black tarry fur, his inability to room with others, and the graze of his teeth, which met the hand of The Chen even when The Chen was trying in a gesture of kindness to feed him a treat. Even though neither of us wanted a name like Rabid Max, we knew we had to be special, or we'd be stored dead in the freezer with just our Numbers attached, rather than the affectionate labels we so longed for.

When they eventually carted off Rabid Max, we didn't think we'd see him again. What a surprise it was to find that Death Jeffery had dried him out and stuffed him and brought him back to the lab to put on a shelf above the desks of The Caretakers, suspended in that pose—as though he came into the world always with his teeth first, jutting out from his head, his mad gaze forever fixated on The Chen. They put a little silver fork in his front paw, as though any of The Caretakers might be his next dinner. Poor Rabid Max. That's what you get when you don't play nice with others. I always liked him, though, admired his spunk, his singlemindedness. Now there was a guy who scared the rats! Boy, I would have liked to have seen their printouts after he'd finished with them! Of the named ones—there were Chip and Dale, who used to bare their revolting ferrety rumps at My Hannah, our Caretaker, when she came in, those crass little monsters. It was a true wonder that they were rehomed and not taxidermied with their asses suspended bald in the air forevermore. And then there's Bandit, who was kind of my second-bestie, and his co-man, Three-Finger—they got named for stealing gloves and other sundries from the cleaning carts in The Alley, which is where we get to chill when they clean our Condos every day. And T-Rex, and Robin Hood, both mighty forces in the lab. We're all named because at one point or another, we did something and got noticed. That's how I really got My Hannah. *I've got my eye on you,* were the first words she said to me shortly after my arrival, and I made it my mission to keep her eye there, on me, whenever possible.

We here in the warren, by that I mean the Laboratory Housing Room, are pretty savvy to the facts and have been since we were kits. Fact No. 1: We're here to serve at the pleasure of The Eyes. The human eyes of The Caretakers and The Researchers, that is, for we know that they are large, that their bodies are long and bulky, that they stand on their hinds while washing us, or talking to us, or taking us out to The Alley while they clean up after us, or setting us up in The Lab Room to scare those insipid rats. The Caretakers, they do jobs I'm grateful they do—some of us, like Hobgoblin, not to mention any names, are real stinkpots, and cleaning up after and playing with us makes them smell unhuman and musky all day long. But all we really see of all of them (or, I should say, all we usually see of them) are their eyes. My Hannah has the most lovely eyes of all: like pools of water, clean and bright. Fact No. 2: We're treated well—very well, in fact—The Caretakers dote on and adore us, My Hannah especially, but all of them, really, do. Although I hate the way that The Eddie talks to some of the other humans; one day I hope they'll fang him up and he'll learn a lesson. And here's Fact No. 3: There are, to our knowledge, only three things that await us—the constant cycle of poking and prodding, of small insertions of viruses, of EKGs—we are, after all, here at the pleasure of Science. And then there's Rabid Max's fate and that of just a few others who have been sacked and then frozen in time, whose stuffed bodies decorate The Caretaker Room and preside in their infinitude of silence over them. There is a pathetic-looking rat, and a bunny, which is just an insult to the rest of us. While I'll admit that they're cute, the bunnies are dumber than rocks, and let it be known that if we were to be charged with intimidating them instead of rats, most of the bunnies would pass out and die rather than bear the scent and twitter of a potent hoblet like me.

Oh! And Fact No. 4: Another fate that awaits us is the possibility of The Bad Hall, the Hall of Disease and Death, the stink of it unlike any other place I have been to in my minute little life. When we were kits, we were all taken at one point or another to The Bad Hall, which has the very particular smell—of surgery, of entrapment, of extremes, of old blood. There's a freezer in there, we know that much, and I suspect that some of our Business are trapped in there forever. I don't know if they died in there or were put there after, but when I am not dreaming of grass, when I am sick with the flus that they sometimes try out on me and I'm fevered in my sleep, I see it, ten feet tall in my mind's eye, that cold, terrible, forever home.

And then, there is the grand fate, the final fact, the lab lottery, the prize—rehoming. That almost *never* happens, but when it does, when I watch the few who have left this way depart for the last time, standing on their hind legs, looking out into the vastness of Grass and Trees that await them—this huge swell arises in my chest, an ache I hardly knew existed. When Chip and Dale got to leave—and they weren't going down The Bad Hall either, where the surgeries happen, where those who Never Came Back were last seen—I hid for a day or two, sullen, moody, not even laughing when Hobgoblin farted in my face and waved his tail to spread it around. We talk about each of these fates almost constantly in The Condos, imagining every possibility, lining up the facts, each detail we know to be true, until I am nearly sick with it. Hobgoblin always says I am a bit melancholic—privately, he calls me Lover Boy as a nickname, which I hate, and which is meant as a teasing term. He is mocking, among other things, my adoration of My Hannah. The truth is, Hobgoblin and I had a certain, shall we say, *rivalry* over My Hannah, who we both knew was devoted more to me than to him. Perhaps it was my scent, which was, I think, less odious to her than that of Hobgoblin, who found the idea of using litter barbaric at best and scraped his ass at the edge of the cage when he was finished with his dailies. He found this amusing; My Hannah clearly found it revolting. I do believe she loved me, in part, for my fastidious nature.

2

So you probably want to know how I got my name. You're probably thinking it is because I am a *devilish little fucker*, which is what The Eddie called me when he first saw me wheeled in here, standing up against all gravity on the cart that brought me inside from the Quarantine Room, the room that doesn't smell of disease and death, but of ammonia and rubbing alcohol and the distant scent of other mammals, none of which I have ever seen in person. I hear they even have monkeys back there, if you can believe it. Monkeys! If they lined those guys up to scare us, I couldn't make any predictions; I might look tough to a rat or a mouse, but to a monkey I probably look like a snack. But back to the naming . . . I'd ask that you consider the whole meaning of the word *Lucifer* before you get all judgmental here: It really means "bringer of the morning star," and I like to think that this has to do with my cheerful disposition, my early and industrious nature. My Hannah named me, and she did so after a slight misunderstanding. She was there as a part of the team whose job it was to poke and to prod us, and we *were* there to be poked and to be prodded, cooperative or no, and I decided, soon as I saw her gentle eyes, heard her sweet voice, that I was willing to subject myself to a certain degree of pain, so as not to become one of the flash-frozen specimens who I knew ended up on The Caretakers' shelves because I'd glimpsed them through the room's window. My Hannah took such fastidious notes about us. My Hannah tucked us, obedient and docile, into our hammocks when she left for the night—and sometimes, when she did, she would tell us a story. My favorite was the one about Goldilocks and the Three Bears. Her gentle voice ascribed each bear his own particular dignity, the way that she ascribed to each of us—to me and to Hobgoblin, to Chip and to Dale, to T-Rex and to Bandit and even to Three-Finger and all the others—our own semblance of dignity. I liked imagining, in those moments, those bears, lying in the perfect little hammocks it was rumored they slept in, in a different land of condos, without needles or night-lights, watching as a tiny Hannah came into their house and ate their bowls of hot kibble. I think My Hannah told us this story to take our minds off the truck, the cold steel, the constant needling now and the poking that was to come. But the story's moral, to my reckoning, was this—get your snacks, get a nap, and get out of the way, before anyone can chase you or take you away. And that is the story that I carried in the smallest pouch that was allowed to be my mind—my mind, not the mind being trained and tested—the nail-sliver, the ant-head, the little blue bead that animates my nights.

So back to my naming. My Hannah was accustomed to staying late in the lab, which was one thing I loved about her. She considered it her job to look after us when we were returned to our Condos after the needles and the poking and prodding. I suppose you could say this was the upside of things for me; her kindness made it easier to withstand the long blood draws, the injections, the cellular mutations I endured in the name of Science. So it didn't surprise me in the least when she stayed late one night for no particular reason, doodling, singing to herself, checking on us with unusual frequency. It was going on the time that Hobgoblin and I usually swing each other, back and forth, playing something My Hannah referred to as "Tippecanoe and Tyler too." But her restlessness gradually made me restless; she let me out for a moment, pet me absently. "Hey there, little one," she said. "It's going to be okay. He's going to call. Yes he is. He is going to call any second now!" Then she put me back. She started to tell us a story about two children lost in the woods, then she disappeared into her own thoughts mid-sentence, as though she had forgotten we were there. Hobgoblin and I were the only ones viably awake; Bandit and Three-Finger had worn themselves out in The Alley that morning, looping themselves in a paper towel tube and rolling around like the dumbasses they are. I should admit that I, too, loved to carouse in The Alley—it was the one place I felt I could let my fur down; we all did, crashing into each other, bumper-ferreting our way into a kind of ecstatic frenzy when the scent of something marvelous began to sweeten our games. It was as though through The Alley we could smell freedom, a sort of freedom somewhere in the far reaches of my mind I knew existed. T-Rex was snoring—he'd taken a recent trip to The Bad Hall lately and was still sleeping off the trauma of having a very faint dose of MERS injected under his skin. His eyes were swollen and red, and he looked less like the brute danger we normally considered him and more like what he truly was, an animal experiment.

"Oh," said My Hannah, to me, I think. "Men are so exasperating." I crept up to the cage rails, I let her know I was listening. She fidgeted with her gloves, with her mask, with her cap, scratching at the hair I was sure she kept underneath. "They act like they like you, then they ignore you, then they bark at you, then they ignore you some more." I was quiet. As a hoblet, I had not been permitted even to see a jill since the moment I left my mother's side, and I had no idea if this was how I would behave or not, nervous, anxious, as though my very life depended on the presence of a jill. "Sometimes," she said, shaking her head, "I just don't know." But just then the door to the lab opened, and The Eddie came in. I could tell it was him by his scent, of course, although his form was much like the other human hobs at the lab: tall, a little rotund, too much kibble, I suppose. His cap was crooked, his gloves too tight. I felt a little fury poking out from my chest.

"Hey," The Eddie said. "You almost finished up here?"

"Yes," she said. "I think so." She was nervous, terribly so; I could see it in her eyes, her hands were shaking. "Are we—I mean, I—I—I mean, what are we doing, then? Are we, um, going . . . out?"

"What are we doing," said The Eddie. "Good question." He walked up behind her, pressed against her. I could swear that she looked back at me—I could swear it!—as though she were worried about what I would see.

Hobgoblin, who had been bonkers just twenty minutes before in his nighttime ruckus, was crashed out in his hammock and showed little interest in awakening; I tried valiantly to arouse him, even nibbling his neck a little. Why? I don't know, I was just as antsy as My Hannah, and my aloneness was vast, unadulterated. I felt like the only ferret in the world. But Hobgoblin was unstirrable. I could hear My Hannah and The Eddie giggling a little. I especially didn't like the smell of him, a kind of musk that made me think of the sweaty little rats we scared shitless, and if you can believe this is true, The Eddie smelled even *worse* than them. And the way he looked at her! As though she were delicious, a morsel to gorge on, a treat. It was appalling. And then he had the gall to tilt in to touch her back, to kiss her neck, to wrap his arms around her, to sway her back and forth. "Dance me, to the end of love," he hummed in her ear to the song that played from the radio on the shelf overhead, and I realized, in that moment, that this was a mating ritual and that *they had done this before*, they knew it well. Oh, and the smell that came up from them as they embraced! Do I need to tell you what envy really feels like?

I guess you could say I went a little wild. In retrospect, I understand now what jealousy can make a hob do. I paced, rapidly; I chewed at the bars of the cage in which we slept; I felt guttural noises coming out of my throat. "What a little devil you are," The Eddie said, and I could swear that this is true—he winked at me—and I could not reach his hand, but if I had been able to, I would have sunk my teeth straight through his fat glove until all manner of blood appeared. Instead, I thrashed about, here and there, lamenting—what was this life, anyway? Living in a brethren of my own kind, with nary a jill around? A fraternity of sad-sack ferrets for whom hunting was just a distant memory, programmed by a great-great-great-great-great, immortalized in the picture in our Housing Room of a tapestry depicting a bunch of peasants out hunting some loathsome rabbits with useless nets and the indispensable assistance of intrepid white outdoorsy and very free ferrets, an image humiliating us in our own impotence?

I am not just fur and bones and blood and teeth! I stamp, waiting to see if My Hannah is looking. *I am real!* But she was already hand in hand with The Eddie, who is already leading her out of the lab. As the door opens, she begins to remove the little blue cap she wears upon her head, and I see a radiant glimpse of her hair as the door shuts behind her, leaving us here with the long hum of the lonely night.

I can only imagine what happened while I paced the cage, alone. My Hobgoblin, when finally awakened, showed little dismay. *Go to sleep*, he said. *Give it a rest. Save yourself—T-Rex says the new drug trial is awful.* I gnashed and turned, I flipped and hurled, I paced. By morning, I was hung over with exhaustion, and that is exactly when My Hannah came through the door, sluicing her gloves on her hands.

"Yes, you are quite the little Lucifer, aren't you?" she said. "You really scared that big bad Eddie."

"Yes, you did. Do you know the story of the big bad wolf, Little Lucifer?" I didn't. "'I'll huff and I'll puff and I'll blow the house down!'" she said. Those pigs! What dumb-dumbs. It took hours before I realized I was the first one she had noticed that morning and that she had told the story, in its full entirety, only to me. And that finally, I had been *named*.

3

For a while things were kind of peaceful. We scared rat after rat. The Researchers took our blood, which wasn't so bad; I didn't even try to bite anyone. We played in The Alley, we sneered at The Newcomers, all numbers and letters, 172G and so forth—those babies! We could have been nicer to them, in retrospect. What did we have to lose? T-Rex recovered, slowly, although he never quite regained his ferocity. What a business we were! But one morning, The Eddie knocked on the glass just behind where we lived, and I could see him shimmying his hips as he carried a metal tray, like The Vik, who we see through the panes of glass bringing coffee in the mornings. "Is it art, or is it life?" The Eddie said loudly, displaying something just out of my line of sight. I stood on my hind legs, shaking a bit as I did, with a growing sense of strain and horror as he lowered the tray in his hands to show it to The Caretakers. "That Jeffrey, man! He's the shit with taxidermy! Check it out!" The Eddie continued, trying repulsively to get My Hannah's attention. My Hannah refused to look, but I could not stop myself, and it was then that I saw that the specimen he was carrying was Three-Finger, who had disappeared some weeks ago under the auspice of surgery. Our beloved fast-handed friend would soon stand on a shelf, suspended in a pose familiar to us, one foot forever fleeing a crime scene, his eyes glassy and fixed on a point far across the room, where sat the three white bunnies, as dumb and frozen in death as they were in life. My Hannah still refused to look in The Eddie's direction, but I could feel the pulse in her hand speed up. She was petting me, soothingly, soothing herself, humming, turning her body so that my line of vision was blocked, trying to distract me from my wild longing to crash into The Eddie for doing this with Three-Finger. Despite her touch, despite her sweet attentions, which I loved but had been before betrayed by, I could not help but look again, and when I did, I saw that The Eddie was dressing Three-Finger in a tiny football jersey, roping a gold chain around his neck, so that he looked much like the humans I saw once on the small screen they brought in to listen to while they cleaned our cages. So they had not only suspended Three-Finger forever in his own fur and skin, one foot forward so that it looked like any moment he would spin around the room under the swinging lights in a fevered get-away dance, but they had made a mockery of him. It was unendurable.

I began to ride out the days buried in the hammock, convinced that I had only moments to live, that Hobgoblin too was just here on loan, that we were momentary features here in the lab, that we would soon join Three-Finger on the shelf. And then came the unthinkable. I was lying in my hammock, ironically resolved to try and enjoy my dinner—it was actually nice in the lab; someone was playing classical music, Stravinsky I think, and I was lulled into a certain musing that perhaps I had escaped the worst of it, that if I just lay around and kept my head down for the rest of my life, I'd be left alone until I died of "natural causes," as I heard them say on occasion, they said it of Old Yeller when he finally kicked the bucket, as natural as it can get if you'd been poked and injected and X-rayed and virused up all of your living days. I would be poked and prodded, of course, but if I kept to myself, didn't make too much trouble, I would not be taxidermied or shoved in the freezer with the others, flattened and cold for the duration. And so there I was, listening to the Stravinsky and thinking about the idea of Grass, how lovely it sounded—*grass, grass,* even the word was a calming one—when I heard My Hannah come in and open each cage, pour in kibble, say a few of her niceties—such niceties!!—and then she would wander to the next one. I watched as she passed by me and Hobgoblin, ignoring us entirely, and a fierce, horrible knot grew in my stomach. We've seen what happens when you get ignored at Food Time, because six hours later, you are wheeled off, down The Hall for blood work or what have you, only the lack of food indicates that you are actually going on past The Lab to The Bad Hall, which smells like terror and death. The few who have returned—Fierce Phil, for example—have told us with certainty that the Freezer there is stockpiled with those who didn't make it. *Your heart can stop in that room, and then you're screwed, man,* he told us when he'd returned, his head lolling about from the anesthesia when he said it. I began to shake uncontrollably, shrieking, shrieking. *I don't want to die! I don't want to die! I don't want to end up in the freezer!* Hobgoblin paced the cage. *Woe be to us, woe be to us! The sky is falling! Woe be to us!* We collided in our mutual horror, then began what could only be called a mutiny, banging the cage over and over, our life-fugue, our death-fugue, with not a human still nearby to hear us. Even if they did hear us, their brains were spiraling on in a different orbit, imagining us as data points, our ferret-y cells mutating in patterns and formations that would save them from the infinitude of errors the humans bring upon themselves.

But our moral uprising amounted only to our own exhaustion. The next morning, I flung myself to the floor, racing, one corner, then another, crashing into Hobgoblin, who was also mounting the surge against our certain deaths, until My Hannah managed to cajole us and bundle us up, handing us one at a time to Death Jeffery, who cradled me, talking sweetly, sweetly, I don't even remember what he said, lulling me, lulling me, although all the while I knew where we were going. Trembling and in terror, we are wheeled in separate carts down the hall. I try not to look around. Death Jeffery is tall, he is kind, but he is a killer, and a taxidermist to boot. Big Bad Wolf. My Hannah is off in a corner, immune to our disappearance, she did not even look me in the eye this morning. The others were still sleeping when they came for Hobgoblin and me, and none of them had seen us depart. No goodbyes. No wishes for a good afterlife. No jokes about freezer burn. Goodbye to Bandit and T-Rex. Goodbye to The Chens and The Viks and to Three-Finger. Goodbye My Hannah. Goodbye to those who have not yet been named. Goodbye Old Death Jeffery. Goodbye Hobgoblin. I hope we are frozen together, at least. I can't bear the idea of dying alone.

I struggled as they lowered me to the table and inserted the needle, my limbs taped down, my breath shallow, my teeth chattering. The light above me hurt my eyes, and I closed them, thinking *grass, grass, grass.* Then I could feel it happening: my arms frozen, my legs frozen, my eyes fixated forever on the shelf in The Bad Room, where a small poster is taped to the wall, a little girl on one side, a mouse on the other, the girl in a hospital bed, some words about animal heroes, my vision blurred. And then it happened. I was locked down in a kind of glass, my heart in glass, the air I used to breathe, glass, the mind that used to beat still, strangely, beating, larger than ever. The last thing I remembered was that the little girl leapt out of a hammock in the Three Bears' house and was never seen again.

4

Come little leaves said the wind one day
Come o'er the meadows with me and play
Put on your dresses of red and gold

For summer has gone and the days grow cold.
Soon as the leaves
Heard the wind's loud call,
Down they came fluttering, one and all;
Over the meadows they danced and flew,
Singing the sad little songs they knew.
Dancing and whirling the little leaves went
Winter had called them and they were content
Soon fast asleep in their earthly beds
The snow lay a coverlet over their heads.

I struggled to move, to open my eyes. My entire self felt bruised, sore, even my eyes hurt, my legs were dead weights, my brain was full of terrycloth, there was a tight feeling in my ass and my balls, and I was swollen and sore. But it became clear to me that I was alive. And that My Hannah was singing. It seemed to be night; there was no telling how long I had been asleep, how long I had been back, what had happened while I was there. My Hannah was resting just outside the cage, but she had one finger inside, petting me, petting my back, very softly, petting Hobgoblin, who was still asleep. When I managed the energy to look over at him, I could see the same swelling and wondered. Where are his balls? Where is his lovely ferrety stink? I could feel the dry sensation of my throat, a great thirst bloomed inside me. My Hannah sang again, a song about a cold mouse, and I fell back asleep for what felt like a long while, with the great relief that I was alive. I dozed off, and when I woke again, My Hannah was still there. The room hummed its middle-of-the-night hum, the blue lights of human progress glowed. My Hannah had fallen asleep, one hand on Hobgoblin's spine. The cap she wore on her head had come loose, and I could see the golden streaks of her hair beneath, and her mask, too, had come just a bit loose from her face. I could see her nose and a glimpse of her cheeks, her breathing, shallow, her soft lips, stopped mid-song. She was so lovely. I fell back asleep for a long while. I woke early, and despite my soreness, my thirst, I put on my most effervescent self—I am, after all, Lucifer, bringer of dawn, the bright morning star—and rolled myself best as I could over to her hand, nudging her awake. "Oh, little one," she said. "I'm so sorry for what you had to go through. But it is over now. When you and Hobgoblin are better, we are going to have so much fun. So much fun." She took a slip of paper from her pocket and pinned it to the outside of the cage so that it faced inward. It was a photograph. I could just make out a dwelling of sorts, surrounded by tufts of something soft. It was almost exactly like the Condos I imagined the Three Bears lived in.

"See here?" she said. "In a few days, you little guys are gonna come home with me. I'm taking you home with me soon as you're better. Go back to sleep, my Luciferlia. Sleep tight for now. Later there will be trees to climb." She sat up, tied her mask tightly, pulled the cap back on her head to cover the loose strands of hair, and stretched up toward the lights that lived in the ceiling. Hobgoblin awoke. *What was that all about?* he asked, dazedly. *Where am I?* I nuzzled him, nestled against him. We stayed like that, two spoons, curled in a tiny percentage of the cage. Death and Taxidermy and the Freezer were real, but none were immediately lurking. The business of soft grass and spring were waiting.

Acknowledgments: Heather Altfeld extends gratitude to Gunnar Theodór for his insightful suggestions on animal literature and Troy Jollimore for his constant support. Lesley Sharp's work on this essay was made possible through generous support from the Radcliffe Institute for Advanced Study at Harvard University; she is also indebted to a wide array of animal technician-caretakers for their generosity of time and expert guidance regarding the lives of laboratory animals. Any errors here are no fault of theirs. Most of all, a special thank you goes out to Sophie, Lucy, Ellie, Alex, and Zookie for their love and their love of animals.

Suggested Reading

For readers interested in other books written from the perspective of animals, see:

Richard Adams. 1977. *The Plague Dogs*. New York: Ballantine Books.

Roberta Scipioni Ball. 2006. "Issues to Consider for Preparing Ferrets as Research Subjects in the Laboratory." ILAR Journal 47(4): 286–90.

Lynda Birke, Arnold Arluke, and Mike Michael. 2007. *The Sacrifice: How Scientific Experiments Transform Animals and People*. West Lafayette, IN: Purdue University Press.

Mikhail Bulgakov. 1968. *Heart of a Dog*. Translated by Mirra Ginsburg. New York: Grove Press.

William Kotzwinkle. 1971. *Doctor Rat*. New York: Open Road Integrated Media, Inc.

For philosophical perspectives on anthropomorphism and animal life, see:

Charles G. D. Roberts. 1953. *The Kindred of the Wild: A Book of Animal Life*. Boston: L.C. Page & Co.

PART 5

Conservation

✿ CHAPTER 17

Read, Respond, Rescue

NATALIE PORTER

My dog, Nico, is a rescue. I have never really felt like I rescued her, though. I didn't find her on the side of the road somewhere, or tied to a tree in the yard of an abandoned house. Nico didn't show up on my doorstep hungry and scared, and I didn't pick her up at my local pound. Truth be told, I got Nico in much the same way as I get many other things in my life, through an online search.

I met Nico on PetFinder, a web-based repository for thousands of homeless dogs across the United States. PetFinder makes it easy to find a dog that suits your lifestyle—to fashion your own creature of comfort, if you will. You start by identifying where you'd like your dog to come from. You can then specify the size, age, and breed you prefer; small, medium or large; puppy, adult, or senior; Chihuahua, Chow Chow, or Catahoula. If you want, you can also select for particular canine characteristics. Say you'd like a housebroken dog who is good with cats and children. Just check the boxes, and PetFinder will generate a list of all the dogs who meet those criteria in your designated area. Think of it like Airbnb, except here it's not the human traveling to her ideal home away from home, but rather the ideal dog traveling to her new "forever home." I was looking for a young, medium-sized, active dog within a fifty-mile radius of my zip code. A picture of Nico (then called "Bella") popped up on my screen. She had a long, lean build; short hair (less shedding, I thought); and the soulful eyes of a hound dog. Her profile said she was a quiet, sweet girl and a great running partner. Check, check, and check. I was sold.

Nico and I quickly jumped into the curious culture of canine companionship, or what some refer to as the canine industrial complex. I devoured books on positive and not-so-positive training methods, which I applied haphazardly to my perplexed but patient pup. We assembled her kit with squeaky toys she picked out herself, different leashes for different activities, feeding toys that satiate *and* stimulate, a bed for lounging and one for sleeping, plus a few bowties for special occasions. Nico and I have run thousands of miles together, driven across the country twice, frequented dog parks and daycares, enrolled in obedience classes, and even engaged in Nosework, a scent and searching sport that comes from police dog training (even if, so far, the only scent she knows is "hot dog").

Through these activities we have learned a lot about each other. But some aspects of Nico's behavior still puzzle me. Why does she duck when people try to pat her on the head? Why does she bark at (seemingly) random men? Why doesn't she drink any water when she's home alone? Why does she bolt at the sight of nail clippers? For the dog enthusiasts I've met, the answer is always the same: "She's a rescue." I now say this myself when I have to explain Nico's quirks to others, linking her current behavior to an unknown but probably unhappy past. This phrase usually elicits a sigh, a knowing nod, and some statement praising me for saving her. I appreciate the sentiment, but, if I'm honest, Nico's adoption felt like an act of canine customization, not salvation.

There was, however, a time in her life when Nico faced impending death; it just occurred long before I met her. So if I didn't rescue Nico, who did? And how did they do it? I've found some answers to these questions at my local animal rescue organization. What follows is a step-by-step guide to rescuing dogs, written by a volunteer for a novice volunteer. If you are a novice, before you dive in, please be warned that this is a *guide*, not an instruction manual. I have learned that while there are some fixed steps in the rescue process, each operation is as unique as the particular dogs and humans involved in it. It's up to you and the dog to read each other and the creatures around you, and up to you to respond in ways that give the dog what she needs to travel to her adoptive home. I have included stories of dogs and humans doing just that: reading and responding to one another. Their stories of success, hiccups, and failure offer some clues into the dos and don'ts of doggie rescue.

Step 1: Intake

There are many ways a dog can find his or her way into your rescue organization. A common one is through an extensive network that links your organization to "high kill" shelters, which euthanize dogs in order to deal with overcrowding. These shelters are common in states that lack spay and neuter laws. If they are linked into the rescue network, each week the shelters will send your organization their "death row lists" in the hope that you can save some dogs from the kill floor.

If your volunteer work includes the task of processing the death row list, my condolences. This will require managing your emotions. You will scroll past profiles of famished and feral dogs, aggressive and anxious dogs, obedient and obstinate dogs, hoarded dogs and stray dogs, dogs whose owners died or dogs whose owners left them in a plastic bag by their neighborhood dumpster. You will see one-eyed dogs and three-legged dogs, injured dogs that cannot walk straight or stand upright. You will also see magnificent dogs. Beautiful, well-behaved dogs betrayed only by old age, the birth of a child, a hole in a fence, or a kink in the tail. Death row does not discriminate; it takes all comers.

I suggest finding a quiet place to do this work, and maybe not a cafe. There is something rather obscene about scanning doggie death row while those around you are enjoying lattes or catching up on gossip. Before you begin, remind yourself that you won't be able to take them all, so use your emotional energy sparingly. Here's a tip: Focus your attention on matching the dog's physical and behavioral characteristics to the intake criteria of your particular organization (as decided by its volunteer board of directors). This work is time-sensitive. You have just a day or two to get these dogs off the kill floor and into a safe place. Scan quickly, and know that there may be dogs you miss by minutes.

Now, some rescue organizations limit their intake to young, healthy, and good-looking specimens with previous experience in home settings. These "plug and play" or "shovel-ready" dogs can be pilfered from death row and placed directly into forever homes. Hooray! Other organizations, however, tackle the hard cases. If your organization falls into the latter category, steel yourself. You will be faced with dogs like Maggie, a gorgeous Chocolate Lab who was once used in dogfights and is scared of humans and other canines. Maggie has learned that human handling leads to fear, pain, and sometimes death. She cowers at the sight of strangers, and if you apply pressure to her collar or try to lead her somewhere, she will resist, crumble, or attempt to escape. Maggie once bolted when a volunteer tried to coax her into a car. She ran through four lanes of oncoming traffic and straight into the woods.

You can't blame Maggie for behaving this way. After all, fleeing from humans was what freed her from the fighting ring and landed her on the path to rescue. But it may be hard to find a foster home for dogs like Maggie, who require extra patience and compassion. This is not because fosters aren't patient or compassionate, but rather because they *are* patient and compassionate. These kind souls open their homes and hearts to countless dogs, and you will be hard-pressed to find a foster who doesn't already have a handful of dogs (and other critters) in their household. Fosters, bless their hearts, are almost always overextended. Their space and finances may be strained by intake, their families may be more or less committed to the work of rescue, and they usually balance their care for dogs with full-time jobs, parenting, and other duties. An additional dog means more walks, more training, more vet visits, and more bodies to bring to adoption events. Fosters may think twice before taking in a dog who cannot be easily added to their menagerie.

So, you've got to protect your fosters, but that doesn't mean you can't nudge them a little. For instance, if you post your chosen death row dogs onto your organization's Facebook page, consider including a photo. Maggie's beseeching eyes would melt the coldest of hearts, and a compassionate foster wouldn't stand a chance. You may even want to tag a foster you know has a soft spot for Labs. Post the image, tag your people, and cross your fingers that one of your fosters can convince her family that an eighth (or tenth or twentieth) dog in the house would be manageable.

Also, be ready to answer questions about Maggie. And don't worry. Your responses can include information that shows how wretched her situation is. Think about each dog while mentally flipping through your catalog of fosters and choose which heartstrings to pull. Remember, too, that volunteers also read each other's comments. So even if a foster posts that she'd totally take Maggie if only her other dog weren't recovering from surgery or hadn't just given birth, take heart. A less burdened foster might read the comment and feel compelled to take her in.

Now, there will be times when a foster fails to rise to the occasion. Don't despair! Your organization probably has some kennel space set aside for dogs that, for one reason or other, have not been placed in a foster home. Dogs like Pauley.

Pauley came to rescue from a high kill shelter in Kentucky, where he had been living for over a year. Where he was before that and what happened to land him there is a mystery. What we do know is that after Pauley was pulled from death row he was placed in a foster home where other dogs also lived.

FIGURE 17.1.   Maggie. Photo by Molly Madison Isenbarger.

Pauley did fine for about a day, until one of the other pups picked a fight with him. In the melee Pauley did not respond to his foster's commands, and when she pulled him away he accidentally "redirected" and bit her in the leg. Poor Pauley was deemed unsafe in the household and sent to the kennel, where for the last six months he has been waiting for a new foster or forever home.

Now, you may be surprised to hear that some dogs have trouble adjusting to a home environment and to life in a family. You might think that the transition from shelter to home, from isolation to integration, would have done Pauley a world of good. Dogs are pack animals, right? Aren't they meant to live with other dogs? And haven't they also evolved to live with humans? Yes, but we don't know if this particular pup has ever lived with humans or dogs, and if so, whether that was a positive or negative experience. All we know is that Pauley, who is about three years old, has spent at least the last eighteen months of his life in a kennel. Imagine for a moment living *half your life* in a box measuring 4 feet by 20 feet, surrounded by chicken wire fencing, flanked by dogs on either side, and subject to the smells and sounds of scores of other captive animals with whom you have zero contact. In your run, you have food, water, possibly a chew toy, and hopefully a blanket or a pallet to lie on. If you are lucky, you get a daily walk so that you don't have to shit where you sleep. These are the conditions that Pauley has learned to live in. He needs to learn (or unlearn) some things before he can be homeward bound. He must be socialized.

Step 2: Socialization

Socialization is the most important part of the rescue process, particularly for those organizations that choose the hard cases over the plug and plays. Basically, socialization is what you do to prepare the pup to live successfully in a home as a family member and companion. Rescue does not prepare dogs for sport, show, or security, and dogs with experience in these worlds must sometimes be modified to fit their new roles.

Kennel pups like Pauley pose two problems for socialization. Problem 1: Pauley has been in a dogfight. If you have a dog that you know has been in a fight, to be on the safe side you have to assume that he's not good with other dogs. When you visit the kennel, take him out for walks alone. In the play yard, make sure he's flying solo. It sounds simple, but remember that you are trying to *socialize*. You don't want to quarantine the guy. If you can, slowly get him used to being around other dogs under controlled conditions. Walk him nearby but not bunched up against another dog. Keep his leash slack. Don't let the dogs get face to face. And watch. Read. Look for signs of agitation or aggression. Is he licking his lips? Growling? Are his teeth bared? Hackles up? Tail erect? Ideally, the dogs will be walking side by side but with some distance between them. If that goes well, start introducing him to other dogs. Why? Because even if a pup like Pauley ends up in a home on his own, he's still going to encounter other dogs, and you want to make sure he's not lunging after them, scaring neighbors and dislocating his handler's shoulder in the process. That is not adoptable behavior!

But there's another reason to push Pauley to engage with other dogs, which is that he might actually get along just fine with them. It's possible that at one time Pauley lived in a home with other dogs. We'll never know for sure, but there are signs that this might be the case. On his walks he heads toward the front doors of homes where dogs live; he's not possessive about food or toys; he doesn't get riled up when other dogs in the kennel bark or lunge at him. But whatever his past, the skills and attitude that Pauley brought with him from his 4 by 20 cell—independence, self-preservation, introversion—do not match the skills he needs to become the kind of pet that can be trusted around other creatures. You want to give him a chance to (re)develop those skills in order to make him more desirable in the eyes of pet finders. The dog who plays nice with others requires fewer lifestyle adjustments and will have a bigger pool of potential adopters. He may also have more fun.

Problem 2: Pauley could not be called off the other dog, and in the middle of the fight he accidentally got his foster in the leg. This is a big problem, because it suggests that Pauley doesn't immediately look to humans for direction, assistance, or affection. He doesn't notice or *respond* to humans. Not yet, anyway. This is not adoptable behavior either. Adopters want a dog that listens to them, and most of the time they also want a reliable friend. Your task is to make pups like Pauley friendly. The first thing you have to do is gather more evidence about the problem. Does the dog ignore you when you say his name? What if you make a noise, whistle, or clap your hands? If he does, try and teach him his name. Say it loudly and in a friendly way, and if he looks at you give him a treat. Choose something "high value" like cheese or hot dogs. You want to show this dog that humans give good things and deserve attention. You can do this on your walks, too. If the pup is pulling ahead, keep him at your side. Say nice things to him. Pet him if he lets you. Think of him as your partner, as part of your pack, and hopefully he'll start to notice. He'll respond and become more social.

Socialization in the foster home is easier. Here, human contact is consistent and the work can go a lot faster. This is especially true for dogs such as Levi, who languish in a kennel. Levi is a 30-pound snow-white basset hound mix who was rejected by his first foster for showing "aggression" toward her other dogs. In just a few weeks at the kennel, Levi dropped several pounds. He just couldn't seem to settle down. He paced up and down his narrow run, scanning the other dogs and the door. He didn't stop for food and rarely did for water. He refused to let the volunteers touch him or take him out for walks. He barked. A lot. He didn't sleep. He cried.

Because of the health risks, a dog like Levi can't stay in the shelter. But just as in Pauley's case, don't assume that the home environment will magically rehabilitate him. In his second foster home, Levi dug. Inside and outside, through mud and grass, carpet and linoleum. He also chewed—not just his toys but also rugs and sofas and blankets. (Some dogs chew their own skin down to the bone.) Levi barked. A lot. He didn't sleep. He cried.

So the home is not a quick fix, but it does provide time and space for problem solving and experimentation. The important thing to do in cases like Levi's is to distinguish between the pup's personality and his problems. Early on, Levi's second foster determined that he is not "aggressive" toward dogs; rather, he is a "rough and tumble" kind of dog. Did you know that dogs have different styles of play? Some of it has to do with breeding, some of it has to do with environment, but the point is that as a socializer your job is to read the dog and determine what's dangerous and what's just a doggone good time.

OK, so what about the urge to pace and bark? You could try some tranquilizers to take the edge off—a controversial move—but you must also try to create conditions that manage the dog's urges. This is tricky business. All dogs dig, chew, and bark, and there are important reasons for them to do so. Socializing a dog for the pet seeker, however, means modifying these behaviors to a level that is agreeable to both pup and person. It's safe to say that a potential adopter would prefer a dog that will not tear her Persian rug to shreds, and although we can never know what it's like to live in Levi's head, if nothing else his weight loss suggests that he is at least somewhat stressed or otherwise uncomfortable.

Now, some doggie behaviorists will tell you that Levi acts the way he does because he feels like he has to fend for himself. He doesn't have an alpha, or a clear role in his pack hierarchy. Such an outlook may work well for the stray dog, hoarded dog, fighting dog, or shelter dog, but it doesn't suit the pet dog. Whatever your ideas about canine companionship, in pet keeping culture ideas about "ownership" and "obedience" generally place canines below their humans—or at least hold them accountable to their humans. That's why pet keepers are often called dog "moms" and "dads." To meet these expectations, the foster's job is to establish herself as someone who Levi will look to her for guidance and assurance. This requires controlling time and space. If dogs like Levi are to function as pets, they need to know where to go and what's expected of them. These two things can transform a dog from anxious and aggressive to calm and collected. Creating a sense of place and a routine makes the dog's life, and therefore his behavior, predictable. Shovel-ready.

Here are some tricks: Set boundaries. Dogs are not allowed on the dining room table (Levi's foster "sister" learned this early on), but they should have beds, crates, and other places to call their own: spots where a dog can take a "time out" when the world gets to be too much. Manage the clock. Feed the dog, walk him, and let him out to do his business at fixed times. He will come to see that his needs are taken care of, on schedule, and that he doesn't have to worry about them. He can relax. He will learn that his human provides, and, because she provides, she is worth paying attention to and responding to. Being a successful human companion means that when the dog does dig himself out of the yard, as Levi did, calling his name will bring him back. If he barks too much, you can tell him to quiet down and he will listen. Housebroken? Responds to commands? Check and check, under the right conditions.

For dogs like Pauley and Levi, socialization means giving up the autonomy they had to develop in a previous life. It will be a difficult road, but there is a payoff: They will be able to travel.

Step 3: Presentation

A socialized dog makes for easier presentation, the next step in the rescue process. Presentation happens in many ways. The Internet is one of them. If you are a tech-savvy person, then I suggest you apply yourself to your organization's website, where you can put up the profiles of all your available animals and link them directly to repositories like PetFinder.

Let's start with the profile photograph. If any of your volunteers have skills in this area, use them. There are two kinds of photos: the portrait and the action shot. The portrait will convey the pup's features brilliantly. I recommend a head and body shot. The headshot is the eye-catcher, the heart-melter. The body shot gives a sense of what you're getting into. Now, those of you who have dogs may be thinking, "Getting my Bam Bam to sit or stand for a portrait? Easier said than done." You're right, but there are some tricks to this. For the headshot, have the foster stand behind the dog and hold her still. She'll be out of sight but her body will be there for comfort. Remember, dogs communicate with their bodies. For the body shot, let the pup roam around first to get comfy. If you are the photographer, arm yourself with treats and toys. Make unfamiliar sounds to get that awww-inspiring head tilt that dogs do so well. Experiment with your tongue and cheeks. Snap your fingers, give a treat. Read the dog. Does she like the whistle or the throat rattle? The peanut butter or jerky? Take note, and use your tools to get a response.

Your other option is the action shot. The advantage here is that you can capture a dog's personality. Getting this shot may seem easier, but make no mistake—it requires a steady hand, lightning-quick reflexes, a tolerance for dirt, and a lot of courage. Go outside. Does the dog like tennis balls? Great! Lie down on your back (don't think about what lurks beneath), have another volunteer throw the ball in the air towards you and snap the pic just as the dog leaps into the air, floppy ears spread out like Dumbo. Whee! Then roll away before she lands on you. Or, have a volunteer dangle a treat above your head. The airborne dog may bowl you over, but the shot will be worth it. Tip: An open mouth and hanging tongue make a dog look happy and friendly. Get the dog worked up and capture that smile. Move in, move in! Those gleaming eyes are best viewed up close. Be warned, though: Your lens will be licked, your clothes will be stained, your back will be sore, and your arms will tremble from the weight of your camera.

Of course, the other part of the profile is equally important: the description. Here you will provide essential information about the dog. This is tricky business, especially in the hard cases. Of course you want to put the pup's best paw forward, but you also have an obligation to be upfront about whatever challenges he might pose for an adopter. Be a wordsmith! Take the dog's unique way of relating to the world and turn it into something manageable, charming even. Is the dog an escape artist? "Sig would love to play in a fenced-in yard." Is the dog bouncing off the walls? "Rockne would fit right into your active family." Is the dog difficult to train? "Hershey would do best with an experienced dog owner." Does she show aggression to strangers? "Electra can be picky about her friends." Is he a barker? "This chatty guy. . . ." You get the idea.

Presentation also happens at the adoption events. Many rescue organizations hold these events for a few hours every weekend at their local pet store. They are taxing. To get through them, both you and the dogs will need strength, stamina, some customer service skills, and an ability to cope with boredom. Sort the dogs into their individual crates and line them up along the aisles for passersby to see. Try to organize them in a consumer-friendly fashion. The smalls with the smalls, etc. Put the ones who don't like other dogs or that have trouble with kids in a spot where they and you can see things coming. Be vigilant! Don't let probing fingers come into contact with snapping canines. Prohibit loose dogs from getting close to your lungers. Never leave a person unattended with a dog. Be ready to ask and answer questions as well. Point adopters to pups who suit their lifestyle. But be upfront and honest, and leave the charming to the dogs.

As with everything, each dog will cope with the adoption event in her own way. Damaged dogs like Maggie may shut down and sleep through the whole thing. Eager puppies like Rockne will jabber until someone pays attention to them. Independent fellas like Pauley will bark at browsers out of boredom, or in the hopes of being let out. Fearful dogs like Sugar will tremble and shake and may require extended lap time to calm their nerves. Some dogs, however, thrive at adoption events. Dogs like Rusty.

Rusty has two big advantages when it comes to presentation. First are his eyes, which are a striking shade of yellow. Rusty uses his eyes to good effect. When you meet him he crouches into the downward dog position, wags his tail, and looks up at you—right into your eyes. When humans and dogs make eye contact, they produce oxytocin, a feel-good hormone. Rusty also hugs. Have you ever been hugged by a dog? Wow! Rusty's hugs bear no resemblance to jumping, a doggie behavior that irritates most humans. Instead, he brings you down to his level with his come-hither eyes, and once you are there he paws his way gently up your body, wraps his front legs around your person, and embraces you. It's like being wrapped in a blanket while gazing into two orbs of pure love and light. Think I'm exaggerating?

FIGURE 17.2. Rusty, embracing a volunteer. Photo by Molly Madison Isenbarger.

Last week a woman came to our adoption event worried that her elderly dog was fading away. When Rusty hugged her, she looked at him, burst into tears, held on tight, and asked if she could take him home. It didn't matter that Rusty had heartworm.

Step 4: Matching

A successful presentation like Rusty's will lead to interest and eventually matching. In this step, you must take your reading and response skills and apply them to task of connecting the right pups with the right people. Do not assume that your interested adopters know what they are doing. Find out.

Take Poe, for instance, a beautiful, young Newfoundland mix. Poe is a stunning dog, and she gets a lot of inquiries from people who are captivated by her profile picture. Many of these people, however, don't bother to read her description. Impulse shoppers, you might say. This is a problem because what the photos don't tell you is that Poe came from a hoarding situation where she lived (survived) with 165 other animals, some outside, some inside, and some functionally feral. For the first ten months of her life, a crucial time for dog socialization, Poe was left outside in a cage where she had virtually no contact with humans or animals. She was helpless to the comings and goings of people and animals, never knowing who belonged, who was in charge, who would feed her, or who would hurt her. Poe became wary. Afraid. And even though she has learned many things in foster care, Poe is still pretty rotten at meeting new people and animals. She's reactive. She barks. Children startle her. She's also young and big and needs to run and play.

Matching pups like Poe requires a lot of explanation and a lot of sussing out. Look first at the application forms. Weed out adopters in the market for a canine commodity (that pretty dog) and focus instead on those in search of companion and everything it entails. Finding a forever home means rejecting any applicants who have surrendered a dog because of a move, because of a marriage, or because of some other lifestyle change. If the applicant has pets, look for their vet's contact information. If it's missing, raise your eyebrows. I can't tell you how many animals have been surrendered because of an illness. Remember, Fido is family: She should fit the adopter's lifestyle, but the adopter must be willing to adjust as needed.

Once you get to the point of meeting adopters, ask dog-specific questions. Do they have experience? How about with dogs that don't like people? Do they entertain houseguests, and if so, what is their plan for Poe? Can they keep up with an 80-pound puppy? Can they afford to feed her? Consider arranging a home visit. Look for some infrastructure: a five-foot fence, a large yard, some playmates, and a few quiet corners for her to feel safe in. Solicit some character references. Read the people and their situation against your dog. Look at how they interact, too; search for smiles, careful movements, kind words, flattened ears, a lax tail, an exposed belly.

Here's a tip: If a good adopter comes to see a specific dog but it's a bad match, don't let him get away! Rack your brain for other possibilities. Poe doesn't like new people, but Rusty adores them, so make an introduction. If they want a younger dog, consider Rockne. A Newfie? Find out who's got one. Mobilize your network. Put out a call on Facebook. Customize their canine. They'll thank you for it and come back for more. Hey, maybe they'll even volunteer to help.

Suggested Readings

On companion and (non-companion) dogs, see:

Raymond Coppinger and Lorna Coppinger. 2016. *What Is a Dog?* Chicago: University of Chicago Press.

Donna Haraway. 2007. *When Species Meet.* Minneapolis: University of Minnesota Press.

Elizabeth Marshall Thomas. 2010. *The Hidden Life of Dogs.* New York: Mariner Books.

On interspecies sociality and the question of reading and responding, see:

Jacques Derrida. 2008. *The Animal That Therefore I Am.* New York: Fordham University Press.

Vinciane Despret. 2004. "The Body We Care For: Figures of Anthropo-Zoo-Genesis." *Body and Society* 10: 111–34.

Paul Nadasdy. 2007. "The Gift in the Animal: The Ontology of Hunting and Human-Animal Sociality." *American Ethnologist* 34: 25–43.

On rescue work and training, see:

Janet Alger and Steven Alger. 2002. *Cat Culture: The Social World of a Cat Shelter.* Philadelphia: Temple University Press.

Vikk Simmons. 2014. *Bonding with Your Rescue Dog: Decoding and Influencing Dog Behavior.* Houston: Ordinary Matters Publishing.

Sophia Yin. 2010. *How to Behave So Your Dog Behaves.* Neptune City, NJ: TFH Publications.

CHAPTER 18

How to Care for a Park with Birds

Birdwatchers' Ecologies in Buenos Aires

Nicholas D'Avella

The following text is written as a letter from an anthropologist (me) to an urban activist from another country, who has written asking for advice on how to protect a neglected park in her home city under threat of private development. Graciela had been told that I have close knowledge about organizations working in defense of the Parque 3 de Febrero, one of Buenos Aires' largest and most well-known parks, and that I might be able to offer a useful perspective on how to protect the park in her home city. In the letter I write to Graciela, I describe a particular episode from my fieldwork and use it as a springboard to discuss how to think about her park as a more-than-natural ecology that exists at the crossroads of plant and animal life, the people who care about them, and the commodification of urban space.

Dear Graciela,

I hope this letter finds you well. I'm not sure how much I have to tell you that will be useful to you—particular situations vary, and I don't have a lot of information about what's going on in your home city. But I can tell you a story about my experience with the Parque 3 de Febrero in Buenos Aires, a story that I think can help us rethink what a park is, and how thinking of parks in these terms might help protect them. My thoughts here come from time I spent with a group called *queremos buenos aires*, a federation of organizations dedicated to issues surrounding the urban environment in Buenos Aires. Several members of queremos buenos aires were also members of other groups, including Asociación Amigos del Lago de Palermo, or Friends of Palermo Lake (one of the large lakes in the Parque 3 de Febrero), and various birdwatching groups in Buenos Aires. Their stories overlap, and it's this overlap I want to tell you about.

On one level, the story of the Parque 3 de Febrero is a story about a group of people who were concerned about public space and wanted to work to keep that public space both well cared for and out of the hands of private interests who wanted to exploit the park to for-profit ends. In this sense, the story of the park has helped me think about the commodification of urban space—the ways that monetary value can encroach upon other ways we value urban life. In my time with queremos buenos aires and the Amigos del Lago, I learned how real estate developers try to claim public land for their private interests—and even about how the city government can be involved with those efforts. In this sense, the work of these organizations is about how a group of people can make more collective forms of value endure in the city in the face of private exploitation of public land. They showed me that it was possible for city residents to band together to prevent the city from turning into one big real estate development scheme.

But if I were to tell the story in this way, it would center on humans, and humans weren't the only ones involved in this struggle. Birds and their environments were also critical actors in saving the park. Through the story I'm going to tell you, I want to suggest that other actors—including nonhumans—might be enrolled in your own efforts to care for the park in your city. Though birds were never front and center in the way that people talked to me about their efforts to defend the Parque 3 de Febrero, as I think back on my time in Buenos Aires I wonder if they weren't actually a pivotal part of the political work that queremos buenos aires and the Amigos del Lago undertook against the commodification of urban space.

I imagine that you might be skeptical about birds as defenders of public parks as you read this! Indeed, sometimes when I tell people that birds are central to urban politics, they respond with the kind of laugh that people laugh when they think something isn't important. But I think birds are more important than they may seem, and I want to make the case to you that birds can be an important part of the politics of public space.

Thinking about birds and the urban ecologies in which they lived was important to members of queremos buenos aires, many of whom considered themselves environmentalists—the name "queremos buenos aires" itself plays with the slippage in Spanish between "we care about Buenos Aires" and the more literal "we want good airs." One thing I learned from the members of queremos buenos aires was the value of thinking about the ecology of the park in a very broad sense—one that contains water, fish, plants, and birds, together with private real estate developers and the (oftentimes shady) institutions in the city government that are responsible for legislating what happens in the park. In the course of their efforts, they expanded their own ideas about the ecology of the park, and I think that hearing this story might encourage you to do the same. I hope an extended example about birds and birdwatchers—and the digital, institutional, and green ecologies they inhabit—can help you and your colleagues deepen your attention to private property and the trouble with ownership and privatization in your own park.

But first, a word about my use of the word *ecology*, since I'm not sure it's what you're used to. In a lot of common usage, *ecology* is a word used to talk about capital-N Nature: a part of the world thought to be untouched by humans. Ecologies, in this sense, are thought to be natural spaces, even if at times they are disturbed by humans. Many of the scholars I've read in my time studying anthropology would critique this idea, however. The idea of a pure nature is itself, they explain, a complicated thing—the product of a way of thinking that arose in a certain time and place (the modern West) in which humans seek to differentiate themselves from the rest of the world: human culture on one side, nature on the other.

While the idea of a pure nature outside of human intervention might at times be useful for supporting conservation efforts, for bird lovers in Buenos Aires, and I think for defenders of parks in other places (like you), it seems important to recognize a different kind of ecology. In part this means rethinking the city as a place that is not opposed to nature, but is instead a place of cohabitation: an ecology itself, in which humans live with animals. Etymologically, the word *ecology* derives from the Greek *oikos*, which my dictionary translates as "house." Perhaps thinking of ecology in this way—a question of where birds dwell—might be a useful way to put a bit of distance between birds' ecology and capital-N Nature. Because in Buenos Aires, birds don't live in "Nature," they live in the city—a city that is also populated by humans. When I talk about birds' ecology, then, I don't just mean birds in all their feathery, wetland-inhabiting glory. I also mean birds as they live in zones of cohabitation with humans. Paying attention to the ecologies in which birds exist in this way helps us stay close to the fact that birds and humans are not separate but live in relation with one another.

I suspect that thinking of your park as an ecology in this sense might be helpful for saving your own park. Does this sound strange to you? Let's see what you think.

Caring for a Park . . .

I want to start by telling you a story from the early days of Amigos del Lago, one of the organizations that was part of queremos buenos aires. I like the story because it shows how concern for the lake helped humans amplify their attention to the urban environment—an attention that included the lake, plants, fish, and birds but also drew in real estate development and urban politics. The story was told to me by Osvaldo, a longtime member of both queremos buenos aires and Amigos del Lago.

It was the late 1980s, and Osvaldo, an avid jogger, used to jog around the lake in the Parque 3 de Febrero. One of the largest and well-known green spaces in the city, the park is known today for its rose garden, its Japanese garden, its man-made lakes, and other amenities typical of the early-twentieth-century French-inspired park design common in Buenos Aires. Back then, however, the park was in a state of disrepair. The state of the Lago de Regatas, or Regatta Lake, was of particular concern. It stank, and trash floated alongside the bodies of dead fish. The grass was not maintained, and cars parked on it all the way up to the lakeshore.

One day, Osvaldo encountered two men who were collecting signatures on a petition to improve the conditions of the park and stopped to talk to them. Over the following months, they formed the group called Amigos del Lago de Palermo. The group continued gathering signatures from park visitors, with demands that Osvaldo described to me twenty years later as primitive: to cut the grass and put some garbage cans around the lake to help control the litter.

But the Amigos also began to look more closely into the smelly, trash-ridden lake. Dug in 1906, it had become home to an unsustainably high population of *Elodea densa* and *Ceratophyllum demersum*, water plants designated invasive in many U.S. states today. Specialists diagnosed a process of rapid eutrophication—the overnourishment of certain plant species—induced by fertilizer runoff. High plant concentrations lead to hypoxia, a lack of oxygen in the water, which, together with other effects like the paucity of sunlight penetrating the vegetative mass, had created an environment that was inhospitable for aquatic fauna. The lack of fish and the quality of the water and the plant life made bird life scarce, too. In other words, the dead fish, the stink, and the lack of birds were related to fertilizer runoff.

At least that's how things appeared at first. But the story went deeper, pulling into the ecology questions of real estate and private development in the park. It turned out that the eutrophication was the result of more than a generalized runoff of fertilizer into the lake. In the southern point of the lake, a drainage pipe was channeling sewage into the lake from two

FIGURE 18.1.   Amigos hug the Lago de Regatas, 1990. Photo courtesy of the Asociación Amigos del Lago de Palermo.

private athletic clubs: the Club Gimnasia y Esgrima and the Club de Caza Mayor. When Osvaldo told me this story, he described this as a critical moment of recognition for the group, in which their attention began to shift and they began to transform their practice of noticing to encompass the private, for-profit developments that were in the park. The Amigos began to think of the lake not just as an isolated entity or as part of a natural environment but as connected to human institutions like the dynamics of private property.

The Amigos took a variety of actions to try to address the lack of care for the lake and the park around it. They wrote letters to government functionaries and to the newspapers. They also organized public acts like an *abrazo al lago*—a giant collective embrace of the lake, calling in all the people they could to gather around the lake holding hands (see figures 18.1 and 18.2). The hug helped draw attention to private development's encroachments onto the public park: "At the time," he told me, "we couldn't actually hug the entire lake. There was a concessionary who had put up a fence, claiming a bit of the lakeshore for themselves. So the hug stopped at that fence." I see the hug as an expression of care but also as a way to channel physical bodies in a space, bringing the Amigos together around a smelly lake and up against a fence making a private land grab in a public park.

The hug and the letters began to gather media attention, building interest in and attention to the lake and its ecology. As a result of the media attention, people began to approach the Amigos with rumors that the lack of care for

FIGURE 18.2. Amigos hug the Lago de Regatas, 1990. Photo courtesy of the Asociación Amigos del Lago de Palermo.

the lake and the park had much deeper roots, implying much more formidable (if less obvious) adversaries than uncut grass and uncollected trash, or even the private athletic clubs. The rumor was that there was a project in works by the government to place half of the park in private concession. "The lake was going to be converted into a motorboat racetrack," Osvaldo told me, "and they were going to build a five-star hotel on one of the plazas of the park. All around the lake, they were going to build stadium seating and food stalls to service the motorboat races that were supposed to happen there. On the islands, which today are avian reserves, they were going to install the sound and illumination towers for the boat races."

That wasn't all. There was to be a shopping plaza, too. The municipal golf course would become part of the hotel as well: sixty hectares of public green space dedicated to private commercial ends. A letter the Amigos wrote to the editor of a major newspaper inquiring about the city's intentions for the park received no official response, but the rumors were confirmed when they received, through unofficial channels, a copy of a draft of the call for proposals for the redevelopment of the park.

As these plans came into view, the lake's state of neglect was cast in a different light. Hardly benign, it instead came to be seen as an active decision, part of a larger and more nefarious plan laying the groundwork for the eventual privatization of the park. If the park were ill cared for, if no one used it, then the case for privatizing it would be that much easier to make.

The Amigos then began to denounce the plan publicly, through a petition that garnered eleven thousand signatures; the news coverage generated enough of a public scandal that the proposal was never put into effect. "We beat the government at a time when the entire country was being privatized," Osvaldo told me. "This was a time when everything started to become private. But because of our efforts, the park didn't enter into concession, the five-star hotel was not built, and the planetarium and the botanical gardens remained public."

As time went on, other cases of land grabs in the park were uncovered, mostly from the private athletic clubs around the park, which had built parking lots, tennis courts, and food concessions on park lands, totaling nearly ten hectares of park space. All of these projects are prohibited under the urban planning code. Discovering each of them depended on the difficult task of compiling plans, decrees, and concessionary documents, work that was often done through the assistance of discreet contacts in the city government. (Work to get the clubs off public land continues today.)

Meanwhile, the Amigos continued to care for and enjoy the park and the lake. In 1994, they began to enlist the assistance of various state institutions to address the lake's troubled ecosystem. Two-thirds of the plant biomass was removed, leaving the remainder to compete with the phytoplankton that greens the water, providing food and habitat for various aquatic fauna. Trash and other solid waste were also removed. A spillway was constructed to bring in fresh water, and the sewage pipe from the clubs was removed.

Animal life began to return to the lake as a result of these efforts. While only three species of avian fauna were present before these interventions, thirty-four began to inhabit the lake, including the rare anhinga, which primarily feeds on chanchitas, one of the many species of fish that were able to reinhabit the lake. The Amigos also noted the presence of the Macá Grande, which nests on floating vegetation near the lakeshore, returning annually to the same nesting place. Tracking these species was enjoyable for the Amigos, and also served to mark their progress cleaning up the lake.

I see the Amigos del Lago as part of what environmentalism might mean in an urban ecology. The lake—and its plants and animals—could not, for the Amigos, be thought about or acted upon as pure Nature. Instead, they had to be considered through their relationship with the dynamics of private property in the park. It wasn't just about water, plants, and animals but also about real estate development, property law, and urban planning. The lake's plants and animals were not incidental to this project of recuperation, but instead provided ongoing objects of care as well as barometers for the effectiveness of that care. The lake thus provided a crucial linking point between plant and animal life and issues of commodification of space relevant to humans as well as to nonhumans.

. . . with Birds!

Now, Graciela, I want to take you back to a memorable encounter I had with a group of swans to deepen the way we think about urban ecologies as zones of cohabitation between humans and birds. I first learned about the swans in an email that Osvaldo sent to the listserv of queremos buenos aires in 2009. It was a message that seemed very simple. It was titled "black-necked swans in Regatta Lake," and the text read: "In the Parque 3 de Febrero, one could enjoy this show without paying admission. These photos were taken on Sunday, June 25, 2009." The message was followed by a dozen pictures of a group of black-necked swans swimming in the lake.

My first instinct was to look at the pictures of swans and move on to things that seemed more important. But the message also gave me pause, in part because it came from Osvaldo—someone I knew well and considered to be a pragmatic, politically minded organizer. The fact that the swan email came from Osvaldo helped me take more seriously the avian attachments of others in the group. For Osvaldo was not the only one involved in urban politics with a passion for birds: When I went to track down his message recently, my keyword search for *aves* (birds) on the listserv came back with five hundred and eighty-nine hits! Birds weren't a focus of my research, but because of this email I began to see them as a key part of a network that I learned to think about differently, in a way that included them within broader practices of the organizations I was working with.

Let's start from the listserv and work our way out, as a way of tracing connections to think about the unique ecology of the black-necked swans Osvaldo wrote about in his email. One way birds made regular appearances on the listserv was through invitations to attend birdwatching outings that were sent out by birdwatching clubs called Clubes de Observadores de Aves (COAs). The messages themselves were typically simple: "Signup is open for an observation trip. Saturday May 19, 9 a.m. COA Caburé and COA RECS, together! Veterinary School, 280 Chorroarín Ave. Meeting place: the flagpole at the entrance." But the simplicity of the invitation belies a more complex ecology that the COAs inhabited—and helped create for birds—in Buenos Aires.

Birdwatchers must have practiced their craft informally in Buenos Aires until recently, when, beginning in the mid-2000s, several COAs were formally founded in neighborhoods in and around Buenos Aires. COAs themselves exist in a far-flung institutional ecology of national and international bird organizations. In Argentina, they are subgroups of the national organization Aves Argentinas, which is in turn affiliated with Birdlife International, an association of avian conservation organizations that can be traced back to the 1920s. The birds that arrived in my inbox were as much a part of this layered institutional ecology as they were inhabitants of the lakes and foliage of Buenos Aires. So you see, Graciela, we already have a complicated ecology in which birds and the humans that care for them telescope out from neighborhoods to international organizations.

If we take a closer look at the practice of birdwatching, we can see that—despite the implications of the name—birdwatching involves much more than watching! On the one hand, it involves physically exploring parts of the city where birds live, a practice that is physically embodied and lush with organic contact—and, I bet, quite a lot of bug spray! But such organic connection doesn't happen alone. Rather, it happens within a highly mediated set of practices that are infused with data-driven, archival passions. Let me explain.

To begin with, many birders are also passionate photo geeks. They are not just interested in seeing birds, they also want to take their pictures. Some go out with simple point-and-shoot cameras (like Osvaldo and his pictures of the swans), while others invest in high-end equipment and expensive telephoto lenses. The website of CoaRECS hosts many images of birds seen in the Ecological Reserve of the Costanera Sur, archiving not only the image but also the bird's species name, its common name, the date of the photo, the name of the photographer, and technical information about the photo, including the kind of camera used, the ISO speed, the aperture, and the exposure time. So we also have a place for digital technology in the ecology we're describing, in the cameras and the images photographers upload.

But the archive that birders produce doesn't stop there. Indeed, many of the invitations to go birding were made with the explicit purpose of gathering data for census work aimed at producing knowledge about the number and kinds of birds that inhabit specific areas. CoaRECS, for example, has conducted twenty-one censuses to date in the reserve. They divide the reserve into sectors and record which species were spotted during each census. Visitors to their website can view the results in a variety of charts that list the birds by common name, scientific name, and family as well as the number of times they were seen. Through the work of the COAs, birds are made to inhabit these charts, refracted through the birders' ethos of data collection and compilation. As the website of CoaRECS explains, in addition to organizing field excursions and giving talks in schools and communities, COAs register species in eBird, a database launched by the Cornell Ornithology Lab and the U.S. National Audubon Society. The work of birders, therefore, in part involves translating birds' organic and feathery appearance into forms of data that can inhabit digital archives. So the birds' and birders' ecology are not just organic (people walking through reserves, in contact with birds) but also institutional (the COAs, Aves Argentinas, the Ornithology Lab, the Audubon Society), as well as digital (the database, the photos, the website).

But the ecology gets even more complicated as we continue to trace the connections. It turns out that the work that birders do is not strictly an instance of human attention to and representation of the avian world. Instead, birders are interested in the various other beings with which birds cohabit in their ecology. To some degree, this means other nonhumans. The website of Aves Argentinas, for example, states that "birds have shown to be effective *indicators of biodiversity*. For this reason, more than twenty years ago the program of Areas Important for the Conservation of Birds (AICAs) arose to protect particular sites of importance recognized by BirdLife and their national affiliates." The protection of these sites, the website continues, could help assure "the survival of a large number of other species of animals and plants." Here, we begin to see that human attention to birds is not directed at birds alone, but birds as part of a broader ecology that includes other species of animals and plants (the biodiversity protected by the AICAs). Birds, in this sense, are not just beings that are observed by birders. Instead, the idea that birds are effective indicators of biodiversity means that birds are not just beings-in-themselves but also *indicators*: They help train attention to the relational webs that are around them and are connected to them. The place of birds, entangled in this ecology, is a way to guide attention: to indicate.

But, as I see it, birds aren't just good indicators of life of other nonhuman species; they can also work as good indicators about human life. As I've already suggested to you, in Buenos Aires, attention to birds' ecologies extends beyond capital-N Nature. This was one lesson from the story about the lake hug and the attention that the polluted lake helped to draw to the plan to redevelop the park as a five-star hotel complex and motorboat racetrack. Here, there's something similar going on. Because birds live in the city, attending to birds' environments means attending to environments shared with humans. Birding organizations in Buenos Aires know this. Take, for example, the mission statement of COA Taguató, which states that their objective is to "help urbanites get to know the birds that surround them, the environments they inhabit, and the conservation problems they face." For this reason, they "don't only observe birds, but *also the anthropic and natural environment*" (*anthropic* means related to human beings). Here, we see that

COAs are interested in more than birds; they also want to know more about how birds and humans relate to one another. It is in this attention that I see the opening for a space of collaboration between the kind of work done by COAs and the work done by other groups, like Amigos del Lago, that are less obviously avian-focused. COAs pay attention to birds, yes. But they are also important nodes through which to bridge environmental politics with the politics of public space. Let me explain.

I mentioned earlier that COAs are based in particular neighborhoods in and around Buenos Aires. There is one dedicated to the ecological reserve bordering Puerto Madero, another in the neighborhoods of Saavedra and Núñez, another in Palermo, still another in Agronomía. This neighborhood specificity serves to connect people's interest in birds with specific urban places: The COA in Saavedra pays attention not only to birds but also to the neighborhood in which they live. In this sense, neighborhood residents aren't just people—they are also birds. Birds' environments and people's environments are drawn together through the neighborhood.

Birdwatching is thus an activity that draws attention to the cohabitation of birds and people in neighborhoods, helping to create shared geographical spaces of ecological commitment and binding concern for bird life and neighborhood life together. Paying attention to birds is a way of attuning to urban ecologies that are always more than capital-N Natural, helping to change the way that people pay attention to urban environments. Indeed, today there is a high level of overlap in the membership and political actions of the COAs and queremos buenos aires and Amigos del Lago. When the city proposed to build a helicopter landing pad near the ecological reserve of the Costanera Sur, CoaRECS was one of the first to sound the alarm about the disturbance it would create for local birds, and queremos buenos aires got involved as well, leveraging a network of organizations in opposition to the construction of the landing pad.

So you see, Graciela, through the efforts of COAs, birds remain central players in a struggle that includes property, real estate, and development. Human actions, like birdwatching expeditions, photography, and avian census-taking are ways of creating shared zones of attention to urban ecologies' pasts and futures, helping to bring to light exceptional and endemic threats to them. They mark the space as a part of ongoing histories of relationality, creating an eventful presence around what could otherwise be thought of as a passive backdrop.

Today, the lake in the Parque 3 de Febrero is a living monument to a future that almost was: The image of the privatized park that hovered at the edge of possibility in the 1990s became firmly installed in the consciousness of the lake's friends. The pictures of the swans Osvaldo sent to the group helped memorialize this history and draw it together with birds' ecology: Osvaldo's comment about the swans providing a show that could be enjoyed "without paying admission" was a wink at the motorboat racetrack, the private athletic clubs, and other efforts at privatizing the lake and its environs that he and other members of the Amigos del Lago prevented from becoming reality. It is within ongoing practices of care for plants, green space in parks, and urban fauna (like the swans) that they heightened their sensitivity to the dark side of the market in urban construction.

So for me, the hug of the lake many years ago and today's birdwatching practices are ways of building a space of political concern, attention, and investment in urban ecologies. They are ecology-making projects, oriented toward a relational space in which urban residents and their organizations incorporate not only the lake and its fauna but also the incursions of private interests and their profitable schemes and toxic discharges. The pictures of swans sit within and help extend ecological attention as part of this practice of care for the lake and the urban ecology in which it exists.

So, one answer to your question about how to save the park in your city might be "Watch birds!" Maybe it's a deceptively simple answer, one that requires an exploded idea of what the practice of watching means and the broad and sprawling ways we can think about birds and their ecologies. I hope that thinking about the park as an ecology in this way can be helpful to you in working to defend your park. I wish you good luck in finding allies—both human and nonhuman—that might be enrolled in your fight.

Saludos, y un abrazo,

Nico

Suggested Readings

On urban ecologies, see

Timothy Choy. 2012. *Ecologies of Comparison: An Ethnography of Endangerment in Hong Kong*. Durham, NC: Duke University Press.

Steve Hinchcliffe and Sarah Whatmore. 2006. "Living Cities: Towards a Politics of Conviviality." *Science as Culture* 15(2): 123–38.

Alex Nading. 2014. *Mosquito Trails: Ecology, Health, and the Politics of Entanglement*. Berkeley: University of California Press.

Melissa Poe, Joyce LeCompte, Rebecca McLain, and Patrick Hurley. 2014. "Urban Foraging and the Relational Ecologies of Belonging." *Social and Cultural Geography* 15(8): 901–19.

On practices and ecologies, see:

Isabelle Stenger. 2005. "Introductory Notes on an Ecology of Practices." *Cultural Studies Review* 11(1): 183–96.

On Nature and its production, see:

Donna Haraway. 1989. *Primate Visions: Gender, Race, and Nature in the World of Modern Science.* New York: Routledge.

Paper Tiger Television Collective. 1987. "Donna Haraway Reads the National Geographies of Primates." New York: Paper Tiger Television. https://www.youtube.com/watch?v=eLN2ToEIlwM.

On translating animal lives, see:

Vinciane Despret. 2016. *What Would Animals Say If We Asked Them the Right Questions?* Translated by Brett Buchanan. Minneapolis: University of Minnesota Press.

On dialogue, social scientists, and ethnography, see:

Helen Verran and Michael Christie. 2011. "Doing Difference Together: Towards a Dialogue with Aboriginal Knowledge Authorities through an Australian Comparative Empirical Philosophical Inquiry." *Culture and Dialogue* 1(2): 21–36.

CHAPTER 19

Introducing Zoo Gorillas

Christena Nippert-Eng

Gorillas are highly social beings. Family troops of western lowland gorillas (the only subspecies living in zoos) consist of one adult male—the silverback—and three to five adult females—a harem—along with the females' immature offspring. In the wild, gorillas get to choose with whom they live. Family troops can be highly dynamic, with females free to convince a silverback to let them join up or to vote with their feet if they do not wish to stay with him. In zoos, however, people play the role of matchmaker and place gorillas into family units by transferring individuals between families and, sometimes, zoos. Zoo gorillas have to go where they are sent, and they have to stay there until people decide otherwise.

The process of introducing a new zoo gorilla to an existing troop is a delicate and sometimes dangerous one, as it is not unusual for the newcomer to be subjected to a fair amount of violence until accepted by the existing troop members. In accredited North American zoos, the first phase of a gorilla introduction requires that keepers quarantine the newcomer for at least one month, to prevent transmission of undetected illness. In the second phase, people may allow the recent arrival to occupy the family troop quarters, alone, in order to get used to the space, keeping the existing (curious and probably increasingly frustrated) troop members elsewhere. By now, existing family members can usually hear and smell the newcomer but may not yet have seen her or him. During these first two phases, keepers may be especially attentive, providing the new arrival with favorite foods and encouragement, in order to help smooth the transition. The third phase of the process typically consists of the visual introduction. At this point, frequently separated by a triple-reinforced glass window, the keepers allow the existing troop members and the newcomer to see each other. After a few days, when the keepers think that everyone has settled down and are used to each other's presence, they may decide to start on the fourth phase. At this point, the newcomer is typically allowed to visit with an existing troop member (sometimes more than one) through a mesh, or fenced, wall. There may even be a small part of the habitat designed for this, called a "Howdy." The Howdy prevents full contact between the gorillas on either side but allows them to become acquainted with each other using all their senses. Gorillas can be quite physical with each other, especially during introductions. The Howdy can serve an incredibly important function, then, prior to the fifth and riskiest phase—that of full, unmediated contact between the newcomer and the existing troop.

When the transferred gorilla is an adult female meant to join a silverback's existing harem, keepers hope that a current troop female will show special interest in befriending the newcomer. This is typically the lowest-status female in the current troop, who is most motivated to seek the possibilities of friendship and alliance with the newcomer. It is vital that someone in the troop helps support the new arrival in the months to come, both emotionally and physically. If all goes well, an existing female troop member will show just such an interest in the newcomer during the third (visual) and fourth (Howdy) phases of the introduction. In that case, keepers may then allow just the newcomer and the welcoming female to have the main part of the habitat to themselves, allowing them (and only them) to have full, unmediated physical contact with each other in the space that they will soon share with the rest of the family. This allows the two females to bond further without threat or distraction, and increases the chances for a successful, complete introduction for everyone. This fictional piece takes place at just such a moment.

Oh my gosh, finally—*finally*—they let me back in. This is so nice. You okay? Watch your head there. You're kind of tall, and these little metal doors can leave quite a bump. I hope you haven't figured that out the hard way. It looks like they're keeping the rest of the group downstairs right now, so I think we have the place to ourselves. Which is really nice.

Come on out, don't be shy. I'll show you around—give you the personal tour. Oh, look! Pumpkin! How is it that you've been getting pumpkin all this time? That's a real treat here. We don't get it very often—only when it starts to turn cold. It's delicious, isn't it? Just give me a minute to finish this up, and

FIGURE 19.1. "Visual Introduction." From the outside yard, a young troop member gets his first look at the newcomer who has been selected to join his family. The adult female sits inside, separated from the juvenile and the rest of his family by a triple layer of safety glass. Photo by John Dominski.

then you can have some, if you want. No? Okay. Well, let's take a walk, then, and I'll show you what's what.

Have you had a good look around while you've been in here by yourself? Most of the time when I've seen you, you've just been sitting either here or over there in that doorway. Hey! Kale! We've got kale today. Usually the Big Guy takes it all. And it's still really crisp. So good. I'm looking for celery, too. I like to eat them together. Go ahead, you can take the rest of that if you want, I'm done.

Holy cow, remember the time I was outside, by that corner of the window, and you were in here, sitting right there? We were having such a nice visit. And you were so sweet, and so scared, and we were having such a nice, quiet time, through the glass. Then BLAMMO!! The Queen Bee herself appears, charges straight across the grass and body-slams the window *right* where you were sitting! She actually knocked me over trying to get at you. Ha! I didn't know she could actually move that fast anymore. She scared the shit out of you—literally, as I remember. But at least *you* were inside! I was *out*side, right next to her! I thought for sure I was gonna get it, just because she couldn't get to you.

You know, when they put me in here, it was just me and the Big Guy at first. I didn't have anyone to be my friend. No one had my back, you know. You don't know how lucky you are. It was just the Big Guy, her, and the kid back then. We've got that other female you've seen now, too, but she came later. But back then, actually, thank goodness I got to meet him alone, first. *He's* fine. Guy's kind of an idiot, actually. He can be really sweet, but he's kind of clueless, you know? Actually, he doesn't really have what it takes. No confidence, really. Previous guy I was with? The kind you never want to leave. You know? Never overreacted, everything easy, you could have a lot of fun because he was totally in charge and knew what he was doing. Not this one. I don't think he really knows what matters. *She* goads him into all kinds of crap. He and I were fine together. Then they let *her* in. She really let me have it. I'm like, screaming, curled up, trying to make myself as small as I can. You know? I'm like, *Okay, okay, I get it! You're it! Number One! No problem! No contest!* Next thing I know, I wake up downstairs with this huge gash across my head and there's, like, this hard string and these tiny bumps all over it. I could stick my finger up to here in the four holes she left in me with those nasty teeth of hers. Felt like I'd been beaten up by at least a gang of three. The people were all being really nice to me. But then they're like, *Time's up—back in you go!* I'm like, *No way—you go in there!* And then when I finally did, you know, the Big Guy wouldn't even look at me. No kidding. Thanks for *nothing*, you big jerk. And the whole time she's sauntering around: *La-dee-da-dee-da. Look at me. Look at my kid. I'm number one.* You'll see. And the minute he even *thinks* about not doing what she wants, she grabs that kid and gets all *Don't forget who's who around here. I'm the mother of your son* on him. He's all googly-eyes at me whenever she's not looking. The moment she pays attention? He's like, *I hate you! You better know your place! Don't even think about doing* anything *unless I say so!* No spine. At all. I don't get it. Anyway, believe me, she's the one running the show. It's not going to be pretty when they let her in. But you'll meet him first—if it's like it was with me—and if they let me stay with you, it'll be two against one, if we need to. And we will, once they let the mom and the kid in here. Then we'll have to join forces for sure. You can't count on him for anything around her.

Here, this is one of my favorite corners. If it gets too warm for you, this is one of the best spots. Nice and cool. You do *not* want to be here when it gets cold out, though. I have a couple favorite spots. Of course, if I want them, they're mine—well, unless she wants them. Or if he does. But if I'm busy or off somewhere else, you should try to get them. I can try to hold on to them for you and let you at least step in when I leave, but you never know how long that will last.

Especially if that little brat comes over. The kid. Or should I say His Highness, the Royal Crown Prince, himself? Probably not a bad kid at heart, but no boundaries. At all. Between his mom and the Big Guy, that kid gets whatever he wants. Do *not* go near him. When—not if—he comes near you and gets in your face—don't look so shocked, I'm not kidding. He will probably even try to take your food. When he does this, just freeze. Don't move, don't even give him a look. You do, and one of his parents will be all over you. I swear—I'm this close to letting him have it. It would be worth it. Someone's got to teach this kid some manners. When he leaves this group, he's going to be in big trouble if they don't start to rein him in. No way any normal gorilla is going to let him behave like that. Well, it takes a troop. A little more time in this place, and I'll be in a good position to insist on a few changes around here, including a little respect from that kid. He's not a baby anymore, it's really just unbelievable. Just watch out for him, okay? Fastest way to a bite and some serious bruises is to just look the wrong way at that kid.

One more piece of advice. That other female you've seen with us, the one who came in after me? Ambition is her middle name. Right now, I'm on top of her. Of course, I hope to keep climbing, myself. I'd love to put that mom in her place one day. But the other one? She's at the bottom right now, and she's going to make sure you take her place. Nothing you can do about it. Between her and all the others, they're going to make sure you're at the bottom of the ladder. I'm sure you know that. But I hope you also know that our best bet is if the three of us stick together. She's a little cranky and keeps mostly to herself, except when she's trying to flirt her way past me. That can be super annoying. But we all have to work together around here. No problem taking on the Big Guy that way. Honestly, if you're ever in a fight, she's the one you want on your side. I'm not kidding. Male, female—this is the one. Hit first and ask questions later, that's her motto. Make sure she's on your side. Give her first pick of everything, get out of her way, all the usual things. If you're feeling brave, you can even try bringing her an occasional treat. Not that that's easy. She's a hoarder, that one. If there's a couple piles of biscuits meant for all of us to share, she'll sneak off to one, stuff her mouth full of them, grab as many as she can carry, and walk on two feet to find a place to sit and gorge herself. It's hard to bring someone a gift when they've already helped themselves to just about everything. Know what I mean?

This is a really great place right here, too. Feel that? Look up. That warm air comes down right here. If you're feeling a little chilly after you come in, this is a great place to warm up. You can see just about everything from here, too, which I like. You don't look like you like the outside much, but maybe you'll change your mind. It can be really nice out there, especially if you want to get away from the family for a bit. He wouldn't let me go out without him for a while, but now he hardly ever stops me. You'll just have to play it by ear, like I did.

One time, I went out—just listen to this, it'll tell you what kind of a kid I'm talking about here. One time, I'm out there, and I'm just minding my own business. Everyone else is inside. Beautiful, cool, sunny day. I was out there for a while, climbing up the fence, getting some of those really tender leaves on top. Nice, right? Then, I start to come back in. All of a sudden, I see the Big Guy starting to head out. He's looking right at me, through the door. He wants to do it. Again. He wanted to do it with me, like, all the time back then—way more than those other two. Anytime—and any*where!* That other guy I was with, before? Strictly nighttime, under the ledge, and quiet as a mouse. This one? Broad daylight, middle of the yard, tons of those outside people watching, laughing, flashing those lights at us. Not that either way is necessarily better than the other. I'm just saying. Be ready to assume the position, anytime, anywhere with this one. So, anyway, there I am outside, minding my own business, and he gets that look, just as I'm about to come back inside. But I'm not in the mood, you know? So I back up, into the yard, and figure I'll just head to the other door. You know, maybe he's not interested enough and will change his mind if I go in the other way. Ha! No. The kid sees what's going on and decides he's going to be daddy's *wing*man! He heads straight for the second door, and sits right down, on the threshold. So *now* what am I going to do? Can't go near the kid, I'll get in trouble. I don't want to go near the dad right now either, though. And I don't want to make a big deal out of it. I'd rather just avoid the issue and go my own way. So I back up and figure I'll just go farther out into the yard and wait a while before I try again. But *then,* the dad starts heading toward me . . . and so does the kid! Now I'm trapped. I've got that little creek and all those logs behind me, the dad on one side—and his miniature highness on the other. So, of course, we wound up doing it again, out there, with the kid—and even his mother—watching us the whole time.

I'm telling you, that kid is something else.

Well, at least they all know by now that the Big Guy is kind of crazy about me. I don't know why, but I count myself lucky in that way, at least. I'm really not interested in him. He wouldn't be my first pick if it were up to me. But it's not, is it? It's not up to you, either. I'm not saying he isn't good-looking, because he is. All I'm saying is, if you're going to lead the troop, then lead the troop. Don't let *her* do it and just pretend you're in charge.

Mostly, I just can't stand that kid right now. *Or* the mom.

How are you at climbing, by the way? I hope you're good at it. Not everyone is when they first get here. You know, you'll be expected to go up. I know you've had the place to yourself for a while now, and every time I've seen you, you've been on the ground. I know, the food's all down here, why go up if you don't have to? But you see how high this place is? And you see those giant wood nesty things on the walls up there? That's for the likes of us. The farther down the hierarchy, the higher up we're expected to go. The mom and the kid get the hammocks, usually that one, right next to the Big Guy's favorite spot, which will be there, you'll see. The rest of us go up. It's good for privacy—except from the kid, of course. He'll just come up and sit right in your space whenever he feels like it. It's outrageous, but honestly, he just doesn't know any better. He's kind of lonely, I think. The mom won't even let the people talk to him—she smacks the fence and makes them stay away, too, whenever they try to play with him even a little bit. Anyway, once you get the hang of it, it's no trouble to carry wood wool and sheets and cardboard up there and make a nice cushy spot for yourself. Of course, the Big Guy will only let you down on the ground if he feels like it. He won't starve you, but he'll make sure everyone else gets to have a go at the good stuff first, and only then will you be allowed down for whatever's left. He's just making a point. I pretty much spent my first couple weeks up there, watching what's going on. That ledge on the right up there is my favorite. It isn't the most comfortable, but it has the best view of the outside. You can see everything—the whole city plus everything going on in the yard and beyond, where the people walk around.

There are a lot of smaller animals that are allowed to go anywhere they want out there, too. When I lived at the other end of the building, with that other guy, he was so funny when it came to those outside animals. They were like his little buddies. One day, he was sitting in the yard, eating lettuce and carrots, and on one side, right next to his big, massive leg, was this little rabbit, and right next to him on the other side was a mama duck. The three of them just sat there together, munching away, soaking up the sun, having a little visit together.

By the way, a word of warning. I don't know if you've ever seen chimps before. That's those guys, right over there. Talk about a pain. The moment we get a little something extra—pumpkins, papier-mâché thingies filled with food, attention, *anything*—they carry on in the worst way. And it's like, if somebody just *looks* at somebody the wrong way over there, the whole place has to know about it. So. Loud. Anyway, if a rabbit goes into their yard, just don't watch, okay? You'll know. They go into, like, their super stealth mode, all super quiet, super organized. Then they circle the poor thing, trap it between them—and then start *shriek*ing like crazy, banging it around until it doesn't move any more. It's awful. They brought their latest victim *inside*. Last week—a beautiful little bunny. *Inside!* And you know what they do afterwards? Uck. Rip it apart. Yep. And then they *eat* it. Blood everywhere! And everybody better get some, or it sets them all off again, shrieking away. Horrible. Just don't watch. I couldn't eat a tomato for a week after the last one.

Okay, well, so you'll get to meet everyone you'll be living with soon enough and start to figure out this side of the equation for yourself. Let me tell you a little bit about the people here. You've met a lot of them already, I'm sure. Probably they've been super nice and stuff while you've been getting used to the place. I can tell you a little bit about what they're like here on a day-to-day basis, when we're all in here together, how's that?

First of all, I've never seen the people come in here when we're in here. Sometimes we're in here and you'll see them out in the yard, putting a whole bunch of food out there. Or maybe the other way around. But as far as I can tell, you're totally safe from people in here—they never come in to whatever space we're in while we're in it.

I will say, though, if you're ever out in the yard or even inside and they call you over? Just go. Even if you can't figure out why they want you, just go. Usually, they just want us to move someplace else. When we come back, there's always fresh food and nesting things, so why not? And variety is the spice of life. We sleep in here and spend most of the day in here, so I'm all for moving around during the day. Anyway, but, you know, they can drop you in your tracks. I've seen it. They've done it to *me*. They have this pipe thing. They try to sneak it behind their backs so you don't see it. But if they bring that thing out and put it up to their mouths, believe me, the next thing you know, you get a sharp pain in your side and you wake up downstairs with a splitting headache. Honestly—if they call you? Just go over. It's way easier that way. As long as the Big Guy says it's okay.

Oh, have you seen these? You can get water here, did you know that? It's hard to figure them out if you haven't seen them before. You stick the tip of your tongue on the end, push this little ball in, then the water comes out. Sometimes those biscuits leave me pretty thirsty. If you put a little water on them, you can soften them and they're easier to chew, by the way. There's one of these on the other side, too, in case the mom decides to hog one. She does that sometimes. We'll be all lined up over here, waiting for a turn on this one, 'cause she's got the kid over there, *playing* with the other one. He gets his sticky little fingers all over it, too. Disgusting.

Actually, the guy I was with before used to wash his hands under one of these spigot things every time before he ate. So funny. It was his thing, you know? The people would show up for afternoon tricks and treats, and he'd make them wait so that he could run over and wash his hands first. They tried tricks and treats outside a couple times, which would have been a refreshing change of pace. But it didn't work. I don't know if they ever figured out it was because he couldn't find a place to wash his hands! Easy-going guy in most ways, but real fussy about that.

So, we've basically got four groups of people here. There's the ones in the green and tan clothes. They're the best. You want to be good to them, because they give us everything we've got in here. In the morning and the afternoon, they're the ones who do tricks and treats with us. Have you ever done that? If not, just watch me. They give you your own person and your own colored shape. Look around for your person and your colored shape, and go over to wherever it is that day. Then they'll start asking you to show them different parts of your body. They use their hands to make a different sign for each part that they want to see. My favorite is when they ask us to stick out our tongues. No—no: My favorite is when they want us to spin around and show them our butts. They touch those little bones on the top. I like the feel of their fingers. When I was really little, they used to carry me around and feed me, you know. One was even, like, my mom. But I haven't seen her in a long time. Even these other green and tan ones used to touch us all the time, through the fence. I played this little finger game with my person. Now, this is the only time I ever get to feel her fingers. You have to wait to hear the whistle after they're done touching you for that trick, though, otherwise you don't know when to turn back around for your treat. Personally, I like those little orange slices. So does the kid, by the way. One time, it was so funny, they asked him to lift his foot and show the bottom of it. He fell right over. The mom was like, *Well, get up. Don't look at me, I'm busy eating.* Which is mostly what she does, anyway.

Anyway, at the end of tricks and treats, it's like this big bonus—whatever's left in the cup, you get it all, all at once. Really fun. I try to see if I can swallow faster than she can give it to me.

Although sometimes, I go reeeeeealllly sloooooow, and chew each piece like, twenty-five times. It makes her laugh. Oh! They give us juice, too. It's tricky—you have to stick your lips out, together, through the fence, and they have to pour it in your mouth for you, just right. That's how that kid gets so sticky. I wish they'd just give us the stupid bottle and let us do it ourselves. But you'll get the hang of it quickly, if you haven't already.

So that's the green and tan people. They're great. Then there's the ones in blue. You see them, you know it's trouble. Even if they pretend they're green and tan people, and don't wear blue that day, you'll get to know who they are—and you know it means someone is sick or someone is going to be sick, soon. They're just bad news. My little sister and I got really sick one time. I remember for a couple days, all we saw were the blue people. Then one day I woke up, feeling better, but my sister was gone. I never saw her again. I still miss her. You remind me of her, you know. She was shy, too. And my brother? Every time he saw this one blue person, he used to throw himself against the glass. He just hated him. That blue guy used to stick a needle in my brother *every* time he saw him. For no reason! It was just mean. I think the blue guy got the point, though, because after a while, he didn't come down here anymore.

Okay, and then there're the ones in the white coats. They're fine. A little cold. But they're the ones who bring the TV over and let us play games in the afternoon. The Big Guy *loves* those games. My last one? Couldn't be bothered. But this one? It's the one thing that seems to get his attention besides food, the mom, and the son. Well, and me. Anyway. He *loves* those TV games. Even though I'm way better at them than he is. No matter how many times he gets the red screen, he just keeps at it. Frankly, I think this guy would do anything for a frozen grape. Maybe that's what it is.

And then there are the outside people. Most of them? Take your pick: awful and rude beyond belief, or incredibly boring. You can be in the middle of a really tense situation with the Big Guy, or having a great game with some little ones, or just relaxing, having a little snack or a nap—doesn't matter. They bang on the glass, yell, make ridiculous monkey noises—from some species *I've* never heard before—and bare their teeth at you. Sometimes I think if it wasn't for this glass, every one of them would try to pick a fight with us. So rude. Was it like this where you came from? Was it glass between you and the outside people? Anyway, they're not all like that. A lot of them are just *boring*. They don't *do* anything. They stop, they loom, and they stare, for like, thirty seconds—and then they walk on. The kids are cute. I don't mind when they stare. They're kids, right? And I love their little hats. Put a cute hat on a kid and I could watch them all morning. There's this one day every year that they try really hard to entertain us, and lots of them wear hats then, and the craziest clothes. The coolest thing is they cover their faces with masks and put them on and take them off for us. The ones who dress up like that get a treat, too, for dressing up for us and walking across our window.

Oh! And we get pumpkins that day! That's one of the times we do. Usually. Not like, for you; well, for us, now.

Yeah. I like hats. One of my brothers was crazy for shoes, though. Women's shoes. And sometimes little kids' shoes. He'd sit by the glass all day, scanning for shoes. He was *crazy* for red ones.

Anyway, I should say that every once in a while, there's an outside person who seems to get it. They come by pretty often and just sit and visit. Like you and I have been doing, through the glass. There's one, I really like her earrings. She always sits down and pulls her hair back so that I can see them. There's another one who sits and draws and shows me what she's doing. There's a guy who sits right over there, too, and shows me pictures of gorillas whenever I come over. I like those kinds. It can be a real thrill when they finally make eye contact with you.

Oh, look! There's my green and tan person. And that's just what I mean about the right kind of eye contact. See how polite? Hey! That's an orange slice! She's got the cup with the fruit in it! Fruit always means they really like whatever you just did. Oh, and there's another person. Is she yours? I bet she is. She's got an orange slice, too! Come on, I'll go first, and don't worry. From now on, I've got your back.

Suggested Readings

For more on western lowland gorillas as a social species, and managing and designing for gorillas in zoos, see:
Christena Nippert-Eng, et al. 2016. *Gorillas Up Close*. New York: Henry Holt.

On the lives of some of the more historically famous zoo gorillas, see:
Nancy Rose Pimm. 2007. *The Heart of the Beast*. New York: Darby Creek Publishing.

On ethnographic observation techniques and zoo gorillas, see:
Christena Nippert-Eng. 2015. *Watching Closely: A Guide to Ethnographic Observation*. Oxford: Oxford University Press. See especially the online companion website with students' gorilla-based homework assignments at http://global.oup.com/us/companion.websites/9780190235529/.

For more on conducting ethnographic fieldwork across a variety of primates, see:
Karen B. Strier. 2013. *Primate Ethnographies*. New York: Routledge.

On best practices and recent research about North American zoo gorillas, see:
The Gorilla Gazette. Available at http://www.gorillagazette.com (This is by keepers, for keepers, and a real insiders' view).

Gorilla Species Survival Plan. Available at http://www.gorillassp.org (The North American AZA gorilla "SSP" outlines concerns and specific plans for maintaining a healthy population of zoo gorillas, including planned transfers of specific individuals between zoos).

Zoo Biology. Jason Watters, Executive Editor, Wiley (peer-reviewed scientific journal with a steady stream of articles on zoo gorillas and both family and bachelor troops).

❦ Contributors

Heather Altfeld is a poet and her first book, *The Disappearing Theatre*, won the Poets at Work Book Prize, selected by Stephen Dunn. Her poems appear in *Narrative Magazine, Pleiades, ZYZZYVA, Poetry Northwest,* and elsewhere. She won the 2017 Robert H. Winner Award and the 2015 Pablo Neruda Prize for Poetry. Her current research and areas of interest include children's literature, anthropology and poetry, and things that have vanished. She lives in Northern California and teaches in the English Department and the Honors Program at California State University, Chico, and is a longtime member of the Community of Writers at Squaw Valley.

Marcus Baynes-Rock is an anthropologist from the University of Notre Dame. He is particularly interested in relations between humans and large carnivores in evolutionary history and contemporary society—which took him to Ethiopia to study urban hyenas. Marcus is currently researching the place of dingoes in past and present Australian societies and the sociocognitive elements of human-dingo relations.

Alex Blanchette is an assistant professor of anthropology and environmental studies at Tufts University. His research examines the ongoing legacy of industrialization, especially as it shapes values and material environments in a post-industrial United States. His forthcoming first book, *Porkopolis,* is an ethnography of labor politics within some of the world's largest corporate meat production facilities.

Catherine E. Bolten is an associate professor of anthropology and peace studies at the University of Notre Dame. She has worked in Sierra Leone on issues related to post-war development, narrative, agriculture, and social change since 2003, and previously conducted research on ethnobotany and ecotourism in Botswana. She is the author of *I Did It to Save My Life: Love and Survival in Sierra Leone*.

Scout Calvert is the data librarian at Michigan State University. Her recent projects have traced the social aspects of data-centric knowledge production in lay communities of genealogists, livestock breeders, and citizen scientists. She also investigates data and metadata practices in libraries and among academic researchers, exploring emerging research methods afforded by new forms of data and informing data policy issues in academic libraries.

Nicholas D'Avella is a Hunt Postdoctoral Fellow and visiting scholar at the Hemispheric Institute of Performance and Politics at New York University. He is an ethnographer of contemporary Argentina with research interests in markets, expert knowledge, and urban ecologies. Both his current and future projects focus on aftermaths of the Argentine economic crisis of 2001. His current book, *Concrete Dreams: Ethnographies of Practice and the Value of Buildings in Post-Crisis Buenos Aires*, is an ethnographic study of a construction boom in the early post-crisis years. His next project, *Developing Economics: Unorthodox Economists in Argentina and Beyond*, is a study of post-neoliberal economic knowledge and policy in Latin American urban financial centers.

Agustín Fuentes is the Edmund P. Joyce C.S.C. Professor of Anthropology at the University of Notre Dame. His current research includes cooperation and community in human evolution, ethnoprimatology and multispecies anthropology, evolutionary theory, and interdisciplinary approaches to human nature(s). He is the author of *Race, Monogamy, and Other Lies They Told You: Busting Myths about Human Nature* and *The Creative Spark: How Imagination Made Humans Exceptional*, and coauthor of *Conversations on Human Nature*.

Ilana Gershon is a professor of anthropology at Indiana University Bloomington. She is interested in how new media affects highly charged social tasks, such as breaking up or hiring in the United States. She has written about how people use new media to end romantic relationships in her book *The Breakup 2.0: Disconnecting over New Media*. Her recent book, *Down and Out in the New Economy: How People Find (or Don't Find) Work Today*, addresses how new media affects hiring in the contemporary American workplace. She has also edited a collection of imagined job manuals, *A World of Work: Imagined Manuals for Real Jobs*. She has no pets and no plants at home.

Andrew Halloran is the director of Chimpanzee Care Services at Save the Chimps. He is the author of *The Song of the Ape*, an investigation of chimpanzee language and communication. Halloran also focuses on the difference between scientific realities (in the form of wild chimpanzee behavior and communication) versus the myths we create about the world around us (manufacturing "talking" apes in laboratories via sign language–trained chimpanzees, gorillas, and orangutans).

Eva Hayward is an assistant professor in gender and women's studies at the University of Arizona, Tucson. She has taught at the University of California, Santa Cruz, the University of New Mexico, Uppsala University (Sweden), Duke University, and the University of Cincinnati. Her research focuses on the study of sensation. She has recently published articles in *Transgender Studies Quarterly, Cultural Anthropology, Parallax, differences, Women's Studies Quarterly*, and *Women and Performance*.

Leslie Irvine is a professor of sociology at the University of Colorado, Boulder. Her research has examined animal selfhood, animal sheltering, gender in veterinary medicine, animals in popular culture, animal abuse, and animal welfare in disasters. Her books include *My Dog Always Eats First: Homeless People and their Animals, Filling the Ark: Animal Welfare in Disasters*, and *If You Tame Me: Understanding our Connection with Animals*. Her articles have appeared in *Society & Animals, Anthrozoös, Gender & Society, Social Problems, The Sociological Quarterly, Qualitative Sociology*, and *Symbolic Interaction*.

Frédéric Keck is a researcher at the Laboratory of Social Anthropology and the director of the Research Department of the Quai Branly Museum. After studying philosophy at the École Normale Supérieure in Paris and anthropology at the University of California, Berkeley, he began researching the history of anthropology and contemporary biopolitical questions. He is the author of *Claude Lévi-Strauss, une introduction; Lucien Lévy-Bruhl, entre philosophie et anthropologie;* and *Un monde grippé*. He is the coeditor of *Des hommes malades des animaux* and *Sentinel Devices*.

Robert G. W. Kirk is a lecturer in medical history and humanities in the Centre for the History of Science, Technology and Medicine (CHSTM) at the University of Manchester (UK). His work examines nonhuman animals in human cultures, particularly nonhuman roles in science, medicine, and technology, as well as the place of animals in history and historical writing. He is currently investigating the interdependence of humans, animals, and health through two projects—"Multispecies Medicine: Biotherapy and the Ecological Vision of Health and Wellbeing" and "The Animal Research Nexus: Changing Constitutions of Science, Health and Welfare"—supported by the Wellcome Trust.

Yasmine Musharbash is a senior lecturer and ARC Future Fellow with the Department of Anthropology at the University of Sydney. Since the 1990s, she has been engaged in participant observation-based research with Warlpiri people in central Australia, focusing on the themes of everyday life, boredom, sleep, the night, and especially, social relations (among Warlpiri people and between Warlpiri people and others including non-Indigenous people, strangers, monsters, and animals). She has published widely, including the ethnography *Yuendumu Everyday: Contemporary Life in Remote Aboriginal Australia* and her most recent coedited volume *Monster Anthropology in Australasia and Beyond*.

Alex Nading is a senior fellow at the Watson Institute for International and Public Affairs at Brown University. He is a medical anthropologist with research specialties in infectious disease and environmental health. His first book, *Mosquito Trails: Ecology, Health, and the Politics of Entanglement*, is an ethnography of community-based dengue fever control in urban Nicaragua. His subsequent work examined ethical debates among scientists, global health organizations, and corporations working to develop dengue vaccines and genetically modified mosquitoes. His current work includes collaborative research on hygiene, sanitation, and quality of life in Managua, and a long-term ethnographic project on an epidemic of chronic kidney disease of unknown causes in Nicaragua's sugar plantation zone.

Nicole C. Nelson is an assistant professor in the History of Science Department at the University of Wisconsin–Madison. She studies the formation and transformation of scientific cultures, particularly in genetics intensive fields. Nicole is currently completing a book based on ethnographic research in an animal behavior genetics laboratory, where scientists were using mice to understand the biology of anxiety and addiction.

Christena Nippert-Eng is a sociologist and professor of informatics at Indiana University Bloomington. She is the author of *Watching Closely: A Guide to Ethnographic Observation*, based on her work helping students learn observation methods by watching zoo gorillas, and the beautifully photographed *Gorillas Up Close*, developed in collaboration with her former students.

Michael Alan Park is a professor of anthropology, emeritus, at Central Connecticut State University. His specialty is evolutionary theory as applied to the human species, past and present. He is the author or coauthor of six anthropology college textbooks and a trade book on evolution. In his retirement he volunteers with a dog rescue organization in Connecticut.

Natalie Porter is an assistant professor of anthropology at the University of Notre Dame. Her research explores how zoonotic disease threats are transforming human-nonhuman relations as well as scientific knowledge production and global public health practice. Natalie is completing a book on avian flu control in Vietnam, which explores health interventions in chicken farms, veterinary laboratories, and meat markets across the country. She spends much of her spare time thinking about, writing about, and playing with dogs.

Aleta Quinn is an assistant professor in philosophy at University of Idaho and a research collaborator at the National Museum of Natural History. Quinn researches the history and philosophy of biology with a focus on organismal biology and taxonomy. She has also trained as a biologist, and is a coauthor on the discovery of the olinguito, the first new carnivore from the Western Hemisphere in thirty-five years.

Sherri Sasnett-Martichuski is a graduate student in sociology at the University of Colorado, Boulder. She was the 2016 recipient of the Herbert Blumer Graduate Student Paper Award for her paper, "The Transgender Experience: In Search of an Authentic Self." She is also the author of "Are the Kids Alright? A Qualitative Study of Adults with Gay and Lesbian Parents," published in the *Journal of Contemporary Ethnography*.

Lesley A. Sharp is the Barbara Chamberlain and Helen Chamberlain Josefsberg '30 Professor of Anthropology at Barnard College and a senior research scientist in Sociomedical Sciences at Columbia University. Her ongoing research addresses moral thought and action in clinical and laboratory contexts. A medical anthropologist by training, she is the author of *Strange Harvest: Organ Transplants, Denatured Bodies, and the Transformed*

Self (which won the New Millennium Book Prize of the Society for Medical Anthropology); *The Transplant Imaginary: Mechanical Hearts, Animal Parts, and Moral Thinking in Highly Experimental Science;* and *Animal Ethos,* a book now in press, which concerns morality in lab animal research and animal activism.

Genese Marie Sodikoff is an associate professor of anthropology at Rutgers University–Newark. Her research has focused on labor hierarchies, biodiversity conservation, human-nonhuman relations, and extinction events in Madagascar. She is currently examining zoonotic disease, focusing on bubonic plague outbreaks and Malagasy funerary practices. She is the author of *Forest and Labor in Madagascar: From Colonial Concession to Global Biosphere* and the editor of *The Anthropology of Extinction: Essays on Culture and Species Death.*

Kaitlin Stack Whitney is a visiting assistant professor at the Rochester Institute of Technology, with a joint appointment in the Science, Technology, and Society (STS) department and the Environmental Science program. Kaitlin's current research blends biology, data science, and science studies to examine the biopolitics of wildlife surveillance and reproductive technologies. She received her doctorate in zoology with an STS minor from the University of Wisconsin–Madison.

Jeannette Vaught holds a doctorate in American studies from the University of Texas. She was formerly an equine veterinary technician, and her work focuses on animals, agriculture, and science. She is at work on a manuscript about the historical biopolitics of reproductive technologies used to create agricultural animals, and is also working on *Locust.*